Property of:
Julia M. Trallo

THE CENTURY VOCABULARY BUILDER

BY
GARLAND GREEVER

AND

JOSEPH M. BACHELOR

APPLETON-CENTURY-CROFTS, INC.
NEW YORK

COPYRIGHT, 1922, BY THE CENTURY CO.
ALL RIGHTS RESERVED, INCLUDING THE
RIGHT TO REPRODUCE THIS BOOK, OR
PORTIONS THEREOF, IN ANY FORM.

COPYRIGHT, 1950, BY GARLAND GREEVER.

593-23

PRINTED IN U. S. A.

To
DANA H. FERRIN
WHOM THIS BOOK OWES MORE
THAN A MERE DEDICATION
CAN ACKNOWLEDGE

PREFACE

You should know at the outset what this book does *not* attempt to do. It does not, save to the extent that its own special purpose requires, concern itself with the many and intricate problems of grammar, rhetoric, spelling, punctuation, and the like; or clarify the thousands of individual difficulties regarding correct usage. All these matters are important. Concise treatment of them may be found in THE CENTURY HANDBOOK OF WRITING and THE CENTURY DESK BOOK OF GOOD ENGLISH, both of which manuals are issued by the present publishers. But this volume confines itself to the one task of placing at your disposal the means of adding to your stock of words, of increasing your vocabulary.

It does not assume that you are a scholar, or try to make you one. To be sure, it recognizes the ends of scholarship as worthy. It levies at every turn upon the facts which scholarship has accumulated. But it demands of you no technical equipment, nor leads you into any of those bypaths of knowledge, alluring indeed, of which the benefits are not immediate. For example, in Chapter V it forms into groups words etymologically akin to each other. It does this for an end entirely practical—namely, that the words you know may help you to understand the words you do not know. Did it go farther—did it ac-

v

count for minor differences in these words by showing that they sprang from related rather than identical originals, did it explain how and how variously their forms have been modified in the long process of their descent—it would pass beyond its strict utilitarian bounds. This it refrains from doing. And thus everything it contains it rigorously subjects to the test of serviceability. It helps you to bring more and more words into workaday harness—to gain such mastery over them that you can speak and write them with fluency, flexibility, precision, and power. It enables you, in your use of words, to attain the readiness and efficiency expected of a capable and cultivated man.

There are many ways of building a vocabulary, as there are many ways of attaining and preserving health. Fanatics may insist that one should be cultivated to the exclusion of the others, just as health-cranks may declare that diet should be watched in complete disregard of recreation, sanitation, exercise, the need for medicines, and one's mental attitude to life. But the sum of human experience, rather than fanaticism, must determine our procedure. Moreover experience has shown that the various successful methods of bringing words under man's sway are not mutually antagonistic but may be practiced simultaneously, just as health is promoted, not by attending to diet one year, to exercise the next, and to mental attitude the third, but by bestowing wise and fairly constant attention on all. Yet it would be absurd to state that all methods of increasing one's vocabulary, or of attaining vigor of physique, are equally valuable. This

PREFACE vii

volume offers everything that helps, and it yields space in proportion to helpfulness.

Aside from a brief introductory chapter, a chapter (number X) given over to a list of words, and a brief concluding chapter, the subject matter of the volume falls into three main divisions. Chapters II and III are based on the fact that we must all use words in combination—must fling the words out by the handfuls, even as the accomplished pianist must strike his notes. Chapters IV and V are based on the fact that we must become thoroughly acquainted with individual words—that no one who scorns to study the separate elements of speech can command powerful and discriminating utterance. Chapters VI, VII, VIII, and IX are based on the fact that we need synonyms as our constant lackeys—that we should be able to summon, not a word that will do, but a word that will express the idea with precision. Exercises scattered throughout the book, together with five of the six appendices, provide well-nigh inexhaustible materials for practice.

For be it understood, once for all, that this volume is not a machine which you can set going and then sit idly beside, the while your vocabulary broadens. Mastery over words, like worthy mastery of any kind whatsoever, involves effort for yourself. You can of course contemplate the nature and activities of the mechanism, and learn something thereby; but also you must work—work hard, work intelligently. As you cannot acquire health by watching a gymnast take exercise or a doctor swallow medicine or a dietician select food, so you cannot become an overlord of words without first fighting battles to subjugate them. Hence this volume is for you less **a labor-saving machine** than a collection and arrangement of materials which you must put together by hand. It assembles everything you need. It tags everything plainly. It tells you just what you must do. In these ways it makes your task far easier. *But the task is yours.* Industry, persistence, a fair amount of common sense—these three you must have. Without them you will accomplish nothing.

Even with them—let the forewarning be candid—you will not accomplish everything. You cannot learn all there is to be learned about words, any more than about human nature. And what you do achieve will be, not a sudden attainment, but a growth. This is not the dark side of the picture. It is an honest avowal that the picture is not composed altogether of light. But as the result of your efforts an adequate vocabulary will some day be yours. Nor will you have to wait long for an earnest of ultimate success. Just as system will speedily transform a haphazard business into one which seizes opportunities and stops the leakage of profits, so will sincere and well-directed effort bring you promptly **and surely into an ever-growing mastery of words.**

CONTENTS

CHAPTER		PAGE
I.	REASONS FOR INCREASING YOUR VOCABULARY	3
II.	WORDS IN COMBINATION: SOME PITFALLS	7
	Tameness	8
	Exercise	10
	Slovenliness	11
	Exercises 12, 13, 14,	15
	Wordiness	15
	Exercises 17, 19,	22
	Verbal Discords	24
	Exercise	26
	1. Abstract vs. Concrete Terms; General vs. Specific Terms	27
	Exercise	29
	2. Literal vs. Figurative Terms	31
	Exercise	33
	3. Connotation	35
	Exercise	36
III.	WORDS IN COMBINATION: HOW MASTERED	40
	Preliminaries: General Purposes and Methods	40
	1. A Ready, an Accurate, or a Wide Vocabulary?	40
	2. A Vocabulary for Speech or for Writing?	43
	The Mastery of Words in Combination	44
	1. Mastery through Translation	44
	Exercise	44
	2. Mastery through Paraphrasing	45
	Exercise	46
	3. Mastery through Discourse at First Hand	46
	Exercise	49

CONTENTS

CHAPTER		PAGE
	4. Mastery through Adapting Discourse to Audience	54
	Exercise	56
IV.	INDIVIDUAL WORDS: AS VERBAL CELIBATES	59
	What Words to Learn First	61
	The Analysis of Your Own Vocabulary	62
	Exercise	65
	The Definition of Words	66
	Exercise	68
	How to Look up a Word in the Dictionary	69
	Exercise	74
	Prying into a Word's Past	75
	Exercise	85
V.	INDIVIDUAL WORDS: AS MEMBERS OF VERBAL FAMILIES	89
	Words Related in Blood	91
	Exercise	93
	Words Related by Marriage	94
	Exercise	97
	Prying into a Word's Relationships	97
	Exercise	103
	Two Admonitions	103
	General Exercise for the Chapter (with Lists of Words Containing the Same Key-Syllables)	105
	Second General Exercise (with Additional Lists)	123
	Third General Exercise	134
	Fourth General Exercise	135
	Latin Ancestors of English Words	135
	Latin Prefixes	140
	Greek Ancestors of English Words	141
	Greek Prefixes	144
VI.	WORDS IN PAIRS	145
	Opposites	146
	Exercise	148

CONTENTS

CHAPTER		PAGE
	Words Often Confused	149
	Exercise	150
	Parallels (with Lists)	158
	Exercise	166
VII.	SYNONYMS IN LARGER GROUPS (1)	176
	How to Acquire Synonyms	178
	Exercise (with Lists)	184
VIII.	SYNONYMS IN LARGER GROUPS (2)	218
	Exercise (with Lists)	218
IX.	MANY-SIDED WORDS	260
	Exercise	262
	Literal vs. Figurative Applications	268
	Exercise	270
	Imperfectly Understood Facts and Ideas	270
	Exercise	272
X.	SUPPLEMENTARY LIST OF WORDS	274
	Exercise	275
XI.	RETROSPECT	285

APPENDICES
1. The Drift of Our Rural Population Cityward (an Editorial) 291
2. Causes for the American Spirit of Liberty (by Edmund Burke) 293
3. Parable of the Sower (Gospel of St. Matthew) 298
4. The Seven Ages of Man (by William Shakespeare) 299
5. The Castaway (by Daniel Defoe) . . 300
6. Reading Lists 307

INDEX 311

THE CENTURY
VOCABULARY BUILDER

CENTURY VOCABULARY BUILDER

I

REASONS FOR INCREASING YOUR VOCABULARY

SOMETIMES a dexterous use of words appears to us to be only a kind of parlor trick. And sometimes it *is* just that. The command of a wide vocabulary is in truth an accomplishment, and like any other accomplishment it may be used for show. But not necessarily. Just as a man may have money without "flashing" it, or an extensive wardrobe without sporting gaudy neckties or wearing a dress suit in the morning, so may he possess linguistic resources without making a caddish exhibition of them. Indeed the more distant he stands from verbal bankruptcy, the less likely he is to indulge in needless display.

Again, glibness of speech sometimes awakens our distrust. We like actions rather than words; we prefer that character, personality, and kindly feelings should be their own mouthpiece. So be it. But there are thoughts and emotions properly to be shared with other people, yet incapable of being revealed except through language. It is only when language is insincere—when it expresses lofty sentiments or generous sympathies, yet springs from designing selfishness—that it justly arouses misgivings. Power over words, like power of any other sort, is for use, not abuse. That it sometimes is abused must not mislead us into thinking that it should in itself be scorned or neglected.

Our contempt and distrust do not mean that our fundamental ideas about language are unsound. Beneath our wholesome dislike for shallow facility and insincerity of speech, we have a conviction that the mastery of words is a good thing, not a bad. We are therefore unwilling to take the vow of linguistic poverty. If we lack the ability to bend words to our use, it is from laziness, not from scruple. We desire to speak competently, but without affectation. We know that if our diction rises to this dual standard, it silently distinguishes us from the sluggard, the weakling, and the upstart. For such diction is not to be had on sudden notice, like a tailor-made suit. Nor can it, like such a suit, deceive anybody as to our true status. A man's utterance reveals what he is. It is the measure of his inward attainment. The assertion has been made that for a man to express himself freely and well in his native language is the surest proof of his culture. Meditate the saying. Can you think of a proof that is surer?

But a man's speech does more than lend him distinction. It does more than reveal to others what manner of man he is. It is an instrument as well as an index. It is an agent—oftentimes indeed it is *the* agent—of his influence upon others. How silly are those persons who oppose words to things, as if words were not things at all but air-born unrealities! Words are among the most powerful realities in the world. You vote the Republican ticket. Why? Because you have studied the issues of the campaign and reached a well-reasoned conclusion how the general interests may be served? Possibly. But nine times in ten it will be because of that *word* Republican. You may believe that in a given instance the Republican cause or candidate is inferior; you may have nothing personally to lose through Republican defeat; yet you squirm and twist and seek excuses for casting a Republican ballot. Such is the power—aye, sometimes the tyranny—of a word. The word *Republican* has not been selected invidiously. *Democrat* would have served as well. Or take religious words—*Catholic, Methodist, Presbyterian, Episcopalian, Baptist, Lutheran,* or what not. A man who belongs, in person or by proxy, to one of the sects designated may be more indifferent to the institution itself than to the word that represents it. Thus you may attack in his presence the tenets of Presbyterianism, for example, but you must be wary about calling the Presbyterian name. *Mother, the flag*—what sooner than an insult coupled with these terms will rouse a man to fight? But does that man kiss his mother, or salute the flag, or pay much heed to either? Probably not. Words not realities? With what realities must we more carefully reckon? Words are as dangerous as dynamite, as beneficent as brotherhood. An unfortunate word may mean a plea rejected, an enterprise baffled, half the world plunged into war. A fortunate word may open a triple-barred door, avert a disaster, bring thousands of people from jealousy and hatred into coöperation and goodwill.

Nor is it solely on their emotional side that men may be affected by words. Their thinking and their esthetic nature also—their hard sense and their personal likes and dislikes—are subject to the same influence. You interview a potential investor; does he accept your proposition or not? A prospective customer walks into your store; does he buy the goods you show him? You enter the drawing room of one of the élite; are you invited again and again? Your words will largely decide—your words, or your verbal abstinence. For be it remembered that words no more than dollars are to be scattered broadcast for the sole reason that you have them. The right word should be used at the right time—and at that time only. Silence is oftentimes golden. Nevertheless there are occasions for us to speak. Frequent occasions. To be inarticulate *then* may mean only embarrassment. It may—some day it will—mean suffering and failure. That we may make the most of the important occasions sure to come, we must have our instruments ready. Those instruments are words. He who commands words commands events—commands men.

II

WORDS IN COMBINATION: SOME PITFALLS

YOU wish, then, to increase your vocabulary. Of course you must become observant of words and inquisitive about them. For words are like people: they have their own particular characteristics, they do their work well or ill, they are in good odor or bad, and they yield best service to him who loves them and tries to understand them. Your curiosity about them must be burning and insatiable. You must study them when they have withdrawn from the throng of their fellows into the quiescence of their natural selves. You must also see them and study them in action, not only as they are employed in good books and by careful speakers, but likewise as they fall from the lips of unconventional speakers who through them secure vivid and telling effects. In brief, you must learn word nature, as you learn human nature, from a variety of sources.

Now in ordinary speech most of us use words, not as individual things, but as parts of a whole—as cogs in the machine of utterance by which we convey our thoughts and feelings. We do not think of them separately at all. And this instinct is sound. In our expression we are like large-scale manufacturing plants rather than one-man establishments. We have at our disposal, not one worker, but a multitude. Hence we are concerned with our employees collectively and with the total production of which they are capable. To be sure, our understanding of them as individuals will increase the worth and magnitude of our output. But clearly we must have large dealings with them in the aggregate.

This chapter and the following, therefore, are given over to the study of words in combination. As in all matters, there is a negative as well as a positive side to be reckoned with. Let us consider the negative side first.

Tameness

Correct diction is too often insipid. There is nothing wrong with it, but it does not interest us—it lacks character, lacks color, lacks power. It too closely resembles what we conceive of the angels as having—impeccability without the warmth of camaraderie. Speech, like a man, should be alive. It need not, of course, be boisterous. It may be intense in a quiet, modest way. But if it too sedulously observes all the *Thou shalt not's* of the rhetoricians, it will refine the vitality out of itself and leave its hearers unmoved.

That is why you should become a disciple of the pithy, everyday conversationalist and of the rough-and-ready master of harangue as well as of the practitioner of precise and scrupulous discourse. Many a speaker or writer has thwarted himself by trying to be "literary." Even Burns when he wrote classic English was somewhat conscious of himself and made, in most instances, no extraordinary impression. But the pieces he impetuously

WORDS IN COMBINATION: SOME PITFALLS

dashed off in his native Scotch dialect can never be forgotten. The man who begins by writing naturally, but as his importance in the publishing world grows, pays more and more attention to felicities—to "style"—and so spoils himself, is known to the editor of every magazine. Any editorial office force can insert missing commas and semicolons, and iron out blunders in the English; but it has not the time, if indeed the ability, to instil life into a lifeless manuscript. A living style is rarer than an inoffensive one, and the road of literary ambition is strewn with failures due to "correctness."

Cultivate readiness, even daring, of utterance. A single turn of expression may be so audacious that it plucks an idea from its shroud or places within us an emotion still quivering and warm. Sustained discourse may unflaggingly clarify or animate. But such triumphs are beyond **the reach of those, whether** speakers or writers, who are **constantly pausing to grope for words**. This does not mean that scrutiny of individual words is wasted effort. Such scrutiny becomes the basis indeed of the more venturesome and inspired achievement. We must serve our apprenticeship to language. We must know words as a general knows the men under him—all their ranks, their capabilities, their shortcomings, the details and routine of their daily existence. But the end for which we gain our understanding must be to hurl these words upon the enemy, not as disconnected units, but as battalions, as brigades, as corps, as armies. Dr. Johnson, one of the most effective talkers in all history, resolved early in life that, always, and whatever topic might be broached, he would on the moment express his thoughts and feelings with as much vigor and felicity as if he had unlimited leisure to draw on. And Patrick Henry, one of the few really irresistible orators, was wont to plunge headlong into a sentence and trust to God Almighty to get him out.

Exercise

1. Study Appendix 1 (The Drift of Our Rural Population Cityward). Do you regard it as written simply, with force and natural feeling? Or does it show lack of spontaneity? —suffer from an unnatural and self-conscious manner of writing? Is the style one you would like to cultivate for your own use?

2. Express, if you can, in more vigorous language of your own the thought of the editorial.

3. Think of some one you have known who has the gift of racy colloquial utterance. Make a list of offhand, homely, or picturesque expressions you have heard him employ, and ask yourself what it is in these expressions that has made them linger in your memory. With them in mind, and with your knowledge of the man's methods of imparting his ideas vividly, try to make your version of the editorial more forceful still.

4. Study Appendix 2 (Causes for the American Spirit of Liberty) as an example of stately and elaborate, yet energetic, discourse. The speech from which this extract is taken was delivered in Parliament in a vain effort to stay England from driving her colonies to revolt. Some of Burke's turns of phrase are extremely bold and original, as "The religion most prevalent in our northern colonies is a refinement on the principle of resistance; it is the dissidence of dissent and the Protestantism of the Protestant religion." Moreover, with all his fulness of diction, Burke could cleave to the heart of an idea in a few words, as "Freedom is to them [the southern slave-holders] not only an enjoyment, but a kind of rank and privilege." Find other examples of bold or concise and illuminating utterance.

5. Read Appendix 3 (Parable of the Sower). It has no special audacities of phrase, but escapes tameness in various ways—largely through its simple earnestness.

6. Make a list of the descriptive phrases in Appendix 4 (The Seven Ages of Man) through which Shakespeare gives life and distinctness to his pictures.

7. Study Appendix 5 (The Castaway) as a piece of homely, effective narrative. (Defoe wrote for the man in the street. He was a literary jack-of-all-trades whom dignified authors of his day would not countenance, but who possessed genius.) It relies upon directness and plausibility of substance and style rather than temerity of phrase. Yet it never sags into tameness. Notice how everyday expressions ("My business was to hold my breath," "I took to my heels") add subtly to our belief that what Defoe is telling us is true. Notice also that such expressions ("the least capful of wind," "half dead with the water I took in," "ready to burst with holding my breath") without being pretentious may yet be forceful. Notice finally the naturalness and lift of the sinewy idioms ("I fetched another run," "I had no clothes to shift me," "I had like to have suffered a second shipwreck," "It wanted but a little that all my cargo had slipped off").

8. Once or twice at least, make a mental note of halting or listless expressions in a sermon, a public address, or a conversation. Find more emphatic wording for the ideas thus marred.

9. To train yourself in readiness and daring of utterance, practice impromptu discussion of any of the topics in Exercise 1, pages 49-51.

Slovenliness

Though we are to recognize the advantage of working in the undress of speech rather than in stiffly-laundered literary linens, though we are not to despise the accessions of strength and of charm which we may obtain from the homely and familiar, we must never be careless. The man whose speech is slovenly is like the man who chews gum—unblushingly commonplace.

We must struggle to maintain our individuality. We must not be a mere copy of everybody else. We must put into our words the cordiality we put into our daily demeanor. If we greeted friend or stranger carelessly, conventionally, we should soon be regarded as persons of no force or distinction. So of our speech and our writing. Nothing, to be sure, is more difficult than to give them freshness without robbing them of naturalness and ease. Yet that is what we must learn to do. We shall not acquire the power in a day. We shall acquire it as a chess or a baseball player acquires his skill—by long effort, hard practice.

One thing to avoid is the use of words in loose, or fast-and-loose, senses. Do not say that owning a watch is a fine proposition if you mean that it is advantageous. Do not say that you trembled on the brink of disaster if you were threatened with no more than inconvenience or comparatively slight injury. Do not say you were literally scared to death if you are yet alive to tell the story.

Exercise

Give moderate or accurate utterance to the following ideas:

The burning of the hen-coop was a mighty conflagration.
The fact that the point of the pencil was broken profoundly surprised me.
We had a perfectly gorgeous time.
It's a beastly shame that I missed my car.
It is awfully funny that he should die.
The saleslady pulled the washlady's hair.
A cold bath is pretty nice of mornings.
To go a little late is just the article.

Another thing to avoid is the use of words in the wrong parts of speech, as a noun for a verb, or an adjective for an adverb. Sometimes newspapers are guilty of such faults; for journalistic English, though pithy, shows here and there traces of its rapid composition. You must look to more leisurely authorities. The speakers and writers on whom you may rely will not say "to burglarize," "to suspicion," "to enthuse," "plenty rich," "real

WORDS IN COMBINATION: SOME PITFALLS

tired," "considerable discouraged," "a combine," or "humans." An exhaustive list of such errors cannot be inserted here. If you feel yourself uncertain in these details of usage, you should have access to such a volume as *The Century Desk Book of Good English*.

EXERCISE

1. For each quoted expression in the preceding paragraph compose a sentence which shall contain the correct form, or the grammatical equivalent, of the expression.

2. Correct the following sentences:

The tramp suicided.
She was real excited.
He gestured angry.
He was some anxious to get to the eats.
All of us had an invite.
Them boys have sure been teasing the canine.

Another thing to avoid is triteness. The English language teems with phrases once strikingly original but now smooth-worn and vulgarized by incessant repetition. It can scarcely be said that you are to shun these altogether. Now and then you will find one of them coming happily as well as handily into your speech. But you must not use them too often. Above all, you must rid yourself of any dependence upon them. The scope of this book permits only a few illustrations of the kinds of words and phrases meant. But the person who speaks of "lurid flames," or "untiring efforts," or "specimens of humanity" —who "views with alarm," or has a "native heath," or is "to the manner born"—does more than advertise the scantness of his verbal resources. He brands himself mentally indolent; he deprives his thought itself of all sharpness, exactness, and power.

Exercise

Replace with more original expressions the trite phrases (italicized) in the following sentences:

Last but not least, we have *in our midst* one who began life *poor but honest.*
After we had *done justice to a dinner* and gathered in the drawing room, we listened *with bated breath* while she *favored us with a selection.*
A goodly number of *the fair sex,* perceiving that *the psychological moment* had come, *applauded him to the echo.*
We were *doomed to disappointment; the grim reaper* had already gathered unto himself *all that was mortal* of our comrade.
No sooner said than done. I soon found myself *the proud possessor* of that for which I had acknowledged *a long-felt want.*
After *the last sad rites* were over and her body was *consigned to earth,* we began talking *along these lines.*
With *a few well-chosen words* he *brought order out of chaos.*
The way my efforts were *nipped in the bud* simply *beggars description.* I am somewhat *the worse for wear. Hoping you are the same,* I remain Yours sincerely, Ned Burke.

Finally, to the extent that you use slang at all, be its master instead of its slave. You have many times been told that the overuse of slang disfigures one's speech and hampers his standing with cultivated people. You have also been told that slang constantly changes, so that one's accumulations of it today will be a profitless clutter tomorrow. These things are true, but an even more cogent objection remains. Slang is detrimental to the formation of good intellectual habits. From its very nature it cannot be precise, cannot discriminate closely. It is a vehicle for loose-thinking people, it is fraught with

WORDS IN COMBINATION: SOME PITFALLS

unconsidered general meanings, it moves in a region of mental mists. It could not flourish as it does were fewer of us content to express vague thoughts and feelings instead of those which are sharply and specifically ours. Unless, therefore, you wish your intellectual processes to be as hazy and haphazard as those of mental shirkers and loafers, you must eschew, not necessarily all slang, but all heedless, all habitual use of it. Now and then a touch of slang, judiciously chosen, is effective; now and then it fulfils a legitimate purpose of language. But normally you should express yourself as befits one who has at his disposal the rich treasuries of the dictionary instead of a mere stock of greasy counterfeit phrases.

Exercise

Replace the following slang with acceptable English:

We pulled a new wrinkle.
He's an easy mark.
Oh, you're nutty.
Beat it.
I have all the inside dope.
You can't bamboozle me.
What a phiz the bloke has!
You're talking through your hat.
We had a long confab with the gink.
He's loony over that chicken.
The prof. told us to vamoose.
Take a squint at the girl with the specs.
Ain't it fierce the way they swipe umbrellas?
Goodnight, how she claws the ivory!
Nix on the rough stuff.
And there I got pinched by a cop for parking my Tin Lizzie.

Wordiness

As a precaution against tameness you should cultivate spontaneity and daring. As a precaution against slovenliness you should cultivate freshness and accuracy. But to display spontaneity, daring, freshness, accuracy you must have or acquire a large stock, a wide range, of words. Now this possession, like any other, brings with it temptation. If we have words, we like to use them. Nor do we wait for an indulgence in this luxury until we have consciously set to work to amass a vocabulary.

Verbosity is, in truth, the besetting linguistic sin. Most people are lavish with words, as most people are lavish with money. This is not to say that in the currency of language they are rich. But even if they lack the means—and the desire—to be extravagant, they yet make their purchases heedlessly or fail to count their linguistic change. The degree of our thrift, not the amount of our income or resources, is what marks us as being or not being verbal spendthrifts. The frugal manager buys his ideas at exactly the purchase price. He does not expend a twenty-dollar bill for a box of matches.

Have words by all means, the more of them the better, but use them temperately, sparingly. Do not think that a passage to be admirable must be studded with ostentatious terms. Consider the Gettysburg Address or the Parable of the Prodigal Son. These convey their thought and feeling perfectly, yet both are simple—exquisitely simple. They strike us indeed as being inevitable—as if their phrasing could not have been other than it is. They have, they are, finality. What could glittering phraseology add to them? Nothing; it could only mar them. Yet Lincoln and the Scriptural writers were not afraid to use big words when occasion required. What they sought was to make their speech adequate without carrying a superfluous syllable.

WORDS IN COMBINATION: SOME PITFALLS

"The sun set" is more natural and effective than "The celestial orb that blesses our terrestrial globe with its warm and luminous rays sank to its nocturnal repose behind the western horizon." Great writers—the true masters—have often held "fine writing" and pretentious speaking up to ridicule. Thus Shakespeare has Kent, who has been rebuked for his bluntness, indulge in a grandiloquent outburst:

> "Sir, in good sooth, in sincere verity,
> Under the allowance of your grand aspéct,
> Whose influence, like the wreath of radiant fire
> On flickering Phoebus' front,—"

No wonder Kent is interrupted with a "What meanest by this?" Sometimes great writers use ornate utterance for humorous effects. Thus Dickens again and again has Mr. Micawber express a commonplace idea in sounding terms which at length fail him, so that he must interject an "in short" and summarize his meaning in a phrase amusing through its homely contrast. But humor based on ponderous diction is too often wearisome. Better say simply "He died," or colloquially "He kicked the bucket," than "He propelled his pedal extremities with violence against the wooden pail which is customarily employed in the transportation of the aquatic fluid."

Exercise

Express these ideas in simpler language:

The temperature was excessive.
The most youthful of his offspring was not remarkable for personal pulchritude.
Henry Clay expressed a preference for being on the right side of public questions to occupying the position of President of the United States of America.

He who passes at an accelerated pace may nevertheless be capable of perusing.

A masculine member of the human race was mounted on an equine quadruped.

But the number of the terms we employ, as well as their ostentatiousness, must be considered. Most of us blunder around in the neighborhood of our meaning instead of expressing it briefly and clearly. We throw a handful of words at an idea when one word would suffice; we try to bring the idea down with a shotgun instead of a rifle. Of course one means of correction is that we should acquire accuracy, a quality already discussed. Another is that we should practice condensation.

First, let us learn to omit the words which add nothing to the meaning. Thus in the sentence "An important essential in cashing a check is that you should indorse it on the back," several words or groups of words needlessly repeat ideas which are expressed elsewhere. The sentence is as complete in substance, and far terser in form, when it reads "An essential in cashing a check is that you should indorse it."

Next, let us, when we may, reduce phrases and even clauses to a word. Thus the clause at the beginning and the phrase at the close of the following sentence constitute sheer verbiage: "Men who have let their temper get the better of them are often in a mood to do harm to somebody." The sentence tells us nothing that may not be told in five words: "Angry men are often dangerous."

Finally, let us substitute phrases or clauses for unneces-

WORDS IN COMBINATION: SOME PITFALLS

sary sentences. The following series of independent assertions contains avoidable repetitions: "One morning I was riding on the subway to my work. It was always my custom to ride to my work on the subway. This morning I met Harry Blake." The full thought may better be embodied in a single sentence: "One morning, while I was, as usual, riding on the subway to my work, I met Harry Blake."

By applying these instructions to any page at hand—one from your own writing, one from a letter some friend has sent you, one from a book or magazine—you will often be able to strike out many of the words without at all impairing the meaning. Another means of acquiring succinct expression is to practice the composition of telegrams and cable messages. You will of course lessen the cost by eliminating every word that can possibly be spared. On the other hand, you must bear it in mind that your punctuation will not be transmitted, and that the recipient must be absolutely safeguarded against reading together words meant to be separated or separating words meant to be read together. That is, your message must be both concise and unmistakably clear.

Exercise

1. Condense the editorial (Appendix 1) by eliminating unnecessary words and finding briefer equivalents for roundabout expressions.

2. Try to condense similarly the Parable of the Sower (Appendix 3) and the Seven Ages of Man (Appendix 4). (The task will largely or altogether baffle you, but will involve minute study of tersely written passages.)

3. Condense the following:

A man whose success in life was due solely to his own efforts rose in his place and addressed the man who presided over the meeting.

A girl who sat in the seat behind me giggled in an irritating manner.

We heard the wild shriek of the locomotive. Any sound in that savage region seemed more terrible than it would in civilized surroundings. So as we listened to the shriek of the locomotive, it sounded terrible too.

I heard what kind of chauffeur he was. A former employer of his told me. He was a chauffeur who speeded in reckless fashion because he was fond of having all the excitement possible.

4. Condense the following into telegrams of ten words or less:

Arrived here in Toledo yesterday morning talked with the directors found them not hostile to us but friendly.

Detectives report they think evidence now points to innocence of man arrested and to former employee as the burglar.

5. The following telegrams are ambiguous. Clarify them.

Jane escaped illness I feared Charley better.

Buy oil if market falls sell cotton.

6. Base a telegraphic night letter of not more than fifty words upon these circumstances:

(a) You have been sent to buy, if possible and as cheaply as possible, a majority of the stock in a given company. You find that many of the stockholders distrust or dislike the president and are willing to sell. Some of these ask only $50 a share for their holdings; the owners of 100 shares want as much as $92; the average price asked is $76. By buying out all the president's enemies, which you can now do beyond question, you would secure a bare majority of the stock. But $92 a share seems to you excessive; that is, you think that by working quietly among the president's friends you can get 100 shares at $77 or thereabouts and thus save approximately $1500. On the other hand, should your dealings with the friends of the president give him premature warning, he might stop the sales by these friends and himself begin buying from his enemies, and thus make your purchase of a majority of the stock impossible. Is the $1500 you would save worth the risk you would be obliged to take? You call for instructions.

(b) You are telegraphing a metropolitan paper the results of a Congressional election. Philput, the Republican candidate,

WORDS IN COMBINATION: SOME PITFALLS

leads in the cities, from which returns are now complete. Wilkins, the Democratic candidate, leads in the country, from only certain districts of which—those nearest the cities—returns have been heard. If the present proportionate division of the rural vote is maintained for the total, Philput will be elected by a plurality of three hundred votes. Philput asserts that the proportions will hold. Wilkins points out, however, that he is relatively stronger in the more remote districts and predicts that he will have a plurality of seven hundred votes. Smallbridge, an independent candidate, is apparently making a better race in the country than in the city, but he is so weak in both places that the ballots cast for him can scarcely affect the outcome unless the margin of victory is infinitesimal.

7. Compress 6a and 6b each into a telegram of not more than ten words.

8. (Do not read this assignment until you have composed the night letters and telegrams called for in 6 and 7.) Compare your first night letter in 6 and your first telegram in 7 with the versions given below. Decide where you have surpassed these versions, where you have fallen short of them.

Night letter: Two factions in company I can buy from enemies president bare majority stock at average seventy-six but hundred of these shares held at ninety-two I could probably get hundred quietly from friends president about seventy-seven but president might detect move and buy majority stock himself wire instructions. (Fifty words.)

Telegram: Wire whether buy safe or risk control saving fifteen hundred. (Ten words.)

A final device for escaping wordiness you will have discovered for yourself while composing telegrams and telegraphic night letters. It is to pass over details not vital to your purpose. Of course you must have due regard for circumstances; details needed for one purpose may be superfluous for another. But all of us are familiar with the person who loses her ideas in a rigmarole of prosaic and irrelevant facts. Such a person is Shakespeare's scatter-brained Dame Quickly. On one occasion this voluble woman is shrilly reproaching Sir

John Falstaff for his indebtedness to her. "What is the gross sum that I owe thee?" he inquires. She might answer simply: "If thou wert an honest man, thyself and the money too. Thou didst promise to marry me. Deny it if thou canst." Instead, she plunges into a prolix recital of the circumstances of the engagement, so that the all-important fact that the engagement exists has no special emphasis in her welter of words. "If thou wert an honest man," she cries, "thyself and the money too. Thou didst swear to me upon a parcel-gilt goblet, sitting in my Dolphin-chamber, at the round table, by a sea-coal fire, upon Wednesday in Wheeson week, when the prince broke thy head for liking his father to a singing-man of Windsor, thou didst swear to me then, as I was washing thy wound, to marry me and make me my lady thy wife. Canst thou deny it? Did not goodwife Keech, the butcher's wife, come in then and call me gossip Quickly? coming in to borrow a mess of vinegar; telling us she had a good dish of prawns; whereby thou didst desire to eat some, whereby I told thee they were ill for a green wound? And didst thou not, when she was gone down stairs, desire me to be no more so familiarity with such poor people; saying that ere long they should call me madam? And didst thou not kiss me and bid me fetch thee thirty shillings? I put thee now to thy book-oath; deny it if thou canst."

Exercise

1. Study the following paragraph, decide which ideas are important, and strike out the details that merely clog the thought:

As I stepped into the room, I heard the clock ticking and that caused me to look at it. It sits on the mantelpiece with some

WORDS IN COMBINATION: SOME PITFALLS

layers of paper under one corner where the mantel is warped. When the papers slip out or we move the clock a little as we're dusting, the ticking stops right away. Of course the clock's not a new one at all, but it's an old one. It has been in the family for many a long year, yes, from even before my father's time. Let me see, it was bought by my grandfather. No, it couldn't have been grandfather that bought it; it was his brother. Oh, yes, I remember now; my mother told me all about it, and I'd forgotten what she said till this minute. But really my grandfather's brother didn't exactly buy it. He just traded for it. He gave two pigs and a saddle, that's what my mother said. You see, he was afraid his hogs might take cholera and so he wanted to get rid of them; and as for the saddle, he had sold his riding-horse and he didn't have any more use for that. Well, it isn't a valuable clock, like a grandfather clock or anything of that sort, though it is antique. As I was saying, when I glanced at it, it read seven minutes to six. I remember the time very well, for just then the factory whistle blew and I remember saying to myself: "It's seven minutes slow today." You see, it's old and we don't keep it oiled, and so it's always losing time. Hardly a day passes but I set it up—sometimes twice a day, as for the matter of that—and I usually go by the factory whistle too, though now and then I go by Dwight's gold watch. Well, anyhow, that tells me what time it was. I'm certain I can't be wrong.

2. Study, on the other hand, The Castaway (Appendix 5) for its judicious use of details. Defoe in his stories is a supreme master of verisimilitude (likeness to truth). As we read him, we cannot help believing that these things actually happened. More than in anything else the secret of his lifelikeness lies in his constant faithfulness to reality. He puts in the little mishaps that would have befallen a man so situated, the things he would have done, the difficulties he might have avoided had he exercised forethought. Though Defoe had little insight into the complexities of man's inner life, he has not been surpassed in his accumulations of naturalistic outer details. These do not cumber his narrative; they contribute to its purpose and add to its effectiveness. In this selection (Appendix 5) observe how plausible are such homely details as Crusoe's seeing no sign of his comrades "except three of their hats, one cap, and two shoes that were not fellows"; as his difficulty in getting aboard the ship again; and as his having his clothes washed away by the rising of the tide. Find half a dozen other such incidents that you consider especially effective.

Verbal Discords

We may pitch our talk or our writing in almost any key we choose. Our mood may be dreamy or eager or hilarious or grim or blustering or somber or bantering or scornful or satirical or whatever we will. But once we have established the tone, we should not—except sometimes for broadly humorous effects—change it needlessly or without clear forewarning. If we do, we create one or the other of two obstacles, or both of them, for whoever is trying to follow what we say. In the first place, we obscure our meaning. For example, we have been speaking ironically and suddenly swerve into serious utterance; or we have been speaking seriously and then incongruously adopt an ironic tone. How are our listeners, our readers to take us? They are puzzled; they do not know. In the second place, we offend—perhaps in insidious, indefinable fashion—the esthetic proprieties; we violate the natural fitness of things. For example, we have been speaking with colloquial freedom, sprinkling our discourse with *shouldn't* and *won't;* suddenly we become formal and say *should not* and *will not.* Our meaning is as obvious as before, but the verbal harmony has been interrupted; our hearers or readers are uneasily aware of a break in the unity of tone.

A speaker or writer is a host to verbal guests. When he invites them to his assembly, he gives each the tacit assurance that it will not be brought into fellowship with those which in one or another of a dozen subtle ways will be uncongenial company for it. He must never be

WORDS IN COMBINATION: SOME PITFALLS

forgetful of this unspoken promise. If he is to avoid a linguistic breach, he must constantly have his wits about him; must study out his combinations carefully, and use all his knowledge, all his tact. He will make due use of spontaneous impulse; but that this may be wise and disciplined, he will form the habit of curiosity about words, their stations, their savor, their aptitudes, their limitations, their outspokenness, their reticences, their affinities and antipathies. Thus when he has need of a phrase to fill out a verbal dinner party, he will know which one to select.

Certain broad classifications of words are manifest even to the most obtuse user of English. *Shady, behead,* and *lying* are "popular" words, while their synonyms *umbrageous, decapitate,* and *mendacious* are "learned" words. *Flabbergasted* and *higgledy-piggledy* are "colloquial," while *roseate* and *whilom* are "literary." *Affidavit, allegro, lee shore,* and *pinch hit* are "technical," while *vamp, savvy, bum hunch,* and *skiddoo* are "slang." It would be disenchanting indeed were extremes of this sort brought together. But offenses of a less glaring kind are as hard to shut out as February cold from a heated house. Unusual are the speeches or compositions, even the short ones, in which every word is in keeping, is in perfect tune with the rest.

For the attainment of this ultimate verbal decorum we should have to possess knowledge almost unbounded, together with unerring artistic instinct. But diction of a kind only measurably inferior to this is possible to us if we are in earnest. To attain it we must study the difference between abstract and concrete terms, and let neither intrude unadvisedly upon the presence or functions of the other; do the same by literal and figurative terms; and instruct ourselves in the nature and significance of connotation.

Before considering these more detailed matters, however, we may pause for a general exercise on verbal harmony.

Exercise

1. Study the editorial in Appendix 1 for unforewarned changes in mood and assemblages of mutually uncongenial words. Rewrite the worst two paragraphs to remove all blemishes of these kinds.

2. Compare Burke's speech (Appendix 2) with Defoe's narrative (Appendix 5) for the difference in tone between them. Does each keep the tone it adopts (that is, except for desirable changes)?

3. Note the changes in tone in the Seven Ages of Man (Appendix 4). Do the changes in substance make these changes in tone desirable?

4. In the following passages, make such changes and omissions as are necessary to unify the tone:

> How I loved to stroll, on those long Indian summer afternoons, into the quiet meadows where the mild-breathed kine were grazing! An old cow that switches her tail at flies and puts her foot in the bucket when you milk her, I absolutely loathe. How I loved to hear the birds sing, to listen to the fall of ripe autumnal apples!

> It wasn't the girl yclept Sally. This girl was not so vivacious as Sally, but she had a mug on her that was a lot less ugly to look at. Gee, when she stood there in front of me with those mute, ineffable, sympathetic eyes of hers, I was ready to throw a duck-fit.

> Old Grimes is dead, that dear old soul;
> We'll never see him more;
> He wore a great long overcoat,
> All buttoned down before.

1. Abstract vs. Concrete Terms; General vs. Specific Terms

Abstract terms convey ideas; concrete terms call up pictures. If we say "Honesty is the best policy," we speak abstractly. Nobody can see or hear or touch the thing *honesty* or the thing *policy;* the apprehension of them must be purely intellectual. But if we say "The rat began to gnaw the rope," we speak concretely. *Rat, gnaw,* and *rope* are tangible, perceptible things; the words bring to us visions of particular objects and actions.

Now when we engage in explanations and discussions of principles, theories, broad social topics, and the like —when we expound, moralize, or philosophize,—our subject matter is general. We approach our readers or hearers on the thinking, the rational side of their natures. Our phraseology is therefore normally abstract. But when, on the other hand, we narrate an event or depict an appearance, our subject matter is specific. We approach our readers or hearers on the sensory or emotional side of their natures. Our phraseology is therefore normally concrete.

You should be able to express yourself according to either method. You should be able to choose the words best suited to make people understand; also to choose the words best suited to make people realize vividly and feel. Now to some extent you will adopt the right method by intuition. But if you do not reinforce your intuition with a careful study of words, you will vacillate from one method to the other and strike crude discords of phrasing. Of course if you switch methods intelligently and of purpose, that is quite another matter. An abstract discussion may be enlivened by a concrete illustration. A concrete narrative or portrayal may be given weight and rationalized by generalization. Moreover many things lie on the borderland between the two domains and may properly be attached to either. Thus the abstraction is legitimate when you say or write: "A man wishes to acquire the comforts and luxuries, as well as the necessaries, of life." The concreteness is likewise legitimate when you say or write: "John Smith wishes to earn cake as well as bread and butter."

In most instances general terms are the same as abstract, and specific the same as concrete. Some subtle discriminations may, however, be made. Of these the only one that need concern us here is that the wording of a passage may not be abstract and yet be general. Suppose, for example, you were telling the story of the prodigal son and should say: "He was very hungry, and could not obtain food anywhere. When he had come to his senses, he thought, 'I should be better off at home.'" This language is not abstract, but it is general rather than specific. When Jesus told the story, he wished to put the situation as poignantly as possible and therefore avoided both abstract and general terms: "And he would fain have filled his belly with the husks that the swine did eat: and no man gave unto him. And when he came to himself, he said, How many hired servants of my father's have bread enough and to spare, and I perish with hunger!" Many a person who shuns abstractions and talks altogether of the concrete things of life, yet traps out circumstance in general rather than specific terms. To do this is always to sacrifice force.

WORDS IN COMBINATION: SOME PITFALLS

Exercise

1. Discuss as abstractly as possible such topics as those listed in Exercise 1, pages 49-51, or as the following:

Is there any such thing as luck?
Is the Golden Rule practicable in the modern business world?
Is modesty rather than self-assertion regarding his own merits and abilities the better policy for an **employee**?
Are substantial, home-keeping girls or girls rather fast and frivolous the more likely to obtain good husbands?
Is it desirable for a young man to take out life insurance?
Is self-education better than collegiate training?
Should one always tell the truth?

2. Discuss as concretely as possible the topics you have selected from 1. Use illustrations drawn from life.

3. Restate in concrete terms such generalizations as the following:

Experience is the best teacher.
Self-preservation is the first law of nature.
To him who in the love of nature holds
Communion with her visible forms, she speaks
A various language.
Necessity is the mother of invention.
The bravest are the tenderest.
Vanity of vanities, all is vanity.
Pride goeth before destruction.
The evil that men do lives after them.

4. Compare the abstract statement "Truths and high ethical principles are received by various men in various ways" with the concrete presentation of the same idea in Appendix 3. Which expression of the thought would be the more easily understood by the average person? Why? Which would you yourself remember the longer? Why?

5. Compare the statement "The second period of a human being's life is that of his reluctant attendance at school" with Shakespeare's picture of the schoolboy in Appendix 4.

6. Burke, near the close of his speech (Appendix 2), presents an idea, first in general terms, and then in specific terms, thus: "No contrivance can prevent the effect of . . . distance in weakening government. Seas roll, and months pass, between the order and the execution, and the want of a speedy explanation of a single point is enough to defeat a whole system." Find else-

where in Burke's speech and in the editorial (Appendix 1) general assertions which may be made more forceful by restatement in specific terms, and supply these specific restatements.

7. State in your own words the general thought or teaching of the Parable of the Prodigal Son. (*Luke* 15: 11-24.)

8. Make the following statements more concrete:

> In front of our house was a tree that at a certain season of the year displayed highly colored foliage.
> A celebrated orator said: "Give me liberty, or give me death!"
> On the table were some viands that assailed my nostrils agreeably and others that put into my mouth sensations of anticipated enjoyment.
> From this window above the street I can hear a variety of noises by day and a variety of different noises by night.
> As he groped through the pitch-dark room he could feel many articles of furniture.

9. State in general terms the thought of the following sentences:

> A burnt child dreads the fire.
> A stitch in time saves nine.
> A cat may look at a king.
> A barking dog never bites.
> If his son ask bread, will he give him a stone?
> If two men ride a horse, one must ride behind.
> Stone walls do not a prison make.
> A merry heart goes all the day.
> Thrice is he armed that hath his quarrel just.
> As the twig is bent, so the tree is inclined.

10. Describe a town as seen from a particular point of view, or at a particular time of day, or under particular atmospheric conditions. Make your description as concrete as possible.

11. Compare your description with this from Stevenson: "The town came down the hill in a cascade of brown gables, bestridden by smooth white roofs, and spangled here and there with lighted windows." Stevenson's sentence contains twenty-five words. How many of them are "color" words? How many "motion" words? How many of the first twenty-five words in your description appeal to one or another of the five senses?

12. Narrate as vividly as possible an experience in your own life. Compare what you have written with the account of Crusoe's escape to the island (Appendix 5). Which narrative is the more concrete? How much?

2. Literal vs. Figurative Terms

Phraseology is literal when it says exactly what it means; is figurative when it says one thing, but really means another. Thus "He fought bravely" is literal; "He was a lion in the fight" is figurative. Literal phraseology as a rule appeals to our scientific or understanding faculties; figurative to our emotional faculties. Here again, as with abstraction and concreteness, you should learn to express yourself by either method.

Both have their advantages and their drawbacks. We all admire the man who has observed, and can state, accurately. It is upon this belief of ours in the literal that Defoe shrewdly traffics. (See Appendix 5.) He does not stir us as some writers do, but he gains our implicit confidence. Dame Quickly, on the contrary, makes egregious use of the literal. (See page 22.) Her facts are accurate, yes; but how strictly, how unsparingly accurate! And how many of them are beside the point! She quite convinces us that the devotee of the literal may be dull.

An advantage of the figurative also is that it may make meanings lucid. Thus when Burke near the close of his discussion (Appendix 2) wishes to make it clear that by a law of nature the authority of extensive empires is slighter in its more remote territories, he has recourse to a figure of speech: "In large bodies, the circulation of power must be less vigorous at the extremities. Nature has said it." More often, however, the function of the figurative is to drive home a thought or a mood of which a mere statement would leave us unmoved—

to make us *feel* it. Thus Burke said of the Americans: "Their love of liberty, as with you, fixed and attached on this specific point of taxing." He added: "Here they felt its pulse, and as they found that beat they thought themselves sick or sound." Had you been one of his Parliamentary hearers, would not that second sentence have made more real and more important the colonial attitude to taxation? The poets of course make frequent and noble use of the figurative. This is how Coleridge tells us that the descent of a tropical night is sudden:

> "The sun's rim dips; the stars rush out;
> At one stride comes the dark."

The words *rush out* and *at one stride comes* convert the stars and the darkness into vast beings or at least vast personal forces; the comparisons are so natural as to seem inevitable; we are transported to the very scene and feel the overwhelming abruptness of the nightfall. But if a figure of speech seems artificial, if it is strained or far-fetched or merely decorative, it subtracts from the effectiveness of the passage. Thus when Tennyson says,

> "When the breeze of a joyful dawn blew free
> In the silken sail of infancy,"

we must stop and ponder before we perceive that what he means is "When I was a happy child." The figure is like an exotic plant rather than a natural outgrowth of the soil; it appears to us something thought up and stuck on; it is a parasite rather than a helper.

Of course, as with abstraction and concreteness, you should develop facility in gliding from literalness to figurativeness and back again. But you are always to

WORDS IN COMBINATION: SOME PITFALLS

remember that your gymnastics are not to militate against verbal concord. You must never set words scowling and growling at each other through injudicious combinations like this: "She was five feet, four and three-quarter inches high, had a small, round scar between her nose and her left cheek-bone, and moved with the lissom and radiant grace of a queen."

Exercise

1. Give the specifications for a house you intend to build.
2. Make a list of comparisons (as to a nest, a haven, a goal) to show what such a house might mean in the life of a man. Expand as many of these comparisons as you can, but do not carry the process to absurd lengths. (In the figure of the nest you may mention the parent birds, their activities, the nestlings; in the figure of the haven you may mention the quiet, sheltered waters in contrast to the turbulent billows outside; in the figure of the goal you may mention the struggle necessary to reach it.)
3. Describe the looks of the house. Use as many figures of speech as you can. If you can find no appropriate figures, at least make your words specific.
4. Give a surveyor's or a tax assessor's or a conveyancer's description of a piece of land. Then describe the land through figures of speech which will vivify its outward appearance or its emotional significance to the owner.
5. Observe that the Parable of the Sower (Appendix 3) is an extended figure of speech. Is the main figure effective? Are its detailed applications effective?
6. The Seven Ages of Man (Appendix 4) is also an extended figure of speech. Does it, as Shakespeare intends, bring vividly to your consciousness the course, motives, stages, evolution of a human being's life? There are several subsidiary figures. Do these add force, definiteness to the picture Shakespeare is drawing at that moment?
7. Observe from Appendix 3, Appendix 4, and the sentences listed under Exercise 9, page 30, that a thing meant to be concrete is likely to be stated figuratively.
8. Examine The Castaway (Appendix 5) for its proportionate use of literal and figurative elements. See Exercise 2, page

23, for a statement of Defoe's purpose. Could he have effected this purpose so well had he employed more figures of speech?

9. Examine Appendix 2 for its use of figures. Are the figures appropriate to the subject matter? Are there enough of them?

10. Galvanize the thought of any sentence or paragraph in the editorial (Appendix 1) by the use of a figure of speech.

11. Summarize or illustrate your opinion on any of the topics listed in Exercise 1, pages 49-51, through the employment of a figure of speech.

12. Are these figures effective?

Man is born unto trouble, as the sparks fly upward.
The flower of our young manhood is scaling the ladder of success.

>   Fair as a star, when only one
>   Is shining in the sky.
>
>   Silence, like a poultice, comes
>   To heal the blows of sound.
>
>   In my head
>   Many thoughts of trouble come,
>   Like to flies upon a plum!

Let me tell you first about those barnacles that clog the wheels of society by poisoning the springs of rectitude with their upas-like eye.

>   The day is done, and the darkness
>   Falls from the wings of night,
>   As a feather is wafted downward
>   From an eagle in his flight.

Yea, though I walk through the valley of the shadow of death, I will fear no evil.

>   Life, like a dome of many-colored glass,
>   Stains the white radiance of eternity.

Mountains stood out like pimples or lay like broken welts across the habitable ground.

>   Life's but a walking shadow, a poor player
>   That struts and frets his hour upon the stage,
>   And then is heard no more; it is a tale
>   Told by an idiot, full of sound and fury,
>   Signifying nothing.

I saw him in Russia, where the infantry of the snow and the cavalry of the wild blast scattered his legions like winter's withered leaves.

13. Recast the following sentences to eliminate the clashing of literal and figurative elements:

Life is like a rich treasure entrusted to us, and to sustain it we must have three square meals a day.

She glanced at the mirror, but did not really see herself. She was trying to puzzle out the right course, and could only see as through a glass darkly.

Arming himself with the sword of zeal and the buckler of integrity, he wrote the letter.

He swept the floor every morning, and was a ray of sunshine in the office. He also emptied the waste baskets and cleaned the cuspidors.

3. Connotation

The connotation of a word is the subtle implication, the emotional association it carries—often quite apart from its dictionary definition. Thus the words *house* and *home* in large measure overlap in meaning, but emotionally they are not equivalents at all. You can say *house* without experiencing any sensation whatever, but if you utter the word *home* it will call back, however slightly, tender and cherished recollections. *Bald heads* and *gray hair* are both indicative of age; but you would pronounce the former in disparaging allusion to elderly persons, and the latter with sentiments of veneration. You would say, of a clodpole that he plays the *fiddle,* but of Fritz Kreisler that he plays the *violin.* And just as you unconsciously adapt words to feelings in these obvious instances, you must learn, on peril of striking false notes verbally, to do so when distinctions are less gross.

Moreover circumstance as well as sentiment may control the connotation of a word. A word or phrase may have a double or triple connotation, and depend upon vocal inflection, upon gesture, upon the words with which it is linked, upon the experience of speaker or hearer, upon time, place, and external fact, or upon other forces outside it for the sense in which it is to be taken. You may be called "old dog" in an insulting manner, or (especially if a slap on the shoulder accompanies the phrase) in an affectionate manner. You may properly say, "Calhoun had logic on his side"; add, however, the words "but his face was to the past," and you spoil the sentence,—for *face* gives a reflex connotation to *side*, slight perhaps and momentary, but disconcerting. Think over the funny stories you have heard. Many of them turn, you will find, on the outcropping of new significance in a phrase because of its environment. Thus the anecdote of the servant who had been instructed to summon the visiting English nobleman by tapping on his bedroom door and inquiring, "My lord, have you yet risen?" and who could only stammer, "My God! ain't you up yet?" Or the anecdote of the minister who in a sermon on the Parable of the Prodigal Son told how a young man living dissolutely in a city had been compelled to send to the pawnbroker first his overcoat, next his suit, next his silk shirt, and finally his very underclothing—"and then," added the minister, "he came to himself." Only by unresting vigilance can you evade verbal discords, if not of this magnitude, at least of much frequency and stylistic harm.

Exercise

1. Note the contrast in emotional suggestion that comes to you from hearing the words:

"Sodium chloride" and "salt"
"A test-tube of H_2O" and "a cup of cold water"

WORDS IN COMBINATION: SOME PITFALLS

The old homestead
Your boarding house
A scene suggesting the intense heat of a midsummer day
Night on the river
The rush for the subway car
The traffic policeman
Your boss
Anything listed in the first part of Exercise 9, page 53.

III

WORDS IN COMBINATION: HOW MASTERED

THE more dangerous pitfalls for those who use words in combination—as all of us do—have been pointed out. The best ways of avoiding these pitfalls have also been indicated. But our work together has thus far been chiefly negative. To be sure, many tasks assigned for your performance have been constructive as well as precautionary; but *the end* held ever before you has been the avoidance of feeble or ridiculous diction. In the present chapter we must take up those aspects of the mastery of words in combination which are primarily positive.

Preliminaries: General Purposes and Methods

Before coming to specific aspects and assignments, however, we shall do well to consider certain large general purposes and methods.

1. A Ready, an Accurate, or a Wide Vocabulary?

First, what kind of vocabulary do we wish to acquire? A facile, readily used one? An accurate one? Or one as nearly as may be comprehensive? The three kinds do

WORDS IN COMBINATION: HOW MASTERED

not necessarily coexist. The possession of one may even hinder and retard the acquisition of another. Thus if we seek a ready vocabulary, an accurate vocabulary may cause us to halt and hesitate for words which shall correspond with the shadings of our thought and emotion, and a wide vocabulary may embarrass us with the plenitude of our verbal riches.

But *may* is not *must*. Though the three kinds of vocabulary may interfere with each other, there is no reason, except superficially, why they should. Our purpose should be, therefore, to acquire not a single kind but all three. We should be like the boy who, when asked whether he would have a small slice of apple pie or a small slice of pumpkin pie, replied resolutely, "Thank you, I will take a large piece of both."

That the assignments in this chapter may help you develop a vocabulary which shall be promptly responsive to your needs, you should perform some of them rapidly. Your thoughts and feelings regarding a topic may be anything but clear, but you must not pause to clarify them. The words best suited to the matter may not be instantly available, but you must not tarry for accessions of language. Stumble, flounder if you must, yea, rearrange your ideas even as you present them, but press resolutely ahead, comforting yourself with the assurance that in the heat and stress of circumstances a man rarely does his work precisely as he wishes. When you have finished the discussion, repeat it immediately—and with no more loitering than before. You will find that your ideas have shifted and enlarged, and that more appropriate words have become available. Further repetitions will assist you the more. But the goal you should set yourself, as you proceed from topic to topic, is the attainment of the power to be at your best in the first discussion. You may never reach this goal, but at least you may approach it.

That the assignments in this chapter may assist you in making your vocabulary accurate, you should perform some of them in another way. When you have selected a topic, you should first of all think it through. In doing this, arrange your ideas as consistently and logically as you can, and test them with your reason. Then set them forth in language which shall be lucid and exact. Tolerate no slipshod diction, no vaguely rendered general meanings. Send every sentence, every word like a skilful drop-kick—straight above the crossbar. When you have done your best with the topic, lay it by for a space. Time is a great revealer of hidden defects, and you must not regard your labors as ended until your achievement is the maturest possible for you. If the quantity of what you accomplish is meager, suffer no distress on that account. The desideratum now is not quantity, but quality.

The assignments in this chapter will do less toward making your vocabulary wide than toward making it facile and precise. To be sure, they will now and then set you to hunting for words that are new. Better still, they will give you a mastery over some of your outlying words—words known to your eyes or ears but not to your tongue. But these advantages will be somewhat incidental. Means for the systematic extension of your verbal domain into regions as yet unexplored by you, are reserved for the later chapters of this book.

2. A Vocabulary for Speech or for Writing?

In the second place, are we to develop a vocabulary for oral discourse or a vocabulary for writing? It may be that our chief impediment or our chief ambition lies in one field rather than in the other. Nevertheless we should strive for a double mastery; we ought to speak well *and* write well. Indeed the two powers so react upon each other that we ought to cultivate both for the sake of either. True, some men, though inexpert as writers, have made themselves proficient as speakers; or though shambling and ineffective as speakers, have made themselves proficient as writers. But this is not natural or normal. Moreover these men might have gleaned more abundantly from their chosen field had they not shut it off from the acres adjacent. Fences waste space and curtail harvests.

The assignments in this chapter are of such a nature that you may perform them either orally or in writing. You should speak and write alternately, sometimes on the same topic, sometimes on topics taken in rotation.

In your oral discussions you should perhaps absent yourself at first from human auditors. A bedstead or a dresser will not make you self-conscious or in any way distract your attention, and it will permit you to sit down afterward and think out the degree of your failure or success. Ultimately, of course, you must speak to human beings—in informal conversations at the outset, in more ambitious ways later as occasion permits.

In your writing you may find it advantageous to make preliminary outlines of what you wish to say. But above all, you must be willing to blot, to revise, to take infinite pains. You should remember the old admonition that easy reading is devilish hard writing.

The Mastery of Words in Combination

These purposes and methods are general. We now come to the specific fields in which we may with profit cultivate words in combination. Of these fields there are four.

1. Mastery through Translation

If you read a foreign language, whether laboriously or with ease, you should make this power assist you to amass a good English vocabulary. Take compositions or parts of compositions written in the foreign tongue, and turn them into idiomatic English. How much you should translate at a given time depends upon your leisure and your adeptness. Employ all the methods—the spontaneous, the carefully perfected, the oral, the written—heretofore explained in this chapter. In your final work on a passage you should aim at a faultless rendition, and should spend time and ransack the lexicons rather than come short of this ideal.

The habit of translation is an excellent habit to keep up. For the study of an alien tongue not only improves your English, but has compensations in itself.

EXERCISE

1. Translate from any accessible book in the foreign language you can read.
2. Subscribe for a period of at least two or three months for a newspaper or magazine in that language, if it is a modern one.

WORDS IN COMBINATION: HOW MASTERED

Translate as before, but give most of your time to rapid oral translation for a real or imaginary American hearer.

3. When you have completed your final written translation of a passage from the foreign language, make yourself master of all the English words you have not previously (1) known or (2) used, but have encountered in your work of translation.

2. Mastery through Paraphrasing

It may be that you are not familiar with a foreign language. At any rate you have some knowledge of English. Put this knowledge to use in paraphrasing; for thus you will enrich your vocabulary and make it surer and more flexible. The process of paraphrasing is simple, though the actual work is not easy. You take passages written in English—the more of them the better, and the more diversified the better—and both reproduce their substance and incarnate their mood in words you yourself shall choose.

You may have a passage before you and paraphrase it unit by unit. More often, however, you should follow the plan adopted by Franklin when he emulated Addison by rewriting the *Spectator Papers*. That is, you should steep yourself in the thought and emotion of a piece of writing, and then lay the piece aside until its wording has faded from your memory, when you should reëmbody the substance in language that seems to you natural and fitting. Much of the benefit will come from your comparing your version, as Franklin did his, with the original. When you perceive that you have fallen short, you should consider the respects wherein your inferiority lies—and should make another attempt, and yet another, and another. When you perceive that in any way you have surpassed the original, you should feel a just pride in your achievement—and should resolve that next time your cause for pride shall be greater still. Even after you have desisted from formal paraphrasing, you should cling to the habit, formed at this time, of observing any notable felicities in whatever you read and of comparing them with the expression you yourself would likely have employed.

Exercise

1. Paraphrase the editorial in Appendix 1. You should improve upon the original. Keep trying until you do.

2. Paraphrase the second paragraph in Burke's speech (Appendix 2). Burke lacked the cheap tricks of the ordinary orator, but his discussions were based upon a comprehensive knowledge of facts, a sympathetic understanding of human nature, a vast depth and range of thought, and a well-meditated political philosophy. In short, he is a model for *elaborated* discussions. Set forth the leading thought of this paragraph; you can give it in fewer words than he employs. But try setting it forth with his full accompaniments of reflection and information; you will be bewildered at his crowding so much into such small compass.

3. Try to rival the pregnant conciseness of the Parable of the Sower (Appendix 3).

4. Paraphrase in prose the Seven Ages of Man (Appendix 4). Catch if possible the mood, the "atmosphere," of each of the pictures painted by Shakespeare. Condense your paraphrase as much as you can.

5. In each of the preceding exercises compare your vocabulary with that of the original as to size, precision, and the grace and ease with which words are put together. Does the original employ terms unfamiliar to you? If so, look up their meaning and make them yours; then observe, when you next paraphrase the passage, whether your mastery of these terms has improved your expression.

3. Mastery through Discourse at First Hand

Models have their use, but you can also work without models. It is imperative that you should. You must learn to discuss, explain, analyze, argue, narrate, and describe for yourself. Here again you should diversify your materials to the utmost, not only that you may become well-rounded and versatile in your ability to set forth ideas and feelings in words, but also that your knowledge and your sensibility may receive stimulation.

It is feasible to begin by discussing or explaining. Most of the intercourse conducted through language consists in either discussion or explanation. Analysis, ordinarily, is almost ignored. Argument is indulged in, and so is description (though less freely), but they are of the bluntest and broadest. Narration—the recounting of incidents of everyday existence—is, however, widely employed.

In your work of discussion or explanation you may seize upon any current topic—industrial, social, political, or what not—that comes into your mind. Or you may make a list of such topics, writing each on a separate piece of paper; may jumble the slips in a hat; and may thus have always at your elbow a collection of satisfactory themes from which you may take one at random. Or you may invest in language of your own selection the substance of an address or sermon you have heard, or give the burden of some important conversation in which you have participated, or explain the tenor of an article you have read. You should of course try to interest your hearers, and above all, you should impart to what you say complete clarity.

In analyzing you should select as your topic a process fairly obscure, the implications of a certain statement or argument, the results to be expected from some action or policy that has been advocated, or the exact matter at issue between two disputants. Any topic for discussion, explanation, or argument may be treated analytically. Your analysis in its final form should be so carefully considered that its soundness cannot be impeached.

In arguing you may take any subject under the sun, from baseball to Bolshevism, for all of them are debated with vehemence. Any topic for discussion or explanation becomes, when approached from some particular angle, material for argument. Thus the initial topic in the exercise that follows is "The aeroplane's future as a carrier of mail." You may convert it into a question for debate by making it read: "The aeroplane is destined to supplant the railroad as a carrier of mail," or "The aeroplane is destined to be used increasingly as a carrier of transcontinental mail." In arguing you may propose for yourself either of two objectives: (1) to silence your opponent, (2) to refute, persuade, and win him over fairly. The achievement of the first end calls for bluster and perhaps a grim, barbaric strength; you must do as Johnson did according to Goldsmith's famous dictum— if your pistol misses fire, you must knock your adversary down with the butt end of it. This procedure, though inartistic to be sure, is in some contingencies the only kind that will serve. But you should cultivate procedure of a type more urbane. Let your very reasonableness be the most potent weapon you wield. To this end you should form the habit of looking for good points on both sides of a question. As a still further precaution against contentiousness you should uphold the two sides successively.

WORDS IN COMBINATION: HOW MASTERED

In narrating you should, as a rule, stick to simple occurrences, though you may occasionally vary your work by summarizing the plot of a novel or giving the gist and drift of big historical events. You should confine yourself, in large part, to incidents in which you have been personally involved, or which you yourself have witnessed, as mishaps, unexpected encounters, bickerings, even rescues or riots. You should omit non-essentials and make the happening itself live for your hearer; if you can so interest him in it that he will not notice your manner of telling it, your success is but the greater.

Finally, in describing you should deal for the most part with beings, objects, and appearances familiar to you. Description is usually hard to make vivid. This is because the objects and scenes are likely to be immobile and (at least when told about) to lack distinctiveness. Try, therefore, to lay hold of the peculiar quality of the thing described, and use words suggestive of color and motion. Moreover be brief. Long descriptions are sure to be wearisome.

Exercise

1. Select topics from the following list for discussion or explanation:

The aeroplane's future as a carrier of mail
The commercial future of the aeroplane
A recent scientific (or mechanical or electrical) invention
A better type of newspaper—its contents and makeup
A better type of newspaper—how it can be secured
The connection between the advertising and news departments of a newspaper—the actual condition
The connection between the advertising and news departments of a newspaper—the ideal
Special features in a newspaper that are popular

A single standard for the sexes—is it possible?
A single standard for the sexes—how it can be attained (or approximated)
Should the divorce laws be made more stringent?
Should a divorced person be prohibited from remarrying?
What further marriage restrictions should be placed upon the physically or mentally unfit?
What further measures should be taken by the cities (states, nation) for the protection of motherhood?
Is the division of men into strongly contrasted groups as to wealth one of nature's necessities, or is it the result of a social and economic system?
Some shortcomings of the labor unions
Are the shortcomings of the labor unions accidental or inherent?
Some ways of bettering the condition of the working classes
How municipal (state, national) bureaus for finding employment for the laborer may become more serviceable
Wrongs committed by big business (or some branch of it)
Should a man's income above a stipulated amount be confiscated by the government?
Income taxes—what exemptions should be granted?
The right basis for business—competition or coöperation?
Are the courts equally just to labor and capital?
How can legal procedure be changed to enable individuals to secure just treatment from corporations without resorting to prolonged and expensive lawsuits?
Where our interests clash with those of Great Britain
How our relations with Great Britain may be further improved
How our relations with Japan may be further improved
How may closer commercial relations with other countries be promoted?
What to do about the railroads and railroad rates
A natural resource that should be conserved or restored
Do high tariffs breed international ill-will?
Should we have a high tariff at this juncture?
To what extent should osteopathy (chiropractic) be permitted (or protected) by law?
What is wrong with municipal government in my city
How woman suffrage affects local government
How to make rural life more attractive
The importance of the rotation of crops
The race problem as it affects my community
The class problem as it affects my community

WORDS IN COMBINATION: HOW MASTERED

The school-house as a social center
How to Americanize the alien elements in our population
To what extent, if at all, should foreign-born citizens of our country be encouraged to preserve their native traditions and culture?
Censorship of the moving picture
Educational possibilities of the moving picture
How to bring about improvement in the quality of the moving picture
The effect of the moving picture upon legitimate drama
A church that men will attend
How young men may be attracted to the churches
How far shall doctrine be insisted upon by the churches?
To what extent shall the church concern itself with social and economic problems?
To what extent, if at all, shall Sunday diversions be restricted?
The advantages of using the free public library
Can the cities give children in the slums better opportunities for physical (mental, moral) development?
Should all cities be required to establish zoölogical gardens, as well as schools, for the children?
How my city might improve its system of public parks
The most interesting thing about the work I am in
Opportunities in the work I am in
The qualities called for in the work I am in
The ideals of my associates
Something I have learned about life
Something I have learned about human nature
A book that has influenced me, and why
A person who has influenced me, and how
My favorite sport or recreation
Why baseball is so popular
What I could do for the people around me
What I should like for the people around me to do for me.

2. Discuss or explain the ideas listed in Exercise 3, page 29.

3. Analyze the debatable questions included in the two preceding exercises or suggested by them. That is, find the issues in each question, and show what each disputant must prove and what he must refute.

4. Analyze the results to be expected from the adoption of some policy or course of action by

A newspaper
A business firm

The city
The farmers
The producers in some business or industry
The consumers
The retail merchants of your city
Some group of reformers
Some social group
Those interested in a social activity, as dancing
Your neighbors
Yourself.

5. Analyze or explain

The testing of seed grain
How to raise potatoes (any other vegetable)
How to utilize and apportion the space in your garden
How to keep an automobile in good shape
How to run an automobile (motor boat)
How to make a rabbit trap
How to lay out a camp
How to catch trout (bass, codfish, tuna fish, lobsters)
How to conduct a public meeting
How a bill is introduced and passed in a legislative body
How food is digested
How to extract oxygen from water
How a fish breathes
How gold is mined
How wireless messages are sent
How your favorite game is played
How to survey a tract of land
How stocks are bought and sold on margins
How public opinion is formed
How a man ought to form his opinions
The responsibility of individuals to society
The responsibility of society to the individual.

6. Argue one side or the other, or the two successively, of queries contained or implied in Exercises 1 and 2.

7. Argue one side or the other, or the two successively, of queries listed in Exercise 1, page 29.

8. Give a narrative of

The earning of your first dollar
How somebody met his match
An amusing incident
An anxious moment
A surprise

WORDS IN COMBINATION: HOW MASTERED 53

The touchdown
That fatal seventh inning
How you got the position
Why you missed the train
When you were lost
Your first trip on the railroad (a motor boat, a merry-go-round, snowshoes, a burro)
A mishap
How Jenkins skated
Your life until the present (a summary)
Something you have heard your father tell
What happened to your uncle
Your partner's (chum's) escapade
Meeting an old friend
Meeting a bore
A conversation you have overheard
When Myrtle eavesdropped
When the girls didn't know Algy was in the parlor
A public happening that interests you
An incident you have read in the papers
An incident from your favorite novel
Backward Ben at the party
Something that happened to you today.

9. Describe

For the mood or general "atmosphere":
   Anything you deem suitable in Exercise 8, pages 38-39
   An old, deserted house
   Your birthplace as you saw it in manhood
   The view from an eminence
   A city as seen from a roof garden by night
   Your mother's Bible
   A barnyard scene
   The lonely old negro at the supper table
   A new immigrant gazing out upon the ocean he has crossed
   The downtown section at closing hour
   A scene of quietude
   A scene of bustle and confusion
   A richly colored scene
   A scene of dejection
   A scene of wild enthusiasm
   A scene of dulness or stagnation.

With attention to homely detail:
   The old living-room
   My aunt's dresses

Barker's riding-horse
The business street of the village
A cabin in the mountains
The office of a man approaching bankruptcy
The Potters' backyard
The second-hand store
The ugliest man.

For general accuracy and vividness:

The organ-grinder
The signs of an approaching storm
The arrival of the train
Mail-time at the village post office
The crowd at the auction
The old fishing-boat
A country fair (or a circus)
The inside of a theater (or a church)
The funeral procession
The political rally
The choir.

4. Mastery through Adapting Discourse to Audience

For convenience, we have heretofore assumed that ideas and emotions, together with such expression of them as shall be in itself adequate and faithful, comprise the sole elements that have to be reckoned with in the use of words in combination. But as you go out into life you will find that these things, however complete they may seem, are not in practice sufficient. Another factor—the human—must have its place in our equation. You do not speak or write in a vacuum. Your object, your ultimate object at least, in building up your vocabulary is to address men and women; and among men and women the varieties of training, of stations, of outlooks, of sentiments, of prejudices, of caprices are infinite. To gain an unbiased hearing you must take persistent cognizance of flesh and blood.

WORDS IN COMBINATION: HOW MASTERED

In adapting discourse to audience you must have a supple and attentive mind and an impressionable and swiftly responsive temperament as well as a wide, accurate, and flexible vocabulary. Unless you are a fool, a zealot, or an incorrigible adventurer, you will not broach a subject at all to which your hearers feel absolute indifference or hostility. Normally you should pick a subject capable of interesting them. In presenting it you should pay heed to both your matter and your manner. You should emphasize for your listeners those aspects of the subject which they will most respond to or most need to hear, whether or not the phases be such as you would emphasize with other auditors. You should also speak in the fashion you deem most effective with them, whether or not it be one to which your own natural instincts prompt you.

Let us say you are discussing conditions in Europe. You must speak in one way to the man who has traveled and in an entirely different way to the man who has never gone abroad—in one way to the well-read man, in an entirely different way to the ignoramus. Let us say you are discussing urban life, urban problems. You must speak in one way to the man who lives in the city, in another to the man who lives in the country. Let us say you are discussing the labor problem. You must speak in one way to employers, in another to employees, possibly in a third to men thrown out of jobs, possibly in a fourth to the general public. Let us say you are discussing education, or literature, or social tendencies, or mechanical principles or processes, or some great enterprise or movement. You must speak in one way to cultivated hearers and in another to men in the street, and if you are a specialist addressing specialists, you will cut the garment of your discourse to their particular measure.

The same principle holds regardless of whether you expound, analyze, argue, recount, or describe. You must always keep a finger on the mental or emotional pulse of those whom you address. But your problem varies slightly with the form of discourse you adopt. In explanation, analysis, and argument the chief barriers you encounter are likely to be those of the mind; you must make due allowance for the intellectual limitations of your auditors, though many who have capacity enough may for some cause or other be unreceptive to ideas. In description you must reckon with the imaginative faculty, with the possibility that your hearers cannot visualize what you tell them—and you must make your words brief. In narration you must vivify emotional torpor; but lest in your efforts to inveigle boredom you yourself should induce it, you must have a wary eye for signals of distress.

Exercise

1. Explain to (a) a rich man, (b) a poor man the blessings of poverty.

2. Discuss before (a) farmers, (b) merchants the idea that farmers (merchants) make a great deal of money.

3. Explain to (a) the initiate, (b) the uninitiate some piece of mechanism, or some phase of a human activity or interest, which you know at first hand and regarding which technical (or at least not generally understood) terms are employed. (The exact subject depends, of course, upon your own observation or experience; you are sure to be familiar with something that most people know hazily, if at all. Bank clerk, chess player, bridge player, stenographer, journalist, truck driver, backwoodsman, mechanic—all have special knowledge of one kind or another and can use the particular terms it calls for.)

WORDS IN COMBINATION: HOW MASTERED

4. Explain to (a) a supporter of the winning team, (b) a supporter of the losing team why the baseball game came out as it did.

5. Discuss before (a) a Democratic, (b) a Republican audience your reasons for voting the Democratic (Republican) ticket in the coming election.

6. Explain to (a) your own family, (b) the man who can lend you the money, why you wish to mortgage your house (any piece of property).

7. Explain to the owner of an ill-conducted business why he should sell it, and to a shrewd business man why he should buy it.

8. Discuss before (a) old men, (b) young men, (c) women the desirability of men's giving up their seats in street cars to women. (Also modify the question by requiring only young men to give up their seats, and then only to old people of either sex, to sick people, or to people with children in their arms.)

9. Explain the necessity of restricting immigration to (a) prospective immigrants, (b) immigrants just granted admission to the country, (c) persons just refused admission, (d) exploiters of cheap labor, (e) ordinary citizens.

10. Discuss the taking out of a life insurance policy with (a) a man not interested, (b) a man interested but uncertain what a policy is like, (c) a man interested and informed but doubtful whether he can spare the money, (d) the man's wife (his prospective beneficiary), whose desires will have weight with him.

11. Discuss the necessity of a reduction in wages with (a) unscrupulous employers, (b) kind-hearted employers, (c) the employees.

12. Advocate higher public school taxes before (a) men with children, (b) men without children.

13. Advocate a further regulation of the speed of automobiles before (a) automobile-owners, (b) non-owners.

14. Urge advocacy of some reform upon (a) a clergyman, (b) a candidate for office.

15. Combat before (a) advertisers, (b) a public audience, (c) a lawmaking body, the defacement of landscapes by advertising billboards.

16. Describe life in the slums before (a) a rural audience, (b) charitable persons, (c) rich people in the cities who know little of conditions among the poor.

17. Describe the typical evening of a spendthrift in a city to (a) a poor man, (b) a miser, (c) the spendthrift's mother, (d) his employer, (e) a detective who suspects him of theft.

18. Describe the city of Washington (any other city) to (a) a countryman, (b) a traveler who has not visited this particular city. (If it is Washington you describe, describe it also for children in whom you wish to inculcate patriotism.)

19. Give (a) a youngster, (b) an experienced angler an account of your fishing trip.

20. Recount for (a) a baseball fan, (b) a girl who has never seen a game, the occurrences of the second half of the ninth inning.

21. Describe a fight for (a) your friends, (b) a jury.

22. Narrate for (a) children, (b) an audience of adults some historical event.

23. Give (a) your partner, (b) a reporter an account of a business transaction you have just completed.

24. Narrate an escapade for (a) your father, (b) your cronies in response to a toast at a banquet with them.

IV

INDIVIDUAL WORDS: AS VERBAL CELIBATES

THUS far we have studied words as grouped together into phrases, sentences, paragraphs, whole compositions. We must now enter upon a new phase of our efforts to extend our vocabulary. We must study words as individual entities.

You may think the order of our study should be reversed. No great harm would result if it were. The learning of individual words and the combining of them into sentences are parallel rather than successive processes. In our babyhood we do not accumulate a large stock of terms before we frame phrases and clauses. And our attainment of the power of continuous iteration does not check our inroads among individual words. We do the two things simultaneously, each contributing to our success with the other. There are plenty of analogies for this procedure. A good baseball player, for instance, tirelessly studies both the minutiæ of his technique (as how to hold a bat, how to stand at the plate) and the big combinations and possibilities of the game. A good musician keeps unremitting command over every possible touch of each key and at the same time seeks sweeping mastery over vast and complex harmonies. So we, if we would have the obedience of our vocabularies, dare not lag into desultory attention to either words when disjoined or words as potentially combined into the larger units of thought and feeling.

We might therefore consider either the individuals first or the groups first. But the majority of speakers and writers pay more heed to rough general substance than to separate instruments and items. Hence we have thought best to begin where most work is going on already—with words in combination.

As you turn from the groups to the individuals, you must understand that your labors will be onerous and detailed. You must not assume that by nature all words are much alike, any more than you assume that all men are much alike. Of course the similarities are many and striking, and the fundamental fact is that a word is a word as a man is a man. But you will be no adept in handling either the one or the other until your knowledge goes much farther than this. Let us glance first at the human variations. Each man has his own business, and conducts it in his own way—a way never absolutely matched with that of any other mortal being. All this you may see. But besides the man's visible employment, he may be connected in devious fashions with a score of enterprises the public knows nothing about. Furthermore he leads a private life (again not precisely corresponding to that of any other), has his hobbies and aversions, is stamped with a character, a temperament of his own. In short, though in thousands of respects he is like his fellows, he has after all no human counterpart; he is a distinct, individual self. To know him, to use him, to count upon his service in whatsoever contingency it might bestead you, you must deem him something more than a member of the great human family. You must cultivate him personally, cultivate him without weariness or stint, and undergo inconvenience in so doing.

Even so with a word. Commonplace enough it may seem. But it has its peculiar characteristics, its activities undisclosed except to the curious, its subtle inclinations, its repugnances, its latent potentialities. There is no precise duplicate for it in all the wide domain of language. To know it intimately and thoroughly, to be on entirely free terms with it, to depend upon it just so far as dependence is safe, to have a sure understanding of what it can do and what it cannot, you must arduously cultivate it. Words, like people, yield themselves to the worthy. They hunger for friendship—and lack the last barrier of reserve which hedges all human communion. Thus, linguistically speaking, you must search out the individuals. You must step aside from your way for the sake of a new acquaintance; in conversations, in sermons, in addresses, in letters, in journalistic columns, in standard literature you must grasp the stranger by the hand and look him straight in the eye. Nor must you treat cavalierly the words you know already. You must study them afresh; you must learn them over and learn them better; you must come to understand them, not only for what they are, but for what they will do.

What Words to Learn First

What, then, is your first task? Somebody has laid down the injunction—and, as always when anything is enjoined, others have given it currency—that each day you should learn two new words. So be it,—but which two? The first two in the dictionary, or hitherto left untouched in your systematic conquest of the dictionary? The first two you hear spoken? The first two that stare at you from casual, everyday print? The first two you can ferret from some technical jargon, some special department of human interest or endeavor? In any of these ways you may obey the behest of these mentors. But are not such ways arbitrary, haphazard? And suppose, after doing your daily stint, you should encounter a word it behooves you to know. What then? Are you to sulk, to withhold yourself from further exertion on the plea of a vocabulary-builder's eight-hour day?

To adopt any of the methods designated would be like resolving to invest in city lots and then buying properties as you encountered them, with no regard for expenditure, for value in general, or for special serviceability to you. Surely such procedure would be unbusinesslike. If you pay out good money, you meditate well whether that which you receive for it shall compensate you. Likewise if you devote time and effort to gaining ownership of words, you should exercise foresight in determining whether they will yield you commensurate returns.

What, then, is the principle upon which, at the outset, you should proceed? What better than to insure the possession of the words regarding which you know this already, that you need them and should make them yours?

The Analysis of Your Own Vocabulary

The natural way, and the best, to begin is with an analysis of your own vocabulary. You are of course

INDIVIDUAL WORDS: AS VERBAL CELIBATES

aware that of the enormous number of words contained in the dictionary relatively few are at your beck and bidding. But probably you have made no attempt to ascertain the nature and extent of your actual linguistic resources. You should make an inventory of the stock on hand before sending in your order for additional goods.

You will speedily discover that your vocabulary embraces several distinct classes of words. Of these the first consists of those words which you have at your tongue's end—which you can summon without effort and use in your daily speech. They are old verbal friends. Numbered with them, to be sure, there may be a few with senses and connotations you are ignorant of—friends of yours, let us say, with a reservation. Even these you may woo with a little care into uncurbed fraternal abandon. With the exception of these few, you know the words of the first class so well that without thinking about it at all you may rely upon their giving you, the moment you need them, their untempered, uttermost service. You need be at no further pains about them. They are yours already.

A second class of words is made up of those you speak on occasions either special or formal—occasions when you are trying, perhaps not to show off, but at least to put your best linguistic foot foremost. Some of them have a meaning you are not quite sure of; some of them seem too ostentatious for workaday purposes; some of them you might have been using but somehow have not. Words of this class are not your bosom friends. They are your speaking acquaintance, or perhaps a little better than that. You must convert them into friends, into prompt and staunch supporters in time of need. That is to say, you must put them into class one. In bringing about this change of footing, you yourself must make the advances. You must say, Go to, I will bear them in mind as I would a person I wished to cultivate. When occasion rises, you must introduce them into your talk. You will feel a bit shy about it, for introductions are difficult to accomplish gracefully; you will steal a furtive glance at your hearer perchance, and another at the word itself, as you would when first labeling a man "my friend Mr. Blank." But the embarrassment is momentary, and there is no other way. Assume a friendship if you have it not, and presently the friendship will be real. You must be steadfast in intention; for the words that have held aloof from you are many, and to unloose all at once on a single victim would well-nigh brand you criminal. But you will make sure headway, and will be conscious besides that no other class of words in the language will so well repay the mastering. For these are words you *do* use, and need to use more, and more freely —words your own experience stamps as valuable, if not indeed vital, to you.

The third class of words is made up of those you do not speak at all, but sometimes write. They are acquaintance one degree farther removed than those of the second class. Your task is to bring them into class two and thence into class one—that is, to introduce them into your more formal speech, and from this gradually into your everyday speech.

The fourth class of words is made up of those you recognize when you hear or read them, but yourself never employ. They are acquaintance of a very distant kind. You nod to them, let us say, and they to you; but there the intercourse ends. Obviously, they are not to be brought without considerable effort into a position of tried and trusted friendship. And shall we be absolutely honest?—some of them may not justify such assiduous care as their complete subjugation would call for. But even these you should make your feudal retainers. You should constrain them to membership in class three, and at your discretion in class two.

Apart from the words in class four, you will not to this point have made actual additions to your vocabulary. But you will have made your vocabulary infinitely more serviceable. You will be like a man with a host of friends where before, when his necessities were sorest, he found (along with some friends) many distant and timid acquaintance.

Outside the bounds of your present vocabulary altogether are the words you encounter but do not recognize, except (it may be) dimly and uncertainly. Some counselors would have you look up all such words in a dictionary. But the task would be irksome. Moreover those who prescribe it are loath to perform it themselves. Your own candid judgment in the matter is the safest guide. If the word is incidental rather than vital to the meaning of the passage that contains it, and if it gives promise of but rarely crossing your vision again, you should deign it no more than a civil glance. Plenty of ways will be left you to expend time wisely in the service of your vocabulary.

Exercise

1. Make a list of the words in class two of your own vocabulary, and similar lists for classes three and four. (To make

a list for class one would be but a waste of time.) Procure if you can for this purpose a loose-leaf notebook, and in the several lists reserve a full page for each letter of the alphabet as used initially. Do not scamp the lists, though their proper preparation consume many days, many weeks. Try to make them really exhaustive. Their value will be in proportion to their accuracy and fulness.

2. Con the words in each list carefully and repeatedly. Your task is to transfer these words into a more intimate list—those in class four into class three, those in three into two, those in two into one. You are then to promote again the words in the lower classes, except that (if your judgment so dictates) you may leave the new class three wholly or partially intact. To carry out this exercise properly you must keep these words in mind, make them part and parcel of your daily life. (For a special device for bringing them under subjection, see the next exercise.)

3. To write a word down helps you to remember it. That is why the normal way to transfer a word from class four into class two is to put it temporarily into the intermediary class, three; you first *see* or *hear* the word, next *write* it, afterwards *speak* it. The mere writing down of your lists has probably done much to bring the words written into the circuit of your memory, where you can more readily lay hold of them. Also it has fortified your confidence in using them; for to write a word out, letter by letter, makes you surer that you have its right form. With many of your words you will likely have no more trouble; they will be at hand, anxious for employment, and you may use them according to your need. But some of your words will still stubbornly withhold themselves from memory. Weed these out from your lists, make a special list of them, copy it frequently, construct short sentences into which the troublesome words fit. By dint of writing the words so often you will soon make them more tractable.

4. Make a fifth list of words—those you hear or see printed, do not understand the meaning of, but yet feel you should know. Obtain and confirm a grasp of them by the successive processes used with words in the preceding lists.

The Definition of Words

Another means of buttressing your command of your present vocabulary is to define words you use or are familiar with.

INDIVIDUAL WORDS: AS VERBAL CELIBATES

Do not bewilder yourself with words (like *and, the*) which call for ingenuity in handling somewhat technical terms, or with words (like *thing, affair, condition*) which loosely cover a multitude of meanings. (You may, however, concentrate your efforts upon some one meaning of words in the latter group.) Select words with a fairly definite signification, and express this as precisely as you can. You may afterwards consult a dictionary for means of checking up on what you have done. But in consulting it think only of idea, not of form. You are not training yourself in dictionary definitions, but in the sharpness and clarity of your understanding of meanings.

About the only rule to be laid down regarding the definition of verbs, adjectives, and adverbs is that you must not define a word in terms of itself. Thus if you define *grudgingly* as "in a grudging manner," you do not dissipate your hearer's uncertainty as to what the word means. If you define it as "unwillingly" or "in a manner that shows reluctance to yield possession," you give your hearer a clear-cut idea in no wise dependent upon his ability to understand the word that puzzled him in the first place.

Normally, in defining a noun you should assign the thing named to a general class, and to its special limits within that class; in other words, you should designate its genus and species. You must take care to differentiate the species from all others comprised within the genus. You will, in most instances, first indicate the genus and then the species, but at your convenience you may indicate the species first. Thus if you affirm, "A cigar is smoking-tobacco in the form of a roll of tobacco-leaves," you name the genus first and later the characteristics of the species. You have given a satisfactory definition. If on the other hand you affirm, "A cigar is a roll of tobacco-leaves meant for smoking," you first designate the species and then merely imply the genus. Again you have given a satisfactory definition; for you have permitted no doubt that the genus is smoking-tobacco, and have prescribed such limits for the species as exclude tobacco intended for a pipe or a cigarette.

In defining nouns by the genus-and-species method, restrict the genus to the narrowest possible bounds. You will thus save the need for exclusions later. Had you in your first definition of a cigar begun by saying that it is tobacco, rather than smoking-tobacco, you would have violated this principle; and you would have had to amplify the rest of your definition in order to exclude chewing-tobacco, snuff, and the like.

Exercise

1. Define words of your own choosing in accordance with the principles laid down in the preceding section of the text.
2. Define the following adjectives, adverbs, and verbs:

Miserable	Rebuke	Wise
Angrily	Rapidly	Boundless
Swim	Paint	Whiten
Haughtily	Surly	Causelessly

3. So define the following nouns as to prevent any possible confusion with the nouns following them in parentheses:

Wages (salary)
Planet (star)
Watch (clock)
Jail (penitentiary)
Vegetable (fruit)
Flower (weed)
Ride (drive)
Truck (automobile)
Reins (lines)
Iron (steel)
Timber (lumber)
Rope (string)

INDIVIDUAL WORDS: AS VERBAL CELIBATES 69

Hail (sleet, snow)
Newspaper (magazine)
Cloud (fog)
Mountain (hill)
Letter (postal card)

Stock (bond)
Street car (railway coach)
Revolver (rifle, pistol, etc.)
Creek (river)

4. While remembering that the following words are of broad signification and mean different things to different people, define them according to their meaning to you:

Gentleman
Honesty
Honor
Generosity
Charity
Modesty

Courage
Beauty
Good manners
A good while
A little distance
Long ago

How to Look Up a Word in the Dictionary

So much for the words which are already yours, or which you can make yours through your own unaided efforts. For convenience we have grouped with them some words of a nature more baffling—words of which you know perhaps but a single aspect rather than the totality, or upon which you can obtain but a feeble and precarious grip. These slightly known words belong more to the class now to be considered than to that just disposed of. For we have now to deal with words over which you can establish no genuine rulership unless you have outside help.

You must own a dictionary, have it by you, consult it carefully and often. Do not select one for purchasing upon the basis of either mere bigness or cheapness. If you do, you may make yourself the owner of an out-of-date reprint from stereotyped plates. What to choose depends partly upon personal preference, partly upon whether your need is for comprehensiveness or compression. If you are a scholar, *Murray's* many-volumed *New English Dictionary* may be the publication for you; but if you are an ordinary person, you will probably content yourself with something less expensive and exhaustive. You will find the *Century Dictionary and Cyclopedia,* in twelve volumes, or *Webster's New International Dictionary* an admirable compilation. The *New Standard Dictionary* will also prove useful. All in all, if you can afford it, you should provide yourself with one or the other of these three large and authoritative, but not too inclusive, works. Of the smaller lexicons *Webster's Collegiate Dictionary, Webster's Secondary School Dictionary,* the *Practical Standard Dictionary,* and the *Desk Standard Dictionary* answer most purposes well.

A dictionary is not for show. You must learn to use it. What ordinarily passes for use is in fact abuse. Wherein? Let us say that you turn to your lexicon for the meaning of a word. Of the various definitions given, you disregard all save the one which enables the word to make sense in its present context, or which fits your preconception of what the word should stand for. Having engaged in this solemn mummery, you mentally record the fact that you have been squandering your time, and enter into a compact with yourself that no more will you so do. At best you have tided over a transitory need, or have verified a surmise. You have not truly *learned* the word, brought it into a vassal's relationship with you, so fixed it in memory that henceforth, night or day, you can take it up like a familiar tool.

This procedure is blundering, farcical, futile, incorrect. To suppose you have learned a word by so cursory a

INDIVIDUAL WORDS: AS VERBAL CELIBATES

glance at its resources is like supposing you have learned a man through having had him render you some temporary and trivial service, as lending you a match or telling you the time of day. To acquaint yourself thoroughly with a word—or a man—involves effort, application. You must go about the work seriously, intelligently.

One secret of consulting a dictionary properly lies in finding the primary, the original meaning of the word. You must go to the source. If the word is of recent formation, and is native rather than naturalized English, you have only to look through the definitions given. Such a word will not cause you much trouble. But if the word is derived from primitive English or from a foreign language, you must seek its origin, not in one of the numbered subheads of the definition, but in an etymological record you will perceive within brackets or parentheses. Here you will find the Anglo-Saxon (Old English), Latin, Greek, French, German, Italian, Scandinavian, or other word from which sprang the word you are studying, and along with this authentic original you may find cognate words in other languages. These you may examine if you care to observe their resemblance to your word, but the examination is not necessary. It could teach you only the earlier or other *forms* of your word, whereas what you are after is the original *meaning*. This too is set down within the brackets; if your search is in earnest, you cannot possible miss it. And having discovered this original meaning, you must get it in mind; it is one of the really significant things about the word.

Your next step is to find the present import of the

word. Look, therefore, through the modern definitions. Of these there may be too many, with too delicate shadings in thought between them, for you to keep all clearly in mind. In fact you need not try. Consider them of course, but out of them seek mainly the drift, the central meaning. After a little practice you will be able to disengage it from the others.

You now know the original sense of the word and its central signification today. The two may be identical; they may be widely different; but through reflection or study of the entire definition you will establish some sort of connection between them. When you have done this, you have mastered the word. From the two meanings you can surmise the others, wherever and whenever encountered; for the others are but outgrowths and applications of them.

One warning will not be amiss. You must not suppose that the terms used in defining a word are its absolute synonyms, or may be substituted for it indiscriminately. You must develop a feeling for *the limits* of the word, so that you may perceive where its likeness to the other terms leaves off and its unlikeness begins. Thus if one of the terms employed in defining *command* is *control,* you must not assume that the two words are interchangeable; you must not say, for instance, that the captain controlled his men to present arms.

Such, abstractly stated, is the way to look up a word in the dictionary. Let us now take a concrete illustration. Starting with the word *tension,* let us ascertain what we can about it in the *Century Dictionary and Cyclopedia.* Our first quest is the original meaning. For this we consult the bracketed matter. There we meet the French,

INDIVIDUAL WORDS: AS VERBAL CELIBATES

Spanish, Portuguese, and Italian kinsmen of the word, and learn that they are traceable to a common ancestor, the Latin *tensio(n)*, which comes from the Latin verb *tendere*. The meaning of *tensio(n)* is given as "stretching," that of *tendere* as "stretch," "extend." Thus we know of the original word that in form it closely resembles the modern word, and that in meaning it involves the idea of stretching.

What is the central meaning of the word today? To acquaint ourselves with this we must run through the definitions listed. Here (in condensed form) they are. (1) The act of stretching. (2) In *mechanics,* stress or the force by which something is pulled. (3) In *physics,* a constrained condition of the particles of bodies. (4) In *statical electricity,* surface-density. (5) Mental strain, stress, or application. (6) A strained state of any kind, as political or social. (7) An attachment to a sewing-machine for regulating the strain of the thread. Now of these definitions (2), (3), (4), and (7) are too highly specialized to conduct us, of themselves, into the highway of the word's meaning. They bear out, however, the evidence of (1), (5), and (6), which have as their core the idea of stretching, or of the strain which stretching produces.

We must now lay the original meaning alongside the central meaning today, in order to draw our conclusions. We perceive that the two meanings correspond. Yet by prying into them we make out one marked difference between them. The original meaning is literal, the modern largely figurative. To be sure, the figure has been so long used that it is now scarcely felt as a figure; its force and definiteness have departed. Consequently we may speak of being on a tension without having in mind at all a comparison of our nervous system with a stretched garment, or with an outreaching arm, or with a tightly strung musical instrument, or with a taut rope.

What, then, is the net result of our investigation? Simply this, that *tension* means stretching, and that the stretching may be conceived either literally or figuratively. With these two facts in mind, we need not (unless we are experts in mechanics, physics, statical electricity, or the sewing-machine) go to the trouble of committing the special senses of *tension;* for should occasion bid, we can —from our position at the heart of the word—easily grasp their rough purport. And from other persons than specialists no more would be required.

Exercise

1. For each of the following words find (a) the original meaning, (b) the central meaning today. (Other words are given in the exercises at the end of this chapter.)

Bias	Supersede	Sly
Aversion	Capital	Meerschaum
Extravagant	Travel	Alley
Concur	Travail	Fee
Attention	Apprehend	Superb
Magnanimity	Lewd	Adroit
Altruism	Instigation	Quite
Benevolence	Complexion	Urchin
Charity	Bishop	Thoroughfare
Unction	Starve	Naughty
Speed	Cunning	Moral
Success	Decent	Antic
Crafty	Handsome	Savage
Usury	Solemn	Uncouth
Costume	Parlor	Window
Presumption	Bombastic	Colleague
Petty	Vixen	Alderman
Queen	Doctor	Engage

INDIVIDUAL WORDS: AS VERBAL CELIBATES 75

Prying Into a Word's Past

To thread with minute fidelity the mazes of a word's former history is the task of the linguistic scholar; our province is the practical and the present-day. But words, like men, are largely what they are because of what they have been; and to turn a gossip's eye upon their past is to procure for ourselves, often, not only enlightenment but also entertainment. This fact, though brought out in some part already, deserves separate and fuller discussion.

In the first place, curiosity as to words' past experience enables us to read with keener understanding the literature of preceding ages. Of course we should not, even so, go farther back than about three centuries. To read anything earlier than Shakespeare would require us to delve too deeply into linguistic bygones. And to read Shakespeare himself requires effort—but rewards it. Let us see how an insight into words will help us to interpret the Seven Ages of Man (Appendix 4).

In line 2 of this passage appears the word *merely*. In Shakespeare's time it frequently meant "altogether" or "that and nothing else." As here used, it may be taken to mean this, or to have its modern meaning, or to stand in meaning midway between the two and to be suggestive of both; there is no way of determining precisely. In line 12 the word *pard* means leopard. In line 18 *saws* means "sayings" (compare the phrase "an old saw"); *modern* means "moderate," "commonplace"; *instances* means what we mean by it today, "examples," "illustrations." (Line 18 as a whole gives us a vivid sense of the justice's readiness to speak sapiently, after the manner of justices, and to trot out his trite illustrations on the slightest provocation.) The word *pantaloon* in line 20 is interesting. The patron saint of Venice was St. Pantaleon (the term is from Greek, means "all-lion," and possibly refers to the lion of St. Mark's Cathedral). *Pantaloon* came therefore to signify (1) a Venetian, (2) a garment worn by Venetians and consisting of breeches and stockings in one. The second sense is preserved, substantially, in our term *pantaloons*. The first sense led to the use of the word (in the mouths of the Venetians' enemies) for "buffoon" and then (in early Italian comedy) for "a lean and foolish old man." It is this stock figure of the stage that Shakespeare evokes. In line 22 *hose* means the covering for a man's body from his waist to his nether-stock. (Compare the present meaning: a covering for the feet and the *lower* part of the legs.) In line 27 *mere* means "absolute." In line 28 *sans* means "without."

Of the words we have examined, only *sans* is obsolete, though *pard, saws,* and *pantaloon* are perhaps not entirely familiar. That is, only one word in the passage, so far as its outward form goes, is completely alien to our knowledge. But how different the matter stands when we consider meanings! The words are words of today, but the meanings are the meanings of Shakespeare. We should be baffled and misled as to the dramatist's thought if we had made no inquiries into the vehicle therefor.

In the second place, to look beyond the present into the more remote signification of words will put us on our guard against the reappearance of submerged or half-

INDIVIDUAL WORDS: AS VERBAL CELIBATES 77

forgotten meanings. We have seen that the word *tension* may be used without conscious connection with the idea of stretching. But if we incautiously place the word in the wrong environment, the idea will be resurrected to our undoing. We associate *ardor* with strong and eager desire. For ordinary purposes this conception of the word suffices. But *ardor* is one of the children of fire; its primary sense is "burning" (compare *arson*). Therefore to pronounce the three vocables "overflowing with ardor" is to mix figures of speech absurdly. We should fall into a similar mistake if we said "brilliant fluency," and into a mistake of another kind (that of tautology or repetition of an idea) if we said "heart-felt cordiality," for *cordiality* means "feelings of the heart." *Appreciate* means "set a (due) value on." We may perhaps say "really appreciate," but scrupulous writers and speakers do not say "appreciate very much." A *humor* (compare *humid*) was once a "moisture"; then one of the four moistures or liquids that entered into the human constitution and by the proportions of their admixture determined human temperament; next a man's outstanding temperamental quality (the thing itself rather than the cause of it); then oddity which people may laugh at; then the spirit of laughter and good nature in general. Normally we do not connect the idea of moisture with the word. We may even speak of "a dry humor." But we should not say "now and then a dry humor crops out," for then too many buried meanings lie in the same grave for the very dead to rest peacefully together.

Even apart from reading old literature and from having, when you use words, no ghosts of their pristine selves rise up to damn you, you may profit from a knowledge of how the meaning of a term has evolved. For example, you will meet many tokens and reminders of the customs and beliefs of our ancestors. Thus *coxcomb* carries you back to the days when every court was amused by a "fool" whose head was decked with a cock's comb; *crestfallen* takes you back to cockfighting; and *lunatic* ("moonstruck"), *disaster* ("evil star"), and "thank your lucky stars" plant you in the era of superstition when human fate was governed by heavenly bodies.

Further, you will perceive the poetry of words. Thus to *wheedle* is to wag the tail and to *patter* is to hurry through one's prayers (paternoster). What a picture of the frailty of men even in their holiness flashes on us from that word *patter!* *Breakfast* is the breaking of the fast of the night. *Routine* (the most humdrum of words) is travel along a way already broken. *Goodby* is an abridged form of "God be with you." *Dilapidated* is fallen stone from stone. *Daisy* is "the day's eye," *nasturtium* (from its spicy smell) "the nose-twister," *dandelion* "the tooth of the lion." A *lord* is a bread-guard.

You will perceive, moreover, that many a dignified word once involved the same idea as some unassuming or even semi-disreputable word or expression involves now. Thus there is little or no difference in figure between understanding a thing and getting on to it; between averting something (turning it aside) and sidetracking it; between excluding (shutting out) and closing the door to; between degrading (putting down a step) and taking down a notch; between accumulating (heaping up) and making one's pile; between taking umbrage (the shadow) and being thrown in the shade; between ejaculating and throwing out a remark; between being on a tension and being highstrung; between being vapid and having lost steam; between insinuating (winding in) and worming in; between investigating and tracking; between instigating (goading on or into) and prodding up; between being incensed (compare *incendiary*) and burning with indignation; between recanting (unsinging) and singing another tune; between ruminating (chewing) and smoking in one's pipe. Nor is there much difference in figure between sarcasm (a tearing of the flesh) and taking the hide off; between sinister (left-handed) and backhanded; between preposterous (rear end foremost) and cart before the horse; between salary (salt-money, an allowance for soldiers) and pin-money; between pedigree (crane's foot, from the appearance of genealogical diagrams) and crowsfeet (about the eyes); between either precocious (early cooked), apricot (early cooked), crude (raw), or recrudescence (raw again) and half-baked. To ponder is literally to weigh; to apprehend an idea is to take hold of it; to deviate is to go out of one's way; to congregate is to flock together; to assail or insult a man is to jump on him; to be precipitate is to go head foremost; to be recalcitrant is to kick.

Again, you will perceive that many words once had more literal or more definitely concrete meanings than they have now. To corrode is to gnaw along with others, to differ is to carry apart, to refuse is to pour back. Polite is polished, absurd is very deaf, egregious is taken from the common herd, capricious is leaping about like a goat, cross (disagreeable) is shaped like a cross, wrong is wrung (or twisted). Crisscross is Christ's cross, attention is stretching toward, expression is pressed out, dexterity is right-handedness, circumstances are things standing around, an innuendo is nodding, a parlor is a room to talk in, a nostril is that which pierces the nose (thrill means pierce), vinegar is sharp wine, a stirrup is a rope to mount by, a pastor is a shepherd, a marshal is a caretaker of horses, a constable is a stable attendant, a companion is a sharer of one's bread.

On the other hand, you will find that many words were once more general in import than they have since become. *Fond* originally meant foolish, then foolishly devoted, then (becoming more general again) devoted. *Nostrum* meant our own, then a medicine not known by other physicians, then a quack remedy. *Shamefast* meant confirmed in modesty (shame); then through a confusion of *fast* with *faced,* a betrayal through the countenance of self-consciousness or guilt. *Counterfeit* meant a copy or a picture, then an unlawful duplication, especially of a coin. *Lust* meant pleasure of any sort, then inordinate sexual pleasure or desire. *Virtue* (to trace only a few of its varied activities) meant manliness, then the quality or attribute peculiar to true manhood (with the Romans this was valor), then any admirable quality, then female chastity. *Pen* meant a feather, then a quill to write with, then an instrument for writing used in the same way as a quill. A *groom* meant a man, then a stableman (in *bridegroom,* however, it preserves the old signification). *Heathen* (heath-dweller), *pagan* (peasant), and *demon* (a divinity) had in themselves no iniquitous savor until early Christians formed their opinion of the people inac-

INDIVIDUAL WORDS: AS VERBAL CELIBATES

cessible to them and the spirits incompatible with the unity of the Godhead. Words betokening future happenings or involving judgment tend to take a special cast from the fears and anxieties men feel when their fortune is affected or their destiny controlled by external forces. Thus *omen* (a prophetic utterance or sign) and *portent* (a stretching forward, a foreseeing, a foretelling) might originally be either benign or baleful; but nowadays, especially in the adjectival forms *ominous* and *portentous*, they wear a menacing hue. Similarly *criticism, censure,* and *doom,* all of them signifying at first mere judgment, have come—the first in popular, the other two in universal, usage—to stand for adverse judgment. The old sense of *doom* is perpetuated, however, in *Doomsday,* which means the day on which we are all to be, not necessarily sent to hell, but judged.

You will furthermore perceive that the exaggerated affirmations people are always indulging in have led to the weakening of many a word. *Fret* meant eat; formerly to say that a man was fretting was to use a vigorous comparison—to have the man devoured with care. *Mortify* meant to kill, then killed with embarrassment, then embarrassed. *Qualm* meant death, but our qualms of conscience have degenerated into mere twinges. Oaths are shorn of their might by overuse; *confound,* once a tremendous malinvocation, may now fall from the lips of respectable young ladies, and *fie,* in its time not a whit less dire, would be scarcely out of place in even a cloister. Words designating immediacy come to have no more strength than soup-meat seven times boiled. *Presently* meant in the present, *soon* and *by and by* meant forthwith.

How they have lost their fundamental meaning will be intelligible to you if you have in ordering something been told that it would be delivered "right away," or in calling for a girl have been told that she would be down "in a minute."

You will detect in words of another class a deterioration, not in force, but in character; they have fallen into contemptuous or sinister usage. Many words for skill or wisdom have been thus debased. *Cunning* meant knowing, *artful* meant well acquainted with one's art, *crafty* meant proficient in one's craft or calling, *wizard* meant wise man. The present import of these words shows how men have assumed that mental superiority must be yoked with moral dereliction or diabolical aid. Words indicating the generality—indicating ordinary rank or popular affiliations—have in many instances suffered the same decline. *Trivial* meant three ways; it was what might be heard at the crossroads or on any route you chanced to be traveling, and its value was accordingly slight. *Lewd* meant belonging to the laity; it came to mean ignorant, and then morally reprehensible. *Common* may be used to signify ill-bred; *vulgar* may be and frequently is used to signify indecent. *Sabotage,* from a French term meaning wooden shoe, has come to be applied to the deliberate and systematic scamping of one's work in order to injure one's employer. *Idiot* (common soldier) crystallizes the exasperated ill opinion of officers for privates. (*Infantry*—an organization of military infants—has on the contrary sloughed its reproach and now enshrines the dignity of lowliness.) Somewhat akin to words of this type is *knave,* which first meant boy, then

INDIVIDUAL WORDS: AS VERBAL CELIBATES

servant, then rogue. Terms for agricultural classes seldom remain flattering. Besides such epithets as *hayseed* and *clodhopper*, contemptuous in their very origin, *villain* (farm servant), *churl* (farm laborer), and *boor* (peasant) have all gathered unto themselves opprobrium; *villain* now involves a scoundrelly spirit, *churl* a contumelious manner, *boor* a bumptious ill-breeding; not one of these words is any longer confined in its application to a particular social rank. Terms for womankind are soon tainted. *Wench* meant at first nothing worse than girl or daughter, *quean* than woman, *hussy* than housewife; even *woman* is generally felt to be half-slighting. Terms affirming unacquaintance with sin, or abstention from it, tend to be quickly reft of what praise they are fraught with; none of us likes to be saluted as *innocent, guileless,* or *unsophisticated,* and to be dubbed *silly* no longer makes us feel blessed. Besides these and similar classes of words, there are innumerable individual terms that have sadly lost caste. An *imp* was erstwhile a scion; it then became a boy, and then a mischievous spirit. A *noise* might once be music; it has ceased to enjoy such possibilities. To live near a piano that is constantly banged is to know how *noise* as a synonym for music was outlawed.

A backward glance over the history of words repays you in showing you the words for what they are, and in having them live out their lives before you. Do you know what an *umpire* is? He is a non (or num) peer, a not equal man, an odd man—one therefore who can decide disputes. Do you know what a *nickname* is? It is an eke (also) name, a title bestowed upon one in addition to his proper designation. Do you know what a *fellow*, etymologically speaking, is? He is a fee-layer, a partner, a man who lays his fee (property) alongside yours. Do you know that *matinée*, though awarded to the afternoon, meant primarily a morning entertainment and has traveled so far from its original sense that we call an actual before-noon performance a morning matinée? Do you know the past of such words as *bedlam, rival, parson, sandwich, pocket handkerchief*? *Bedlam*, a corruption of *Bethlehem*, was a hospital for the insane in London; it came to be a general term for great confusion or discord. *Rivals* were formerly dwellers—that is, neighboring dwellers—on the bank of a stream; disputes over water-rights gave the word its present meaning. A *person* or *parson*, for the two were the same, was a mask (literally, that through which the sound came); then an actor representing a character in a play; then a representative of any sort; then the representative of the church in a parish. A *sandwich* was a stratification of bread and meat by the Earl of Sandwich, who was so loath to leave the gaming table that he saved time by having food brought him in this form. A *kerchief* was originally a cover for the head, and indeed sundry amiable, old-fashioned grandmothers still use it for this purpose. Afterward people carried it in their hands and called it a *handkerchief;* and when they transferred it to the pocket, they called it a *pocket handkerchief* or pocket hand head-cover. A scrutiny of such words should convince you that the reading of the dictionary, instead of being the dull occupation it is almost proverbially reputed to be, may become an occupation truly fascinating. For

INDIVIDUAL WORDS: AS VERBAL CELIBATES

clustered about the words recorded in the dictionary are inexhaustible riches of knowledge and of interest for those who have eyes to see.

EXERCISE

1. For each of the following words look up (a) the present meaning if you do not know it, (b) the original meaning, (c) any other past meanings you can find.

Exposition	Corn	Cattle
Influence	Sanguine	Turmoil
Sinecure	Waist	Shrew
Potential	Spaniel	Crazy
Character	Candidate	Indomitable
Infringe	Rascal	Amorphous
Expend	Thermometer	Charm
Rather	Tall	Stepchild
Wedlock	Ghostly	Haggard
Bridal	Pioneer	Pluck
Noon	Neighbor	Jimson weed
Courteous	Wanton	Rosemary
Cynical	Street	Plausible
Grocer	Husband	Allow
Worship	Gipsy	Insane
Encourage	Clerk	Disease
Astonish	Clergyman	Boulevard
Realize	Hectoring	Canary
Bombast	Primrose	Diamond
Benedict	Walnut	Abominate
Piazza	Holiday	Barbarous
Disgust	Heavy	Kind
Virtu	Nightmare	Devil
Gospel	Comfort	Whist
Mermaid	Pearl	Onion
Enthusiasm	Domino	Book
Fanatic	Grotesque	Cheat
Auction	Economy	Illegible
Quell	Cheap	Illegitimate
Sheriff	Excelsior	Emasculate
Danger	Dunce	Champion
Shibboleth	Calico	Adieu
Essay	Pontiff	Macadamize
Wages	Copy	Stentorian

86 CENTURY VOCABULARY BUILDER

Quarantine	Puny	Saturnine
Buxom	Caper	Derrick
Indifferent	Boycott	Mercurial
Gaudy	Countenance	Poniard
Majority	Camera	Chattel.

2. The following words are often used loosely today, some because their original meaning is lost sight of, some because they are confused with other words. Find for each word (a) what the meaning has been and (b) what the correct meaning is now.

Nice	Awful	Atrocious
Grand	Horrible	Pitiful
Beastly	Transpire	Claim
Weird	Aggravate	Uncanny
Demean	Gorgeous	Elegant
Fine	Noisome	Mutual (in "a mutual
Lovely	Cute	friend")
Stunning	Liable	Immense.

3. The following sentences from standard English literature illustrate the use of words still extant and even familiar, in senses now largely or wholly forgotten. The quotations from the Bible and Shakespeare (all the Biblical quotations are from the King James Version) date back a little more than three hundred years, those from Milton a little less than three hundred years, and those from Gray and Coleridge, respectively, about a hundred and seventy-five and a hundred and twenty-five years. Go carefully enough into the past meanings of the italicized words to make sure you grasp the author's thought.

And now abideth faith, hope, charity, these three; but the greatest of these is *charity*. (1 *Corinthians* 13:13)
I *prevented* the dawning of the morning. (*Psalms* 119:147)
Our eyes *wait* upon the Lord our God. (*Psalms* 123:2)
The times of this ignorance God *winked* at. (*Acts* 17:30)
And Jesus said, Somebody hath touched me; for I perceive that *virtue* is gone out of me. (*Luke* 8:46)
To judge the *quick* and the dead. (1 *Peter* 4:5)
Be not wise in your own *conceits*. (*Romans* 12:16)
In maiden meditation, *fancy*-free. (Shakespeare: *A Midsummer Night's Dream*)
Is it so *nominated* in the bond? (Shakespeare: *The Merchant of Venice*)
Would I had met my *dearest* foe in heaven. (Shakespeare: *Hamlet*)

INDIVIDUAL WORDS: AS VERBAL CELIBATES 87

The *extravagant* and *erring* spirit. (Said of a spirit wandering from the bounds of purgatory. Shakespeare: *Hamlet*)

The *modesty* of nature. (Shakespeare: *Hamlet*)

It is a nipping and an *eager* air. (Shakespeare: *Hamlet*)

Security

Is mortals' chiefest enemy. (Shakespeare: *Macbeth*)

Most *admired* disorder. (Shakespeare: *Macbeth*)

Upon this *hint* I spake. (From the account of the wooing of Desdemona. Shakespeare: *Othello*)

This Lodovico is a *proper* man. A very handsome man. (Shakespeare: *Othello*)

Mice and rats and such small *deer*. (Shakespeare: *King Lear*)

This is no sound

That the earth *owes*. (Shakespeare: *The Tempest*)

Every shepherd *tells* his *tale*. (Milton: *L'Allegro*)

Bring the *rathe* primrose that forsaken dies. (*Rathe* survives only in the comparative form *rather*. Milton: *Lycidas*)

Can honor's voice *provoke* the silent dust? (Gray: *Elegy*)

The *silly* buckets on the deck. (Coleridge: *The Ancient Mariner*)

4. In technical usage or particular phrases a former sense of a word may be embedded like a fossil. The italicized words in the following list retain special senses of this kind. What do these words as thus used mean? Can you add to the list?

To *wit*
Might and *main*
Time and *tide*
Christmas*tide*
Sad bread
A bank *teller*
To *tell* one's *beads*
Aid and *abet*
Meat and drink
Shop*lifter*
Fishing-*tackle*
Getting off *scot*-free
An *earnest* of future favors
A *brave* old hearthstone
Confusion to the enemy!
Giving aid and *comfort* to the enemy
Without *let* or hindrance

A *let* in tennis
*Quick*lime
Cut to *the quick*
Neat-foot oil
To *sound in* tort (Legal phrase)
To bid one God*speed*
I had as *lief* as not
The child *favors* its parents
On *pain* of death
Widow's *weeds*
I am *bound* for the Promised Land
To *carry* a girl to a party (Used only in the South)
To give a person so much *to boot*.

5. Each of the subjoined phrases contradicts itself or repeats

CENTURY VOCABULARY BUILDER

its idea clumsily. The key to the difficulty lies in the italicized words. What is their true meaning?

A weekly *journal*
Ultimate end
Final *ultimatum*
Final *completion*
Previous *preconceptions*
Nauseating seasickness
Join together
Descend down
Prefer better
Argent silver
Completely *annihilate*
Unanimously by all
Most *unique* of all
The other *alternative*
Endorse on the back
Incredible to believe
A *criterion* to go by
An *appetite* to eat
A *panacea* for all ills

Popular with the people
Biography of his life
Autobiography of his own life
Vitally alive
A new, *novel*, and ingenious explanation
Mutual dislike for each other
Omniscient knowledge of all subjects
A *material* growth in mental power
Peculiar faults of his own
Fly into an *ebullient* passion
To *saturate* oneself with gold and silver
Elected by *acclamation* on a secret ballot.

INDIVIDUAL WORDS: AS MEMBERS OF VERBAL FAMILIES

OUR investigation into the nature, qualities, and fortunes of single words must now merge into a study of their family connections. We do not go far into this new phase of our researches before we perceive that the career of a word may be very complicated. Most people, if you asked them, would tell you that an individual word is a causeless entity—a thing that was never begotten and lacks power to propagate. They would deny the possibility that its course through the world could be other than colorless, humdrum. Now words thus immaculately conceived and fatefully impotent, words that shamble thus listlessly through life, there are. But many words are born in an entirely normal way; have a grubby boyhood, a vigorous youth, and a sober maturity; marry, beget sons and daughters, become old, enfeebled, even senile; and suffer neglect, if not death. In their advanced age they are exempted by the discerning from enterprises that call for a lusty agility, but are drafted into service by those to whom all levies are alike. Indeed in their very prime of manhood their vicissitudes are such as to make them seem human. Some rise in the world some sink; some start along the road of grandeur or obliquity, and then backslide or reform. Some are social climbers, and mingle in company where verbal dress coats are worn; some are social degenerates, and consort with the ragamuffins and guttersnipes of language. Some marry at their own social level, some above them, some beneath; some go down in childless bachelorhood or leave an unkempt and illegitimate progeny. And if you trace their own lineage, you will find for some that it is but decent and middle-class, for some that it is mongrelized and miscegenetic, for some that it is proud, ancient, yea perhaps patriarchal.

It is contrary to nature for a word, as for a man, to live the life of a hermit. Through external compulsion or internal characteristics a word has contacts with its fellows. And its most intimate, most spontaneous associations are normally with its own kindred.

In our work hitherto we have had nothing to say of verbal consanguinity. But we have not wholly ignored its existence, for the very good reason that we could not. For example, in the latter portions of Chapter IV we proceeded on the hypothesis that at least some words have ancestors. Also in the analysis (page 72 ff.) of the dictionary definition of *tension* we learned that the word has, not only a Latin forebear, but French, Spanish, Portuguese, and Italian kinsmen as well. One thing omitted from that analysis would have revealed something further—namely, that the word has its English kinfolks too. For the bracketed part of the dictionary definition mentions two other English words, *tend* and *tense*, which from their origin involve the same idea as that of *tension* —the idea of stretching.

INDIVIDUAL WORDS: OF VERBAL FAMILIES

Now words may be akin in either of two ways. They may be related in blood. Or they may be related by marriage. Let us consider these two kinds of connection more fully.

Words Related in Blood

As an illustration of blood kinships enjoyed by a native English word take the adjective *good*. We can easily call to mind other members of its family: goodly, goodish, goody-goody, good-hearted, good-natured, good-humored, good-tempered, goods, goodness, goodliness, gospel (good story), goodby, goodwill, goodman, goodwife, good-for-nothing, good den (good evening), the Good Book. The connection between these words is obvious.

Next consider a group of words that have been naturalized: scribe, prescribe, ascribe, proscribe, transcribe, circumscribe, subscriber, indescribable, scribble, script, scripture, postscript, conscript, rescript, manuscript, nondescript, inscription, superscription, description. It is clear that these words are each other's kith and kin in blood, and that the strain or stock common to all is *scribe* or (as sometimes modified) *script*. What does this strain signify? The idea of writing. The *scribes* are a writing clan. Some of them, to be sure, have strayed somewhat from the ancestral calling, for words are as wilful—or as independent—as men. *Ascribe,* for example, does not act like a member of the household of writers, whatever it may look like. We should have to scrutinize it carefully or consult the record for it in that verbal Who's Who, the dictionary, before we could understand how it came by its scribal affiliations honestly. But once we begin to reflect or to probe, we find we have not mistaken its identity. *Ascribe* is the offspring of *ad* (to) and *scribo* (write), both Latin terms. It originally meant writing to a person's name or after it (that is, imputing to the person by means of written words) some quality or happening of which he was regarded as the embodiment, source, or cause. Nowadays we may saddle the matter on him through oral rather than written speech. That is, *ascribe* has largely lost the writing traits. But all the same it is manifestly of the writing blood.

The *scribes* are of undivided racial stock, Latin. Consider now the *manu,* or *man,* words which sprang from the Latin *manus,* meaning "hand." Here are some of them: manual, manœuver, mandate, manacle, manicure, manciple, emancipate, manage, manner, manipulate, manufacture, manumission, manuscript, amanuensis. These too are children of the same father; they are brothers and sisters to each other. But what shall we say of legerdemain (light, or sleight, of hand), maintain, coup de main, and the like? They bear a resemblance to the *man's* and *manu's,* yet one that casual observers would not notice. Is there kinship between the two sets of words? There is. But not the full fraternal or sororal relation. The *mains* are children of *manus* by a French marriage he contracted. With this French blood in their veins, they are only half-brothers, half-sisters of the *manu's* and the *man's*.

Your examination of the family trees of words will be practical, rather than highly scholastic, in nature. You need not track every word in the dictionary to the den of its remote parentage. Nor need you bother your head

INDIVIDUAL WORDS: OF VERBAL FAMILIES

with the name of the distant ancestor. But in the case of the large number of words that have a numerous kindred you should learn to detect the inherited strain. You will then know that the word is the brother or cousin of certain other words of your acquaintance, and this knowledge will apprise you of qualities in it with which you should reckon. To this extent only must you make yourself a student of verbal genealogy.

Exercise

(Simple exercises in tracing blood relationships among words are given at the end of the chapter. Therefore the exercises assigned here are of a special character.)

1. Each of the following groups is made up of related words, but the relationship is somewhat disguised. Consult the dictionary for each word, and learn all you can as to (a) its source, (b) the influence (as passing through an intermediate language) that gave it its present form, (c) the course of its development into its present meaning.

Captain
Capital
Decapitate
Chef
Chieftain

Cavalry
Chivalry

Camera
Chamber

Serrated
Sierra

Influence
Influenza

Isolate
Insular

Cathedral
Chaise
Chair
Shay

Camp
Campaign
Champion

Inept
Apt

Inimical
Enemy

Espionage
Spy

Governor
Gubernatorial

Guardian
Ward

Guarantee
Warrant

Incipient
Receive

Poor
Pauper

Work
Wrought
Playwright

2. The variety of sources for modern English is indicated by the following list. Do not seek for blood kinsmen of these particular words, but think of all the additional words you can that have come into English from Indian, Spanish, French, any other language spoken today.

Alphabet (Greek)
Folio (Latin)
Boudoir (French)
Binnacle (Portuguese)
Anger (Old Norse)
Isinglass (Low German)
Slogan (Celtic)
Polka (Polish)
Shekel (Hebrew)
Algebra (Arabic)
Puttee (Hindoo)
Boomerang (Australian)
Potato (Haytian)
Guano (Peruvian)
Renegade (Spanish)
Piano (Italian)
Car (Norman)
Rush (German)
Sky (Icelandic)
Yacht (Dutch)
Hussar (Hungarian)
Samovar (Russian)
Chess (Persian)
Tea (Chinese)
Kimono (Japanese)
Tattoo (Tahitian)
Voodoo (African)
Skunk (American Indian)
Buncombe (American)

Words Related by Marriage

That words marry and are given in marriage, is too generally overlooked. Any student of a foreign language, German for instance, can recall the thrill of discovery and the lift of reawakened hope that came to him when first he suspected, aye perceived, the existence of verbal matrimony. For weeks he had struggled with words that apparently were made up of fortuitous collocations of letters. Then in some beatific moment these huddles of letters took meaning; in instance after instance they represented, not a word, but words—a linguistic household. Let them be what they might—a harem, the domestic establishment of a Mormon, the dwelling-place of verbal polygamists,—he could at last see order in their relationships. To their morals he was indifferent, absorbed as he was in his joy of understanding.

INDIVIDUAL WORDS: OF VERBAL FAMILIES

In English likewise are thousands of these verbal marriages. We may not be aware of them; from our very familiarity with words we may overlook the fact that in instances uncounted their oneness has been welded by a linguistic minister or justice of the peace. But to read a single page or harken for thirty seconds to oral discourse with our minds intent on such states of wedlock is to convince ourselves that they abound. Consider this list of everyday words: somebody, already, disease, vineyard, unskilled, outlet, nevertheless, holiday, insane, resell, schoolboy, helpmate, uphold, withstand, rainfall, deadlock, typewrite, football, motorman, thoroughfare, snowflake, buttercup, landlord, overturn. Every term except one yokes a verbal husband with his wife, and the one exception (*nevertheless*) joins a uxorious man with two wives.

These marriages are of a simple kind. But the nuptial interlinkings between families of words may be many and complicated. Thus there is a family of *graph* (or write) words: graphic, lithograph, cerograph, cinematograph, stylograph, telegraph, multigraph, seismograph, dictograph, monograph, holograph, logograph, digraph, autograph, paragraph, stenographer, photographer, biographer, lexicographer, bibliography, typography, pyrography, orthography, chirography, calligraphy, cosmography, geography. There is also a family of *phone* (or sound) words: telephone, dictaphone, megaphone, audiphone, phonology, symphony, antiphony, euphonious, cacophonous, phonetic spelling. It chances that both families are of Greek extraction. Related to the *graphs* —their cousins in fact—are the *grams:* telegram, radiogram, cryptogram, anagram, monogram, diagram, logogram, program, epigram, kilogram, ungrammatical. Now a representative of the *graphs* married into the *phone* family, and we have graphophone. A representative of the *phones* married into the *graph* family, and we have phonograph. A representative of the *grams* married into the *phone* family, and we have gramophone. A representative of the *phones* married into the *gram* family, and we have phonogram. Of such unions children may be born. For example, from the marriage of Mr. Phone with Miss Graph were born phonography, phonographer, phonographist (a rather frail child), phonographic, phonographical, and phonographically.

Intermarriage between the *phones* and the *graphs* or *grams* is a wedding of equals. Some families of words, however, are of inferior social standing to other families, and may seek but not hope to be sought in marriage. Compare the *ex's* with the *ports*. An *ex,* as a preposition, belongs to a prolific family but not one of established and unimpeachable dignity. Hence the *ex's,* though they marry right and left, lead the other words to the altar and are never led thither themselves. Witness exclude, excommunicate, excrescence, excursion, exhale, exit, expel, expunge, expense, extirpate, extract; in no instance does *ex* fellow its connubial mate—it invariably precedes. The *ports,* on the other hand, are the peers of anybody. Some of them choose to remain single: port, porch, portal, portly, porter, portage. Here and there one marries into another family: portfolio, portmanteau, portable, port arms. More often, however, they are wooed than themselves do the pleading: comport, purport, report, disport, transport, passport, deportment, importance, opportunity, importunate, inopportune, insupportable. From our knowledge of the two families, therefore, we should surmise that if any marriage is to take place between them, an *ex* must be the suitor. The surmise would be sound. There is such a term as *export*, but not as *portex*.

Now it is oftentimes possible to do business with a man without knowing whether he is a man or a bridal couple. And so with a word. But the knowledge of his domestic state and circumstances will not come amiss, and it may prove invaluable. You may find that you can handle him to best advantage through a sagacious use of the influence of his wife.

Exercise

1. For each word in the lists on pages 74 and 85 determine (a) whether it is single or married; (b) if it is married, whether the wedding is one between equals.

2. Make a list of the married words in the first three paragraphs of the selection from Burke (Appendix 2). For each of these words determine the exact nature and extent of the dowry brought by each of the contracting parties to the wedding.

Prying Into a Word's Relationships

Hitherto in our study of verbal relationships we have usually started with the family. Having strayed (as by good luck) into an assembly of kinsmen, we have observed the common strain and the general characteristics, and have then "placed" the individual with reference to these. But we do not normally meet words, any more than we meet men, in the domestic circle. We meet them and greet them hastily as they hurry through the tasks of the day, with no other associates about them than such as chance or momentary need may dictate. If we are to see anything of their family life, it must be through effort we ourselves put forth. We must be inquisitive about their conjugal and blood relationships.

How, then, starting with the individual word, can you come into a knowledge of it, not in its public capacity, but in what is even more important, its personal connections? You must form the habit of asking two questions about it: (1) Is it married? (2) Of what family or families was it born? If you can get an understanding answer to these two questions, an answer that will tell you what its relations stand for as well as what their name is, your inquiries will be anything but bootless.

Let us illustrate your procedure concretely. Suppose you read or hear the word *conchology*. It is a somewhat unusual word, but see what you can do with it yourself before calling on the dictionary to help you. Observe the word closely, and you will obtain the answer to your first question. *Conchology* is no bachelor, no verbal old maid; it is a married pair.

Your second and more difficult task awaits you; you must ascertain the meaning of the family connections. With Mr. Conch you are on speaking terms; you know him as one of the shells. But the utmost you can recall about his wife is that she is one of a whole flock of *ologies*. What significance does this relationship possess? You are uncertain. But do not thumb the dictionary yet. Pass in mental review all the *ologies* you can assemble. Wait also for the others that through the unconscious operations of memory will tardily straggle in. Be on the lookout for *ologies* as you read, as you listen. In time you will muster a sizable company of them. And you will draw a conclusion as to the meaning of the blood that flows through their veins. *Ology* implies speech or study. *Conchology,* then, must be the study of conches.

Your investigations thus far have done more than teach you the meaning of the word you began with. They have brought you some of the by-products of the study of verbal kinships. For you no longer pass the *ologies* by with face averted or bow timidly ventured. You have become so well acquainted with them that even a new one, wherever encountered, would flash upon you the face of a friend. But now your desires are whetted. You wish to find out how much you *can* learn. You at last consult the dictionary.

Here a huge obstacle confronts you. The *ologies,* like the *ports* (page 96), are a haughty clan; they are the wooed, rather than the wooing, members of most marital households that contain them. Now the marriage licenses recorded in the dictionary are entered under the name of the suitor, not of the person sought. Hence you labor under a severe handicap as you take the census of the *ologies.* Let us imagine the handicap the most severe possible. Let us suppose that no *ology* had ever been the suitor. Even so, you would not be entirely baffled. For you could look up in the dictionary the *ologies* you yourself had been able to recall. To what profit? First, you could verify or correct your surmise as to what the *ological* blood betokens. Secondly, you could perhaps obtain cross-references to yet other *ologies* than those you remembered.

CENTURY VOCABULARY BUILDER

But you are not reduced to these extremities. The *ologies,* arrogant as they are, sometimes are the applicants for matrimony, and the marriage registry of the dictionary so indicates. To be sure, they do not, when thus appearing at the beginning of words, take the form *ology.* They take the form *log.* But you must be resourceful enough to keep after your quarry in spite of the omission of a vowel or two. Also from some lexicons you may obtain still further help. You may find *ology, logy, logo,* or *log* listed as a combining form, its meaning given, and examples of its use in compounds cited.

By your zeal and persistence you have now brought together a goodly array of the *ologies*—all or most, let us say, of the following: conchology, biology, morphology, phrenology, physiology, osteology, histology, zoology, entomology, bacteriology, ornithology, pathology, psychology, cosmology, eschatology, demonology, mythology, theology, astrology, archeology, geology, meteorology, mineralogy, chronology, genealogy, ethnology, anthropology, criminology, technology, doxology, anthology, trilogy, philology, etymology, terminology, neologism, phraseology, tautology, analogy, eulogy, apology, apologue, eclogue, monologue, dialogue, prologue, epilogue, decalogue, catalogue, travelogue, logogram, logograph, logotype, logarithms, logic, illogical. (Moreover you may have perceived in some of these words the kinship which exists in all for the *loquy* group—see page 128.) Of course you will discard some items from this list as being too learned for your purposes. But you will observe of the others that once you know the meaning of *ology,* you are likely to know the whole word. Thus from your study

INDIVIDUAL WORDS: OF VERBAL FAMILIES

of *conchology* you have mastered, not an individual term, but a tribe.

In *conchology* only one element, *ology*, was really dubious at the outset. Let us take a word of which both elements give you pause. Suppose your thought is arrested by the word *eugenics*. You perhaps know the word as a whole, but not its components. For by looking at it and thinking about it you decide that its state is married, that it comprises the household of Mr. Eu and his wife, formerly Miss Gen. But you cannot say offhand just what kind of person either Mr. Eu or the erstwhile Miss Gen is likely to prove.

Have you met any of the *Eu's* elsewhere? You think vaguely that you have, but cannot lay claim to any real acquaintance. To the dictionary you accordingly betake yourself. There you find that Mr. Eu is of a family quite respectable but not prone to marriage. *Euphony, eupepsia, euphemism, euthanasia* are of his retiring kindred. The meaning of the *eu* blood, so the dictionary informs you, is well. The *gen* blood, as you see exemplified in gentle, general, genital, engender, carries with it the idea of begetting, of producing, of birth, or (by extension) of kinship. *Eugenics,* then, is an alliance of well and begotten (or born).

Your immediate purpose is fulfilled; but you resolve, let us say, to make the acquaintance of more of the *gens,* whose number you have perceived to be legion. You are duly introduced to the following: genus, generic, genre, gender, genitive, genius, general, Gentile, gentle, gentry, gentleman, genteel, generous, genuine, genial, congeniality, congener, genital, congenital, engender, generation, progeny, progenitor, genesis, genetics, eugenics, pathogenesis, biogenesis, ethnogeny, palingenesis, unregenerate, degenerate, monogeny, indigenous, exogenous, homogeneous, heterogeneous, genealogy, ingenuous, ingenious, ingénue, engine, engineer, hygiene, hydrogen, oxygen, endogen, primogeniture, philoprogeniture, miscegenation. Some of these are professional rather than social; you decide not to leave your card at their doors. Others have assumed a significance somewhat un*gen*-like, though the relationship may be traced if you are not averse to trouble. Thus *engine* in its superficial aspects seems alien to the idea of born. But it is the child of *ingenious* (innate, inborn); *ingenious* is the inborn power to accomplish, and *engine* is the result of the application of that power. Whether you care to bother with such subtleties or not, enough *gens* are left to make the family one well worth your cultivation.

Thus by studying two words, *conchology* and *eugenics*, you have for the first time placed yourself on an intimate footing with three verbal families—the *ologies*, the *eu's*, and the *gens*. Observe that though you studied the *ologies* apart from the *eu's* and the *gens*, your knowledge—once you have acquired it—cannot be kept pigeonholed, for the *ologies* have intermarried with both the other families. Hence you on meeting *eulogy* can exclaim: "How do you do, Mr. Eu? I am honored in making your acquaintance, Mrs. Eu—I was about to call you by your maiden name; for I am a friend of your sister, the Miss Ology who married Mr. Conch. And you too, Mr. Eu—I cannot regard you as a stranger. I have looked in so often on the family of your brother—the Euphony family,

I mean. What a beautiful literary household it is! Yet it has been neglected by the world—yea, even by the people who write. Well, the loss is theirs who do the neglecting." And *genealogy* you can greet with an equal parade of family lore: "Don't trouble to tell me who you are. I am hob and nob with your folks on both sides of the family, and my word for it, the relationship is written all over you. Mr. Gen, I envy you the pride you must feel in the prominence given nowadays to the *eugenics* household. And it must delight you, Miss Ology-that-was, that connoisseurs are so keenly interested in *conchology*. How are Grandfather Gen and Grandmother Ology? They were keeping up remarkably the last time I saw them." Do you think words will not respond to cordiality like this? They will work their flattered heads off for you!

Exercise

1. For each of the following words (a) determine what families are intermarried, (b) ascertain the exact contribution to the household by each family represented, and (c) make as complete a list as possible of cognate words.

Reject	Oppose	Convent
Defer	Omit	Produce
Expel		

2. Test the extent of the intermarriages among these words by successively attaching each of the prefixes to each of the main (or key) syllables. (Thus re-ject, re-fer, re-pel, etc.)

Two Admonitions

In tracing verbal kinships you must be prepared for slight variations in the form of the same key-syllable. Consider these words: wise, wiseacre, wisdom, wizard, witch, wit, unwitting, to wit, outwit, twit, witticism, witness, evidence, providence, invidious, advice, vision, visit, vista, visage, visualize, envisage, invisible, vis-à-vis, visor, revise, supervise, improvise, proviso, provision, view, review, survey, vie, envy, clairvoyance. Perhaps the last six should be disregarded as too exceptional in form to be clearly recognized. And certainly some words, as *prudence* from *providentia,* are so metamorphosed that they should be excluded from practical lists of this kind. But even in the words left to us there are fairly marked divergences in appearance. Why? Because the key-syllable has descended to us, not through one language, but through several. As good verbal detectives we should be able to penetrate the consequent disguises; for *wis, wiz, wit, vid, vic,* and *vis* all embody the idea of seeing or knowing.

On the other hand, you must take care not to be misled by a superficial resemblance into thinking two unrelated key-syllables identical. Let us consider two sets of words. The first, which is related to the *tain* group (see page 121), has a key-syllable that means holding: tenant, tenement, tenure, tenet, tenor, tenable, tenacious, contents, contentment, lieutenant, maintenance, sustenance, countenance, appurtenance, detention, retentive, pertinacity, pertinent, continent, abstinence, continuous, retinue. The second has a key-syllable that means stretching: tend, tender, tendon, tendril, tendency, extend, subtend, distend, pretend, contend, attendant, tense, tension, pretence, intense, intensive, ostensible, tent, tenterhook, portent, attention, intention, tenuous, attenuate, extenuate, antenna, tone, tonic, standard. The form of the key-syllable for the first set of words is usually *ten, tent,* or *tin;* that for

INDIVIDUAL WORDS: OF VERBAL FAMILIES

the second *tend, tens, tent,* or *ten.* You may therefore easily confuse the two groups until you have learned to look past appearances into meanings. Thenceforth the holdings and the stretchings will be distinct in your mind —will constitute two great families, not one. Of course individual words may still puzzle you. You will not perceive that *tender,* for example, belongs with the stretchings until you go back to its primary idea of something stretched thin, or that *tone* has membership in that family until you connect it with the sound which a stretched chord emits.

General Exercise for the Chapter

Each of the key-syllables given below is followed by (1) a list of fairly familiar words that embody it, (2) a list of less familiar words that embody it, (3) several sentences containing blank spaces, into each of which you are ultimately to fit the appropriate word from the first list. (The existence of the two lists will show you that learned words may have commonplace kinfolks.)

First, however, you are to study each word in both lists for (1) its exact meaning, (2) the influence of the key-syllable upon that meaning, (3) any variation of the key-syllable from its ordinary form. (A few words have been introduced to show how varied the forms may be and yet remain recognizable.)

Also, as an aid to your memory, you are to copy each list, underscoring the key-syllable each time you encounter it.

(The lists are practical, not meticulously academic. In many instances they contain words derived, not from a single original, but from cognates. No list is exhaustive.)

Ag, act, ig (carry on, do, drive): (1) agent, agitate, agile, act, actor, actuate, exact, enact, reaction, counteract, transact, mitigate, navigate, prodigal, assay, essay; (2) agenda, pedagogue, synagogue, actuary, redact, castigate, litigation, exigency, ambiguous, variegated, cogent, cogitate.

Sentences (inflect forms if necessary; for example, use the past tense, participle, or infinitive of a verb instead of its present tense): It was —— into law. The legislators had been —— by honest motives, but the popular —— was immediate. The —— of the mining company refused to let us proceed with the ——. Nothing could —— the offense. The father was ——, the son ——. The student handed in his —— at the —— time designated. Though —— enough on land, he could not —— a ship. The —— by missing his cue so —— the manager that his good work thereafter could not —— the ill impression.

Burn, brun, brand (burn): (1 and 2 combined) burn, burnish, brunette, brunt, bruin, brand, brandish, brandy, brown.

Sentences: He plucked a —— from the ——. The —— hair of the —— was so glossy it seemed ——. He —— his sword and bore the —— of the conflict. After drinking so much —— he saw snakes in his imagination, he staggered off into the woods and met Old —— in reality.

Cad, cas, cid (fall): (1) cadence, decadent, case, casual, casualty, occasion, accident, incident, mischance, cheat; (2) casuistry, coincide, occidental, deciduous.

Sentences: The period was a —— one. He gave but —— attention to the —— of the music. On this —— an —— befell him. To the general it was a mere —— that his —— were heavy. As a result of this —— he was accused of trying to —— them.

Cede, ceed, cess (go): (1) cede, recede, secede, concede, intercede, procedure, precedent, succeed, exceed, success, recess, concession, procession, intercession, abscess, ancestor, cease, decease; (2) antecedent, precedence, cessation, accessory, predecessor.

Sentences: He —— the existence of a —— that justified such ——. The delegate —— his authority when he consented to —— the territory. He would not —— from his position or —— for mercy. At —— the pupils —— in forming a ——. His —— was suffering from an —— at the time the Southern states ——. His agony —— only with his ——.

Ceive, ceit, cept, cip, cap(t) (take): (1) receive, deceive, perceive, deceit, conceit, receipt, reception, perception, inception, conception, interception, accept, except, precept, municipal, participate, anticipate, capable, capture, captivate, case (chest, covering), casement, incase, cash, cashier, chase, catch, prince, forceps, occupy; (2) receptacle, recipient, incipient, precipitate, accipiter, capacious, incapacitate.

Sentences: Though she —— the officers, she did not prevent the —— of the fugitive. He —— that the man was very ——. The mayor skilfully —— the alderman and proposed that —— bonds be issued. The sight of the money —— him and he quickly gave me a ——. He uttered musty ——, which were not always given a friendly ——. From the —— of the movement he plotted to —— the leadership in it. The —— took part in the ——, but failed to —— any of the game.

Cide, cis(e) (cut, kill): (1) decide, suicide, homicide, concise, precise, decisive, incision, scissors, chisel, cement; (2) parricide, fratricide, infanticide, regicide, germicide, excision, circumcision, incisors, cesura.

Sentences: He could not —— whether to make the —— with a —— or a pair of ——. There was —— evidence that he was the ——. In a few —— sentences he explained why his friend could never have been a ——. The prim old lady had very —— manners of speech.

Cur, course (run): (1) current, currency, incur, concur, occurrence, cursory, excursion, course, discourse, intercourse, recourse; (2) curriculum, precursor, discursive, recurrent, concourse, courier, succor, corridor.

Sentences: He —— in the request that payment be made in ——. The —— was so strong that the —— by steamer had to be abandoned. In the —— of his remarks he had —— to various shifts and evasions. By his —— with one faction, though it was but ——, he —— the enmity of the other. It was a disgraceful ——.

Dic, dict (speak, say): (1) dedicate, vindicate, indication, predicament, predict, addict, verdict, indict, dictionary, dictation, jurisdiction, vindictive, contradiction, benediction, ditto, condition; (2) abdicate, adjudicate, juridical, diction, dictum, dictator, dictaphone, dictograph, edict, interdict, valedictory, malediction, ditty, indite, ipse dixit, on dit.

Sentences: The man —— to drugs was —— for —— treatment of his wife, and the —— were that the —— would be against him. He said, on the contrary, that his character would be ——. The attorney for the defense —— that the judge would rule that the matter did not lie within his ——. This would leave the prosecution in a ——. But the prosecution issued a strong —— of this theory, and said —— were favorable for proving the man guilty.

Duce, duct (lead): (1) induce, reduce, traduce, seduce, introduce, reproduce, education, deduct, product, production, reduction, conduct, conductor, abduct, subdue; (2) educe, adduce, superinduce, conducive, ducat, duct, ductile, induction, aqueduct, viaduct, conduit, duke, duchy.

Sentences: We —— the company to —— the fare. They —— ten cents from the wages of each man, an average —— of four per cent. They —— us when they say we have wilfully lessened ——. The highwaymen —— the ——. If you have an ——, you can —— an idea in other words.

Error (wander): (1) error, erroneous, erratic, errand; (2) errata, knight errant, arrant knave, aberration.

INDIVIDUAL WORDS: OF VERBAL FAMILIES 109

Sentences: That —— fellow came on a special —— to tell us we had made an ——. And his statement was —— at that!

Fact, fic(e), fy, fect, feat, feit (make, do): (1) fact, factory, faction, manufacture, satisfaction, suffice, sacrifice, office, difficult, pacific, terrific, significant, fortification, magnificent, artificial, beneficial, verify, simplify, stupefy, certify, dignify, glorify, falsify, beautify, justify, infect, perfect, effect, affection, defective, feat, defeat, feature, feasible, forfeit, surfeit, counterfeit, affair, fashion; (2) factor, factotum, malefaction, benefaction, putrefaction, facile, facsimile, faculty, certificate, edifice, efficacy, prolific, deficient, proficient, artifice, artificer, beneficiary, versification, unification, exemplification, deify, petrify, rectify, amplify, fructify, liquefy, disaffect, refection, comfit, pontiff, ipso facto, de facto, ex post facto, au fait, fait accompli.

Sentences: The opposing —— by incredible —— had found it —— to take over the —— of the goods. By this —— it —— what goodwill the owner of the —— had for it, but it won the —— of the public. The owner, though seemingly —— at first, soon —— a scheme to make the success of the enterprise more ——. By an —— lowering of the price of his own goods and by —— that those of his rivals were ——, he hoped to —— the public mind with unjust suspicions. But all this did not ——. In truth the —— of it was the hastening of his own —— and a —— heightening of the public —— toward his rivals. His directors, seeing that his policy had failed to —— itself, met in his —— and urged him to take a more —— attitude.

Fer (bear, carry): (1) transfer, prefer, proffer, suffer, confer, offer, referee, deference, inference, indifferent, ferry, fertile; (2) referendum, Lucifer, circumference, vociferate, auriferous, coniferous, pestiferous.

Sentences: With real —— to their wishes he —— to —— the goods by ——. The —— of the sporting writers was that the —— was —— to his duties. After —— apart, the farmers —— the use of their most —— acres for this experiment. To be mortal is to ——.

Fide (trust, believe, have faith): (1) fidelity, confide, confident, diffident, infidel, perfidious, bona fide, defiance, affiance; (2) fiduciary, affidavit, fiancé, auto da fé, Santa Fé.

Sentences: He was —— that the man was an ——. He had —— in a —— rascal. He had been —— for years and had proved his ——. Though we are somewhat —— in making it, you may be sure it is a —— offer. His attitude toward his father is one of gross ——.

Grade, gress (walk, go): (1) grade, gradual, graduate, degrade, digress, Congress, aggressive, progressive, degree; (2) gradation, Centigrade, ingress, egress, transgression, retrogression, ingredient.

Sentences: His failure to —— from college made him feel ——, especially as his cronies all received their ——. The engine lost speed —— as it climbed the long ——. I —— to remark that some members of —— are more —— than ——.

Hab, hib (have, hold): (1) habit, habitation, inhabitant, exhibit, prohibition, ability, debit, debt; (2) habituate, habiliment, habeas corpus, cohabit, dishabille, inhibit.

Sentences: The —— of the island —— an —— to live without permanent ——. It was his —— to glance first at the —— side of his ledger, as he was much worried about his ——. Most women favor ——.

Hale, heal, hol, whole (sound): (1) hale, hallow, Hallowe'en, heal, health, unhealthy, healthful, holy, holiday, hollyhock, whole, wholesome; (2) halibut, halidom.

INDIVIDUAL WORDS: OF VERBAL FAMILIES

Sentences: Though he lived in a —— climate, he was ——. The food was ——, the man —— and hearty. He did not think of a —— as ——. We had —— in our garden almost until ——. He wept at hearing the —— name of his mother. For a —— month the wound refused to ——.

It (go): (1) exit, transit, transition, initial, initiative, ambition, circuit, perishable; (2) itinerant, transitory, obituary, sedition, circumambient.

Sentences: The —— was broken. It was his —— shipment of —— goods, and they suffered a good deal in ——. His —— was to be regarded as a man of great ——. His —— was less effective than his entrance.

Ject (throw): (1) eject, reject, subject, project, objection, injection, dejected, conjecture, jet, jetty; (2) abject, traject, adjective, projectile, interjection, ejaculate, jetsam, jettison.

Sentences: With —— mien he watched the waves lash the ——. His scheme was —— to much ridicule and then ——, and he himself was —— from the room. From a pipe that —— from the corner of the building came a —— of dirty water. He could only —— what their —— was. The —— brought immediate relief.

Jud, jur, just (law, right): (1) judge, judicious, judicial, prejudice, jurist, jurisdiction, just, justice, justify; (2) judicature, adjudicate, juridical, jurisprudence, justiciary, de jure.

Sentences: The eminent —— said the matter did not lie within his ——. Though —— in most matters, he admitted to —— in this. The —— said he would comment in an unofficial rather than a —— way. She could not —— her suspicions. He was not only —— himself, but devoted to ——.

Junct (join): (1) junction, juncture, injunction, disjunctive, conjugal, adjust; (2) adjunct, conjunction, subjunctive, conjugate.

112 CENTURY VOCABULARY BUILDER

Sentences: A —— force had entered their —— relationships. At this —— he gave the —— that disturbances should cease. The tramp halted at the —— to eat his lunch and —— his knapsack.

Jure (swear): (1 and 2 combined) juror, jury, abjure, adjure, conjurer, perjury.

Sentences: They —— their loyalty. He —— them to remember their duty as ——. The —— held the —— guilty of ——.

Leg, lig, lect (read, choose, pick up): (1) elegant, illegible, college, negligent, diligent, eligible, elect, select, intellect, recollect, neglect, lecturer, collection, coil, cull; (2) legend, legion, legacy, legate, delegate, sacrilegious, dialect, lectern, colleague, lexicon.

Sentences: In —— he listened to the —— and took an occasional note in an —— hand. She —— an —— costume. They —— the only man who was ——. He did not —— to take up the ——. He was —— rather than ——. Her mind was too —— to —— all the circumstances.

Lig (bind): (1 and 2 combined) ligament, ligature, obligation, ally, alliance, allegiance, league, lien, liable, liaison, alloy.

Sentences: It was a pleasure that knew no ——. To belong to the —— carries ——. In studying anatomy you learn all about —— and ——. The two nations were in ——. We may be sure of their ——. We will take a —— upon your property. As a —— officer he was —— for the equipment which our —— reported lost.

Luc, lum, lus (light): (1) lucid, translucent, luminous, illuminate, luminary, luster, illustrate, illustrious; (2) lucent, Lucifer, lucubration, elucidate, pellucid, relume, limn.

INDIVIDUAL WORDS: OF VERBAL FAMILIES 113

Sentences: The —— author spoke very ——. He gave us a —— explanation of a very abstruse subject. The material was —— even to the rays of the feeblest of the heavenly ——. He —— his theory by the following anecdote. This deed added —— to his fame.

Mand (order): (1 and 2 combined) mandate, mandamus, mandatory, demand, remand, countermand, commandment.

Sentences: The superior court issued a writ of ——. The case was —— to the lower court. His instructions were not discretionary, but ——. At your —— the —— has been issued. The —— promptly —— the orders of the offending officer.

Mit, mis, mise (send): (1) permit, submit, commit, remit, transmit, mission, missile, missionary, remiss, omission, commission, admission, dismissal, promise, surmise, compromise, mass, message; (2) emit, intermittent, missive, commissary, emissary, manumission, inadmissible, premise, demise.

Sentences: The —— could only —— why so many of his people had not attended ——. The —— contained a —— that no one would be held ——. The request was —— that he would please ——. He —— to his —— without a protest. A —— was appointed to investigate whether the territory should be granted —— as a state. His —— was such as to —— him to tarry if he chose.

Move, mote, mob (move): (1) move, movement, removal, remote, promote, promotion, motion, motive, emotion, commotion, motor, locomotive, mob, mobilize, automobile, moment; (2) immovable, motivate, locomotor ataxia, mobility, immobile, momentum.

Sentences: The next —— was his, and his —— was profound. The —— of the —— from across the alley enabled the —— to surge in a threatening —— toward the rear of the building. At this —— the —— was great. The officer whose —— had seemed so —— was now enabled to —— strong forces for the campaign. The —— began a slow —— forward. His exact —— was not known.

Pass, path (suffer): (1) passion, passive, impassive, impassioned, compassion, pathos, pathetic, impatient, apathy, sympathy, antipathy; (2) passible, impassible, dispassionate, pathology, telepathy, hydropathy, homeopathy, allopathy, osteopathy, neuropathic, pathogenesis.

Sentences: With an —— countenance he spoke of the —— of our Lord. The —— of the story moved her to ——. He allowed his —— no further expression than through that one —— shrug. With a —— smile he settled back into dull ——. His plea was ——.

Ped, pod (foot): (1) pedal, pedestrian, pedestal, expedite, expediency, expedition, quadruped, impediment, biped, tripod, chiropodist, octopus, pew; (2) centiped, pedicle, pedometer, velocipede, sesquipedalian, antipodes, podium, polypod, polyp, Piedmont.

Sentences: A —— suggested that we could —— matters by each mounting a ——. The loss of the —— was a serious —— to the rider of the bicycle. The —— had me place my foot on an artist's ——. The purpose of this nautical —— was to capture a live ——. The —— of having so large a —— for the statue had not occurred to us. A —— scarcely recognizable as human occupied my ——.

Pell, pulse (drive): (1) dispel, compel, propeller, repellent, repulse, repulsive, impulse, compulsory, expulsion, appeal; (2) appellate, interpellate.

Sentences: After the —— of the attack, the mists along the lowlands were ——. His manner was ——, even ——. The revolutions of the —— soon —— the boatmen to shove farther off. After his —— he —— for a rehearing of his case. The act was ——, but he felt an —— toward it anyhow.

INDIVIDUAL WORDS: OF VERBAL FAMILIES

Pend, pense, pond (hang, weigh): (1) pending, impending, independent, pendulum, perpendicular, expenditure, pension, suspense, expense, pensive, compensate, ponder, ponderous, preponderant, pansy, poise, pound; (2) pendant, stipend, appendix, compendium, propensity, recompense, indispensable, dispensation, dispensary, avoirdupois.

Sentences: The veterans felt great —— while action regarding their —— was ——. We shall —— you. An arm of it stood in a position —— to the —— mass. He knew that fate was ——, and he watched the —— swing back and forth slowly. He gave a —— argument in favor of the —— of the money. There is ——, that's for thoughts. Let us —— the question whether the —— is needful. She was a woman of rare social ——. Penny-wise, ——-foolish.

Pet (seek): (1 and 2 combined) petition, petulant, impetus, impetuous, perpetuate, repeat, compete, competent, appetite, centripetal.

Sentences: A great —— force keeps the planets circling about the sun. The complaints of a —— woman led him to —— for the prize. The sexual —— leads men to —— the race. The —— was pronounced upon —— authority to be ill drawn up. With —— wrath he —— the assertion. The —— became noticeably weaker.

Ply, plic, plicate (fold): (1) ply, reply, imply, plight, suppliant, explicit, implicit, implicate, supplicate, duplicate, duplicity, complicate, complicity, accomplice, application, plait, display, plot, employee, exploit, simple, supple; (2) pliant, pliable, replica, explication, inexplicable, multiplication, deploy, triple, quadruple, plexus, duplex.

Sentences: We —— the thief's —— with questions. He —— that others were —— with him. The king —— to the

―― that such ―― must never be ―― in the realm thereafter. It would be a ―― matter to ―― the order. The manager had ―― confidence in his ――. She admired his courage in this ――, perceived his ―― in the crime, and deplored his participation in the ――. They ―― him for an ―― promise that mercy would be shown. She was in a ――, for she had not had time to arrange her hair in its usual broad ――. He was ―― of body. The ―― was refused.

Pose, pone (place): (1) expose, compose, purpose, posture, position, composure, impostor, postpone, post office, positive, deposit, disposition, imposition, deponent, opponent, exponent, component; (2) depose, impost, composite, apposite, repository, preposition, interposition, juxtaposition, decomposition.

Sentences: The ―― said he would ―― the manner in which the cashier had made away with the ――. The true ―― of the ―― was now known, yet he retained his ――. For you to make yourself an ―― of these wild theories is an ―― on your friends. The closing hour at the ―― is ―― thirty minutes on account of the rush of Christmas mail. He was ―― that his ―― had ―― the letter. One of the ―― elements in his ―― was gloom.

Prise, prehend (seize): (1) prize, apprise, surprise, comprise, enterprise, imprison, comprehend, apprehension; (2) reprisal, misprision, reprehend, prehensile, apprentice, impregnable, reprieve.

Sentences: He had no ―― as to what the ―― would ――. His ―― was so great that he could scarcely ―― the fact that the ―― was his. The judge ―― them of the likelihood that they would be ――.

Prob (prove): (1 and 2 combined) probe, probation, probate, probity, approbation, reprobate, improbable.

Sentences: The young ―― was placed on ――. The will was brought into the ―― court. It is ―― that such ―― as his will win the ―― of evil-doers.

INDIVIDUAL WORDS: OF VERBAL FAMILIES

Rupt (break): (1 and 2 combined) rupture, abrupt, interrupt, disrupt, eruption, incorruptible, irruption, bankrupt, rout, route, routine.

Sentences: The volcano was in ——. Though ——, he remained ——. The —— of the barbarians —— these reforms. The organization was —— after having already been put to ——. The —— he had chosen led to a —— in their relationships. It was —— work.

Sed, sid(e), sess (seat): (1) sedulous, sedentary, supersede, subside, preside, reside, residue, possess, assessment, session, siege; (2) sediment, insidious, assiduous, subsidy, obsession, see (noun), assize.

Sentences: The —— was so small that he scarcely noticed he —— it. The officer was —— in making the —— upon every tax-payer fair. During the —— Congress remained in ——. He —— in the city and has a —— occupation. When the officer who —— is firm, such commotions will quickly ——. He —— the disgraced commander.

Sequ, secu, sue (follow): (1) sequel, sequence, consequence, subsequent, consecutive, execute, prosecute, persecute, sue, ensue, suitor, suitable, pursuit, rescue, second; (2) obsequies, obsequious, sequester, inconsequential, non sequitur, executor, suite.

Sentences: On the —— day they continued the ——. In the —— chapter of the —— the heroine is ——. The —— of events is hard to follow. The —— was that her brother began to —— her ——. The district attorney —— six —— offenders, but thought it useless to bring any —— offender to trial. It was a —— occasion.

Shear, share, shore (cut, separate): (1 and 2 combined) shear, sheer, shred, share, shard, scar, score, (sea)shore, shorn, shroud, shire, sheriff.

118 CENTURY VOCABULARY BUILDER

Sentences: The —— had on his face a —— made by a —— thrown at him. In that —— it is an old custom for every one to —— in the —— of the sheep. There was, instead of the usual ——, a —— cliff that rose from the sea. All —— as the freshman was, he had hardly a —— of his former dignity. The —— was very one-sided. A —— of mist was about him.

Sign (sign): (1) sign, signal, signify, signature, consign, design, assign, designate, resignation, insignificant; (2) ensign, signatory, insignia.

Sentences: He —— his approval of the ——. The disturbance caused by his —— was ——. He —— no reason for —— those particular men. As he could not write his own ——, I —— the document for him. It was a —— defeat.

Solve, solu (loosen): (1) solve, resolve, dissolve, solution, dissolute, resolute, absolute; (2) solvent, absolution, indissoluble, assoil.

Sentences: On account of his —— course he had given his parents many a problem to ——. He —— the powder in a cupful of water and —— to give it to the patient. This —— of the difficulty did not win the —— approval of his employer. The obstacles were many, but he was ——.

Spec(t), spic(e) (look): (1) spectator, spectacle, suspect, aspect, prospect, expect, respectable, disrespect, inspection, speculate, special, especial, species, specify, specimen, spice, suspicion, conspicuous, despise, despite, spite; (2) specter, spectrum, spectroscope, prospector, prospectus, introspection, retrospect, circumspectly, conspectus, perspective, specie, specification, specious, despicable, auspices, perspicacity, frontispiece, respite.

Sentences: His —— was conducted in such a manner as to show the utmost ——. In —— she noticed an odor of ——. From his —— you would have taken him to be a —— of wild animal. The —— was better than we had —— it to be.

INDIVIDUAL WORDS: OF VERBAL FAMILIES

Though you have no —— fondness for children, you will enjoy the —— of them playing together. The —— did not —— what underhand tactics some of the players were resorting to. In —— of all this, we made a —— showing. The —— is one you cannot ——. —— this —— of matters, she did not —— the cause of her ——, but let him —— what it might be.

Spire, spirit (breathe, breath): (1 and 2 combined) spirit, spiritual, perspire, transpire, respire, aspire, conspiracy, inspiration, expiration, esprit de corps.

Sentences: At the —— of a few days it —— that a —— had actually been formed. The —— of the division was such that every man —— to meet the enemy forthwith. He was a man of much —— and marked powers of ——. As he lay there, he merely —— and ——; he had no thought whatsoever of things ——.

Sta, sti(t), sist (stand): (1) stand, stage, statue, stall, stationary, state, reinstate, station, forestall, instant, instance, distance, constant, withstand, understand, circumstance, estate, establish, substance, obstacle, obstinate, destiny, destination, destitute, substitute, superstition, desist, persist, resist, insist, assist, exist, consistent, stead, rest, restore, restaurant, contrast; (2) stature, statute, stadium, stability, instable, static, statistics, ecstasy, stamen, stamina, standard, stanza, stanchion, capstan, extant, constabulary, apostate, transubstantiation, status quo, armistice, solstice, interstice, institute, restitution, constituent, subsistence, pre-existence, presto.

Sentences: The —— of the motion was that the student who had been expelled should be ——. He —— in his —— resolution to go on the ——. She could not —— the pleas of —— people. He —— her to alight at the ——. In an —— you shall —— what the —— was that drove me to tempt —— thus. We had gone but a little —— when I perceived by the hungry working of his jaws that his —— was the —— in the next block. No —— could cause him to ——. She was —— in a —— at the bazaar.

Stead (place): (1 and 2 combined) stead, steadfast, instead, homestead, farmstead, roadstead, bestead.

Sentences: —— of resting in a harbor, the ships were tossed about in an open ——. Little did it —— him to cling to the old ——. A —— nestled by the highway. To be known as —— now stood him in good ——.

Strict, string, strain (bind): (1) district, restrict, strictly, stringent, strain, restrain, constrain; (2) stricture, constriction, boa constrictor, astringent, strait, stress.

Sentences: We —— them by means of —— regulations. He —— them to this course by his mere example. He attended —— to his duties. You should not —— your pleasures in this way. The —— of long effort was telling on him.

Tact, tang, tain, ting, teg (touch): (1) tact, contact, intact, intangible, attain, taint, stain, tinge, contingent, integrity, entire, tint; (2) tactile, tactual, tangent, distain, attaint, attainder, integer, disintegrate, contagion, contaminate, contiguous.

Sentences: His appointment is —— upon his removing this —— from his name. His —— is such that no —— with evil could leave any —— upon him. The contents were ——. With —— he hopes to —— the —— approval of his auditors. It was a dark ——. The reason is ——.

Tail (cut): (1 and 2 combined) detail, curtail, entail, retail, tailor, tally.

Sentences: He held the property in ——. He kept the reckoning straight by means of —— cut in a shingle. He resolved to —— expenses by visiting the —— less often. We need not go into ——. The profit lies in the difference between wholesale and —— prices.

INDIVIDUAL WORDS: OF VERBAL FAMILIES

Tain (hold—for related *ten* group see page 104): (1 and 2 combined) detain, abstain, contain, obtain, maintain, entertain, pertain, appertain, sustain, retain.

Sentences: Village life and things —— thereto I shall willingly —— from. I —— that precepts of this kind in no sense —— to public morals. If the gentleman can —— the consent of his second, the chair will —— the motion as he restates it. Though your forces may —— heavy losses, they must —— their position and —— the enemy.

Term, termin (end, bound): (1 and 2 combined) term, terminus, terminal, terminate, determine, indeterminate, interminable, exterminate.

Sentences: At the —— of the railroad stands a beautiful —— station. The manner in which we may —— the agreement remains ——. He —— that rather than yield he would make the negotiations ——. During the second —— they —— all the rodents about the school.

Tort (twist): (1) torture, tortoise, retort, contort, distortion, extortionate, torch, (apple)tart, truss, nasturtium; (2) tort, tortuous, torsion, Dry Tortugas.

Sentences: By the light of the —— he saw a —— fowl by the fireside and a —— in the cupboard. The —— of his countenance was due to the —— he was undergoing. ——ing his face into a very knowing look, he —— that a man with a —— in his buttonhole and —— shell glasses on his nose had leered at the girls as he passed.

Tract, tra(i) (draw): (1) tract, tractor, intractable, abstracted, retract, protract, detract, distract, attractive, contractor, trace, trail, train, trait, portray, retreat; (2) traction, tractate, distraught, extraction, subtraction.

Sentences: In an —— manner he drove the —— across a large —— of ground. He —— his gaze at the —— girl. The —— was now willing to —— his statement that in the house as it stood there was no —— of departure from the specifications. Down the weary —— of the pioneer dashes the palatial modern ——. To be —— was one of his ——. The artist —— her as in a —— state. The —— of his forces —— but little from his fame.

Vene, vent (come): (1) convene, convenient, avenue, revenue, prevent, event, inventor, adventure, convention, circumvent; (2) venire, venue, parvenu, advent, adventitious, convent, preventive, eventuate, intervention.

Sentences: The legislature —— in order to pass a measure regarding the public ——. At the —— the wily old politician was able to —— his enemies. The —— saw no means of —— this infringement of his patent right. In that —— we are likely to have an ——. Through the long, shaded —— they strolled together.

Vert, vers(e) (turn): (1) avert, divert, convert, invert, pervert, advertize, inadvertent, verse, aversion, adverse, adversity, adversary, version, anniversary, versatile, divers, diversity, conversation, perverse, universe, university, traverse, subversive, divorce; (2) vertebra, vertigo, controvert, revert, averse, versus, versification, animadversion, vice versa, controversy, tergiversation, obverse, transverse, reversion, vortex.

Sentences: Though he carried a large —— of goods, he was —— to —— them. He had —— forgotten that it was his wedding ——. The —— was on —— subjects. They —— a broad area where nothing had been done to —— the danger that threatened them. With —— stubbornness he held to his —— of the story. He held that the reading of —— is —— of masculine qualities. His professors at the —— soon —— him to new social and economic theories. Her husband was such a —— creature that she resolved to secure a ——. Americans are the most —— people in the ——. The anecdote —— his —— himself. Her answer not only was ——; it revealed her ——. He had undergone grave —— in his time.

Vince, vict (conquer): (1 and 2 combined) evince, con-

INDIVIDUAL WORDS: OF VERBAL FAMILIES 123

vince, province, invincible, evict, convict, conviction, victorious.

Sentences: He was —— that the campaign against the rebels in the —— could not be ——. He —— a lively interest in my theory that the fugitive could not be ——. He felt an —— repugnance to —— the man, and this in spite of his —— that the man was guilty.

Voc, voke (call, voice): (1) vocal, vocation, advocate, irrevocable, vociferous, provoke, revoke, evoke, convoke; (2) vocable, vocabulary, avocation, equivocal, invoke, avouch, vouchsafe.

Sentences: He was a —— —— of the measure, but no sooner was the order issued than he wished it ——. In —— the assembly he —— the enthusiasm of his followers. That he should give —— utterance to this thought —— me; but the words, once spoken, were ——.

Volve, volute (roll, turn): (1) involve, devolve, revolver, evolution, revolutionary, revolt, voluble, volume, vault; (2) circumvolve, convolution, convolvulus.

Sentences: It —— upon me to put down the ——. In this —— the heroine is —— and the hero handy with a ——. He was —— in a —— uprising. He had laid the papers away in a ——. The —— of civilization is a tedious story.

Second General Exercise

Copy both sections (the first consists of fairly familiar terms, the second of less familiar terms) of each of the following word-groups. Find the key-syllable, underscore it in each word, observe any modifications in its form. Decide for yourself what its meaning is; then verify or correct your conclusion by reference to the dictionary. Study the influence of the key-syllable upon the meaning of each separate word; find the word's original signification, its present signification. Add to each word-group as many cognate words as you can (1) think of for yourself, (2) find in the dictionary by looking under the key-syllable. Fill the blanks in the sentences after each word-group with terms chosen from the first section of words in that group.

(1) Animosity, unanimous, magnanimity; (2) animus, animadvert, equanimity.

Sentences: It was the —— opinion that to so noble a foe —— should be shown. The spiteful man continued to display his ——.

(1) Annual, annuity, anniversary, perennial, centennial, solemn; (2) superannuate, biennial, millennium.

Sentences: The amateur gardener made the —— discovery that the plant was a ——. The —— celebration of the great man's birth took a —— and imposing form in our city. By a happy coincidence the increase in his —— came on his wedding ——.

(1) Audit, auditor, auditorium, audience, inaudible, obey; (2) aurist, auricular, auscultation.

Sentences: His voice may not have been ——, but it certainly did not fill the ——. Not one —— in all that vast —— but was willing to —— his slightest suggestion. He was not willing that they should —— his accounts.

(1) Automatic, automobile, autocrat, autobiography; (2) autograph, autonomy.

Sentences: The —— dictated to his secretary the third chapter of his ——. The habit of changing gear properly in an —— becomes almost ——.

(1) Cant, descant, incantation, chant, enchant, chanticleer, accent, incentive; (2) canto, canticle, cantata, recant, chantry, chanson, precentor.

Sentences: He —— upon this topic in a queer, foreign ——. Such utterances are mere sanctimonious ——; I had rather listen to the —— of a voodoo conjurer. The little girl from the city was —— with the crowing of ——. The —— of the choir somehow gave him the —— to try again.

INDIVIDUAL WORDS: OF VERBAL FAMILIES

(1) Cent, per cent., century, centennial; (2) centenary, centime, centurion, centimeter, centigrade.

Sentences: For nearly a —— this family has been living on a small —— of its income. I wouldn't give a —— for —— honors; I want my reward now.

(1) Chronic, chronological, chronicle; (2) chronometer, synchronize, anachronism.

Sentences: It is a —— record of changing activities and —— ills. This page is a —— of athletic news.

(1) Corps, corpse, corporal, corpulent, corporation, incorporate; (2) corpus, habeas corpus, corporeal, corpuscle, Corpus Christi.

Sentences: The —— gentleman said he did not believe in —— punishment. The hospital —— carried the —— into the office of a great ——. He resolved to —— this idea into the reforms he was introducing.

(1 and 2 combined) Creed, credulous, credential, credit, accredit, discredit, incredible.

Sentences: He was not so —— as to suppose that his —— would be accepted and his statements —— without some investigation. It is to his —— that he refused to be bound by his former religious ——. That such —— has been heaped upon him is ——.

(1) Crescent, increase, decrease, concrete, recruit, accrue, crew; (2) crescendo, excrescence, accretion, increment.

Sentences: The —— now had —— evidence that military life was not altogether pleasant. In the olden days on the sea deaths from scurvy might bring about a dangerous —— in the size of the ——. His courage —— with the profits that —— to him. The —— moon rode in the sky.

(1) Cure, secure, procure, sinecure, curious, inaccurate; (2) curate, curator.

> *Sentences:* Occupying the position for a while will —— you of the notion that it is a ——. He was —— to know so a bookkeeper had managed to —— so high a salary. He —— the equipment required.

(1 and 2 combined) Indignity, indignation, undignified, condign, deign, dainty.

> *Sentences:* We must not be too —— about visiting —— punishment upon those responsible for this ——. He did not —— to express his ——. It was an —— act.

(1) Durable, endure, during, duration, obdurate; (2) durance, duress, indurate, perdurable.

> *Sentences:* —— the whole interview she remained ——. It is a —— cloth; it will —— all sorts of weather. The session was one of prolonged ——.

(1) Finite, infinite, define, definite, confine, final, in fine, unfinished; (2) definitive, infinitesimal.

> *Sentences:* One cannot —— the ——. He —— himself to purely —— topics. —— it was a —— offer and the —— one he expected to make. The bridge is still ——.

(1) Flexibility, inflexible, deflect, inflection, reflection, reflex; (2) circumflex, genuflection.

> *Sentences:* The —— influence of this act was great. I did not like the —— of his voice. After some —— he decided to remain ——. He was not to be —— from his purpose. I could but admire the —— of her tones.

(1) Fluent, affluent, influence, influenza, superfluous, fluid, influx, flush (rush of water), fluctuate; (2) confluent, mellifluous, flux, reflux, effluvium, flume.

INDIVIDUAL WORDS: OF VERBAL FAMILIES

Sentences: When you —— the basin, an —— of water fills it again. He is an —— man and a —— writer. When I had ——, the doctor gave me a disgusting —— to drink. The wind must have an —— in making the waves —— as they do. Any more would be ——.

(1) Fort, forte, effort, comfort, fortitude, fortify, fortress; (2) aqua fortis, pianoforte.

Sentences: The defenders of the —— held out with great ——. Though a —— or two stood at important passes, the border was not really ——. His —— was not public speaking. It was only by an —— that he could —— them.

(1) Fraction, infraction, fracture, fragility, fragment, suffrage, frail, infringe; (2) diffract, refractory, frangible.

Sentences: It was in the course of his —— of the rules that he suffered the —— of his collar-bone. He told the committee of ladies that he was as fond of —— as of ——. It is hardly a proof of —— that he is so willing to —— upon the rights of others. The —— scaffolding bent and swung as he trod it.

(1 and 2 combined) Fugitive, fugue, refuge, subterfuge, centrifugal.

Sentences: Closing his eyes as if to listen better to the —— was a little —— of his. The upward movement of the missile was arrested by the —— attraction of the earth. The —— took —— in an abandoned barn.

(1) Refund, confound, foundry, confuse, suffuse, profuse, refuse, diffuse; (2) fusion, effusion, transfuse.

Sentences: With —— cheeks and —— utterance he made a —— apology. The amount we lost through the defective work at your —— should be —— to us. Such a blow might —— but not —— him. He —— the appointment.

(1) Belligerent, gesture, suggest, congested, digestion, register, jest; (2) gerund, congeries.

Sentences: As he stopped before the cash —— he gave a —— which showed that his —— was none too good. His look was ——, but he lightly made a ——. Amid the —— traffic she stopped to —— that pink would be more becoming than lavender.

(1) Relate, translate, legislate, elation, dilated, dilatory; (2) collate, correlate, prelate, oblation, superlative, ablative.

Sentences: With —— eyes he —— the passage for me. The —— was very —— in agreeing upon the measure to be passed. He —— the story with pride and ——.

(1) Locate, locality, locomotive, dislocate; (2) locale, allocate, collocation.

Sentences: In trying to —— the mine as near the fissure as possible he fell and —— his hip. It was the only —— in that entire ——.

(1) Soliloquy, loquacious, loquacity, colloquial, eloquent, obloquy, circumlocution, elocution; (2) magniloquent, grandiloquent, ventriloquism, interlocutor, locutory, allocution. (For related *log* and *ology* words see page 100.)

Sentences: —— always, he indulged at this time in a great deal of ——. Though it was mere ——, yet there was something —— about it. Amid all this —— he managed to rid himself of a good deal of —— regarding Standish. Hamlet's —— on suicide is a famous passage.

(1) Allude, elude, delude, ludicrous, illusory, collusion; (2) prelude, postlude, interlude.

Sentences: Such evidence is ——, and belief in it is ——. He —— to a possible —— between them. The more credulous ones he ——, and the skeptical he manages to ——.

INDIVIDUAL WORDS: OF VERBAL FAMILIES

(1) Metrical, thermometer, barometer, pedometer, diametrically, geometry; (2) millimeter, chronometer, hydrometer, trigonometry, pentameter.

Sentences: He was careful to consult both the —— and the ——. He always wore a —— on these trips. The two were —— opposed to each other. The poet has great —— skill. —— is an exact science.

(1) Monotone, monotonous, monoplane, monopoly, monocle, monarchy, monogram, monomania; (2) monosyllable, monochrome, monogamy, monorail, monograph, monolith, monody, monologue, monad, monastery, monk.

Sentences: His eye held a ——, his gold ring bore a —— seal, and his voice was a stilted ——. One thing I hate about a —— is the —— reference to everything as his majesty's. He had a —— of the trade in his town. He is suffering, not from madness, but from ——.

(1) Mortal, immortality, mortify, post mortem, mortgage, morgue; (2) mortmain, moribund, à la mort.

Sentences: After a hasty —— examination, the body was taken to the ——. She was —— at this reminder of the —— on her father's property. The —— shall put on ——.

(1 and 2 combined) Mutual, mutation, permutation, commute, transmute, immutable, moult.

Sentences: As he —— that morning he reflected upon the —— and combinations of fortune. We suffer the —— of this worldly life, but ourselves are not ——. God's love is ——, and our love for each other should be ——. Birds when they —— are weakened in body and depressed in spirit.

(1) Native, prenatal, innate, nature, unnatural, naturalize, nation, pregnant, puny; (2) denatured, nativity, cognate, agnate, nascent, renascence, née.

Sentences: It was some —— influence, he thought, that gave him his —— physique. It was a —— reply, but its heartlessness was ——. He was not —— to the country, but ——. —— in his —— was the love of his own ——.

(1) Note, notion, notable, notice, notorious, cognizant, incognito, recognize, noble, ignoble, ennoble, ignore, ignorance, ignoramus, reconnoiter, quaint, acquaintance; (2) notary, notation, connotation, cognition, prognosticate, reconnaissance, connoisseur.

Sentences: In complete —— of the enemy's position, he decided that he would —— it. —— himself, he was —— of what was going on about him. You must —— the conduct of such an ——. His —— with this —— gentleman ——him. He —— but would not —— this —— fellow. The —— is a —— one. He could but —— how —— his brother had become.

(1) Panacea, panoply, panorama, pantomime, pan-American, pandemonium; (2) pantheist, pantheon.

Sentences: Arrayed in all the —— of savages, they acted the scene out in ——. From this point the —— of the countryside unrolled itself before him. It is no —— for human ills; any supposition that it is will lead to ——. It is a —— movement.

(1) Peter, petrify, petrol, stormy petrel, petroleum, saltpeter, pier; (2) petrology, parsley, samphire.

Sentences: As he walked along the ——, he observed the flight of the ——. The English name for gasoline is ——. —— is used in the manufacture of gunpowder. He was almost —— at hearing of this enormous stock of ——. The crowing of the cock caused —— to weep bitterly.

(1 and 2 combined) Petty, petite, petit jury, petit larceny, petticoat, pettifogger.

Sentences: Charged with ——, he was tried by the ——. The contemptible —— hid behind the —— of his wife. She was a winsome maiden, dainty and ——. It is a —— fault.

(1 and 2 combined) Philosophy, philanthropy, Philadelphia, bibliophile, Anglophile.

Sentences: His —— was generous, but his —— was not profound. That queer old —— hangs to the library like a cater-

INDIVIDUAL WORDS: OF VERBAL FAMILIES

pillar. It was the love of humankind that caused Penn to name the city ——. Most Americans are not ——.

(1 and 2 combined) Cosmopolitan, metropolitan, politics, policy, police.

Sentences: Those who engage in —— lack, as a rule, a —— outlook. It is merely —— intolerance of towns and villages. The —— of the mayor was to increase the —— force.

(1 and 2 combined) Potential, potency, potentate, impotent, omnipotent, plenipotentiary.

Sentences: So far from being ——, we possess a —— difficult to estimate. The —— sent an ambassador ——. A —— solution of the problem is this. —— God.

(1) Impute, compute, dispute, ill repute, reputation, disreputable; (2) putative, indisputable.

Sentences: She could not —— the cost. There was some —— as to the cause of his ——. Let them —— to me what motives they will. Though somewhat ——, he was extremely solicitous about his ——.

(1) Abrogate, arrogate, interrogate, arrogant, derogatory, prerogative; (2) surrogate, rogation, prorogue.

Sentences: In an —— manner he —— these —— to himself. To —— authority is to give opportunity for remarks —— to one's reputation. He skilfully —— the witness.

(1) Salmon, sally, assail, assault, insult, consult, result, exultation, desultory; (2) salient, salacious, resilient.

Sentences: After the —— the firing was ——. The defenders —— out and —— us, but the —— of this effort only added to our ——. We sat there watching the —— leap over the waterfall and —— about our arrangements for taking them. To accept the remark as an —— is to acknowledge the speaker as an equal.

(1) Science, conscience, unconscious, prescience, omniscience, nice; (2) sciolist, adscititious, plebiscite.

Sentences: By his —— understanding of the issues he was able to gain a reputation for ——. We thought he possessed ——, but he seemed —— of his erudition. Except under the sharp necessities of ——, he was ruled by a —— thoroughly tender.

(1) Sect, section, non-sectarian, dissect, insect, intersection, vivisection, segment, sickle; (2) bisect, trisect, insection, sector, secant.

Sentences: He stood at the —— of the roads, leaning on the shank of a sharp ——. The foreman of the —— gang is a member of our ——. The boy was —— an —— with a butcher knife he had previously used to cut for himself a large —— of the Sunday cake. It is a —— movement. He defended the —— of animals.

(1) Sense, consent, assent, resent, sentimental, dissension, sensation, sensibility, sentence, scent, nonsense; (2) sentient, consensus, presentiment.

Sentences: A woman of her —— would shrink from a —— of this sort. He —— in a single, crisp ——. To be —— is to be guilty of ——. He had the good —— to —— to this course. He —— such —— and the causes that produced them. A hound hunts by ——.

(1) Despond, respond, correspond, corespondent, sponsor; (2) sponsion, spouse, espouse.

Sentences: She —— that her husband had been —— with the ——. The —— of the movement could as yet see no reason to ——.

(1 and 2 combined) Structure, instructor, construct, obstruct, destructive, misconstrue, instrument.

Sentences: The student —— the intentions of his ——. He resolved to —— every effort to complete the ——. The —— was one that might easily be turned to —— work. They —— a grandstand overlooking the racetrack.

INDIVIDUAL WORDS: OF VERBAL FAMILIES

(1) Terrace, territory, subterranean, inter, terrier; (2) terrene, tureen, terrestrial, terra cotta, Mediterranean, terra firma, parterre.

Sentences: The ―― was tearing a great hole in the ―― in order to ―― a bone. He found rich ―― deposits. The discoverers laid claim to the entire ――.

(1) Thesis, parenthesis, antithesis, anathema, theme, epithet, treasure; (2) hypothesis, synthesis, metathesis.

Sentences: To set two ideas in ―― to each other makes both more vivid. By way of ―― he informed me that the subject was ―― to his father. On this ―― he can summon a host of picturesque ――. The ―― is one you will find it hard to establish. He was seeking Captain Kidd's buried ――.

(1 and 2 combined) Tumor, tumidity, tumult, tumulus, contumacy.

Sentences: The ―― of his joints was due to rheumatism. His ―― led to a ―― of opposition. So excited was he at the discovery of the ―― that he did not permit the ―― on his hand to restrain him from beginning the excavation.

(1 and 2 combined) Turbid, disturb, perturbation, turbulence, imperturbable, trouble.

Sentences: His ―― manner gave no hint of the ―― within him. The ―― sweep of the stream caused her not the slightest ――. Do not ―― yourself with the thought that you are putting me to any ――.

(1 and 2 combined) Pervade, invade, evasion, vade mecum.

Sentences: He promised that there would be no ―― of payments. Byron's *Childe Harold* was my ―― during my travels in Switzerland and Italy. The fragrance of heliotrope ―― the room. You must not ―― my privacy like this.

(1) Avail, prevail, prevalent, equivalent, valiant, validity, invalid, invalidate; (2) valetudinarian, valediction, valence.

Sentences: The —— of the agreement has been thoroughly established. Our cause is just, and must ——. It is —— to admitting that the terms are now ——. It was a —— act and —— the concessions previously wrested from us. The —— impression is that mere ingenuity will not ——.

(1) Virtue, virile, virgin, virtually; (2) virago, virtuoso, triumvir.

Sentences: It was —— a new arrangement. It is —— soil. To be —— and daring is every boy's dream. —— is its own reward.

(1) Revive, survival, convivial, vivid, vivify, vivacious, vivisection; (2) vive (le roi), qui vive, bon vivant, tableau vivant.

Sentences: He has a —— manner, a —— spirit. The —— of the opposition to the —— of animals is very marked. You cannot —— a dead cause or scarcely —— memories of it. The —— coloring of her cheeks was a sure sign of health, or of skill.

Third General Exercise

Find the key-syllable (in a few instances the key-syllables) of each of the following words. How does it affect the meaning of the word? Does it appear, perhaps in disguised form, in any of the words immediately preceding or following? Can you bring to mind other words that embody it?

Innovation	Denomination	Dandelion	Efflorescent
Commonwealth	Ignominy	Trident	Arbor vitæ
Welfare	Synonym	Indenture	Consider
Wayfarer	Patronymic	Contemporary	Constellation
Adjournment	Parliament	Disseminate	Disaster
Rival	Dormitory	Annoy	Suburb
Derivation	Demented	Odium	Address
Arrive	Presumptuous	Desolate	Dirigible
Denunciation	Indent	Impugn	Dirge

INDIVIDUAL WORDS: OF VERBAL FAMILIES

Indirectly	Rapture	Quiet	Hilarious
Desperate	Exasperate	Requiem	Exhilarate
Inoperative	Complacent	Acquiesce	Rudiment
Benevolent	Dimension	Ambidextrous	Erudite
Voluntary	Commensurate	Inoculate	Mark
Offend	Preclude	Divulge	Marquis
Enumerate	Cloister	Proper	Libel
Dilapidate	Turnpike	Appropriate	Libretto
Request	Travesty	Omnivorous	Vague
Exquisite	Atone	Voracious	Vagabond
Exonerate	Incarnate	Devour	Extravagant
Approximate	Charnal	Escritoire	Souse
Insinuate	Etiquette	Mordant	Saucer
Resurgence	Rejuvenate	Remorse	Oyster
Insurrection	Eradicate	Miser	Ostracize

Fourth General Exercise

With a few exceptions like the hale—heal group on page 110, most verbal families of straight English or of Germanic-Scandinavian-English descent are easily recognizable as families. Witness the *good* family on page 91 and the *stead* family on page 120. The families in which kinship may be overlooked are likely to be of Latin or Greek ancestry, though perhaps with a subsequent infusion of blood from some other foreign language, as French. Hitherto our approach to verbal families has been through the descendants, or through that quality in their blood which holds them together. But we shall also profit from knowing something of the founders of these families—from having some acquaintance with them as individuals. Below (in separate lists) the more prominent of Latin and of Greek progenitors are named, their meaning is given, and two or three of their living representatives (not always direct descendants) are designated. Starred words are those whose progeny has not been in good part assembled in the preceding pages; for these words you should assemble all the living representatives you can. (Inflectional forms are given only where they are needed for tracing English derivatives.)

Latin Ancestors of English Words

Latin word	Meaning	English representatives
Ago, actum	do, rouse	agile, transact
*Alius	other	alias, inalienable

CENTURY VOCABULARY BUILDER

Latin word	Meaning	English representatives
*Alter	other	alteration, adultery
*Altus	high	altitude, exalt
*Ambulo	walk	perambulator, preamble
*Amicus	friend	amicable, enemy
*Amo, amatum	love	inamorata, amateur, inimical
*Anima	life	animal, inanimate
Animus	mind	animosity, unanimous
Annus	year	annuity, biennial
*Aqua	water	aquarium, aqueduct
Audio, auditum	hear	audience, audit
*Bellum	war	rebel, belligerent
*Bene	well	benefit, benevolence
*Bonus	good	bonanza, bona fide
*Brevis	short	abbreviate, unabridged
Cado, casum	fall	cadence, casual
Caedo, cecidi, caesum	cut, kill	suicide, incision
Cano, cantum	sing	recant, chanticleer
Capio, captum	take, hold	capacious, incipient
*Caput, capitis	head	cape (Cape Cod), decapitate, chapter, biceps
Cedo, cessum	go	concede, accessory
Centum	hundred	per cent., centigrade
*Civis	citizen	civic, uncivilized
*Clamo	shout	acclaim, declamation
*Claudo, clausum	close, shut	conclude, recluse, cloister, sluice
Cognosco (see Nosco)		
*Coquo, coxi, coctum	cook	decoction, precocious
*Cor, cordis	heart	core, discord, courage
Corpus	body	corpse, incorporate
Credo, creditum	believe	creed, discreditable
Cresco, cretum	grow	crescendo, concrete, accrue
*Crux, crucis	cross	crucifix, excruciating
Cura	care	curate, sinecure
Curro, cursum	run	occur, concourse
*Derigo, directum	direct	dirge, dirigible, address
*Dexter	right, right hand	ambidextrous, dexterity
Dico	speak, say	abdicate, verdict
*Dies	day	diary, quotidian

INDIVIDUAL WORDS: OF VERBAL FAMILIES

Latin word	Meaning	English representatives
Dignus	worthy, fitting	dignity, condign
Do, datum	give	condone, data
*Doceo, doctum	teach	document, doctor
*Dominus	lord	dominion, danger
*Domus	house	domicile, majordomo
*Dormio	sleep	dormant, dormouse
Duco	lead	traduce, deduction
*Duo	two	dubious, duet
Durus	hard	durable, obdurate
Eo, itum	go	exit, initial
Error, erratum	wander	erroneous, aberration
Facio, feci, factum	make, do	manufacture, affect, sufficient, verify
Fero, latum	carry	transfer, relate
Fido	trust, believe	confide, perfidious
Finis	end	confine, infinity
Flecto, flexum	bend	reflection, inflexible
Fluo, fluxum	flow	influence, reflux
Fortis	strong	fortress, comfort
Frango, fractum	break	infringe, refraction
*Frater	brother	fraternity, fratricide
Fugio, fugitum	flee	centrifugal, fugitive
Fundo, fusum	pour	refund, profuse, fusion
Gero, gestum	carry	belligerent, gesture, digestion
Gradior, gressus	walk	degrade, progress
*Gratia	favor, good-will, pleasure	ingratiate, congratulate, disgrace
*Grex, gregis	flock	segregate, egregious
Habeo, habitum	have, hold	habituate, prohibit
Itum (see *Eo*)		
Jacio, jeci, jactum	throw, hurl	reject, interjection
Jungo, junctum	join	conjugal, enjoin, juncture
Juro	swear	abjure, perjury
Jus, juris	law, right	justice, jurisprudence
Judex (from *jus dico*)	judge	judgment, prejudice
*Juvenis	young	rejuvenate, juvenilia
Latum (see *Fero*)		
*Laudo, laudatum	praise	allow, laudatory
Lego, lectum	read, choose	elegant, lecturer, dialect
*Lex, legis	law	privilege, illegitimate, legislature

Latin word	Meaning	English representatives
*Liber	book	libel, library
*Liber	free	liberty, deliberate
Ligo	bind	obligation, allegiance, alliance
*Linquo, lictum	leave	delinquent, relict, derelict
*Litera	letter	illiterate, obliterate
Locus	place	collocation, dislocate
Loquor, locutus	speak	soliloquy, elocution
Ludo, lusum	play	prelude, illusory
Lux, lucis / Lumen, luminis	light	lucid, luminary
*Magnus	great	magnate, magnificent
*Malus	bad, evil	malaria, malnutrition
Mando	order	mandatory, commandment
Manus	hand	manual, manufacture
*Mare	sea	maritime, submarine
*Mater	mother	maternal, alma mater
*Medius	middle	mediocre, intermediate
*Mens	mind	mental, demented
*Miror	wonder	mirror, admirable
Mitto, missum	send	commit, emissary
*Mordeo, morsum	bite	mordant, morsel, remorse
Mors, mortis	death	mortal, mortify
Moveo, motum	move	remove, locomotive
*Multus	many	multiform, multiplex
Muto, mutatum	change	transmute, immutable, moult
Nascor, natus	be born	renascence, cognate
*Nihil	nothing	nihilism, annihilate
*Nomen, nominis	name	denomination, renown
*Norma	rule	abnormal, enormous
Nosco, notum / Cognosco, cognitum	know	notation, incognito
*Novus	new	novelty, renovate
*Nuntio	announce	denounce, renunciation
*Opus, operis	work	magnum opus, inoperative
*Pater	father	patrician, patrimony
Patior, passus	suffer	impatient, passion
Pello, pulsum	drive	propeller, repulse
Pendeo, pensum	hang	pendulum, appendix
Pendo, pensum	weigh	compendium, expense
Pes, pedis	foot	expedite, biped

INDIVIDUAL WORDS: OF VERBAL FAMILIES

Latin word	Meaning	English representatives
Peto	seek	impetus, compete
*Plaudo, plausum	clap, applaud	explode, plausible
*Plecto, plexum	braid	perplex, complexion
*Pleo, pletum	fill	complement, expletive
*Plus, pluris	more	surplus, plural
Plico, plicatum	fold	reply, implicate
Pono, positum	place	opponent, deposit
Porto	carry	report, porter
Potens, potentis	powerful	impotent, potential
Prendo, prehensum	seize	comprehend, apprise
*Primus, primatis	first	primary, primate
Probo, probatum	prove	improbable, reprobate
*Pugno	fight	impugn, repugnant
Puto	think	impute, disreputable
*Quaero, quaesitum	seek	require, inquest, exquisite
*Rapio, raptum	seize	enraptured, surreptitious
*Rego, rectum	rule, lead	region, erect
*Rideo, risum	laugh	deride, risible
Rogo, rogatum	ask	prorogue, abrogate
Rumpo, ruptum	break	disrupt, eruption
Salio, saltum	leap	salient, insult
*Sanguis	blood	sang froid, ensanguined
Scio, scitum	know	prescience, plebiscite
Scribo, scriptum	write	prescribe, manuscript, escritoire
Seco, sectum	cut	secant, dissect
Sedeo, sessum	sit	supersede, obsession
Sentio, sensum	feel	presentiment, consensus
Sequor, secutus	follow	sequence, persecute, ensue
Signum	sign	insignia, designate
*Solus	alone	solitude, desolate
Solvo, solutum	loosen	solvent, dissolute
*Somnus	sleep	somnambulist, insomnia
*Sono	sound	consonant, resonance
*Sors, sortis	lot	sort, assortment
Specio, spectum	look	despicable, suspect
Spiro, spiratum	breathe	perspire, conspiracy
*Spondeo, sponsum	promise	respond, espouse
Sto, steti, statum	stand	constant, establish
Sisto, stiti, statum	cause to stand	consistent, superstition
Stringo, strictum	bind	stringent, restrict

Latin word	Meaning	English representatives
Struo, structum	build	construe, destruction
Tango, tactum	touch	intangible, tact
Tempus, temporis	time	temporize, contemporary
Tendo, tensum	stretch	distend, intense
Teneo, tentum	hold	tenure, detention
*Tento	try	tentative, attempt
Terminus	end, boundary	terminal, exterminate
Terra	earth	territory, inter
Torqueo, tortum	twist	distort, tortuous
Traho, tractum	draw	extract, subtraction
Tumeo, tumidum	swell	tumor, contumacy
Turba	tumult, crowd	turbulent, disturb
*Unus	one	unify, triune, onion
*Urbs	city	urbane, suburban
Vado, vasum	go	pervade, invasion
Valeo, validum	be strong	prevail, invalid
Venio, ventum	come	intervene, adventure
Verto, versum	turn	divert, adverse
*Verus	true	verdict, veracity
*Via	way	obviate, impervious, trivial
Video, visum	see	provide, revise
Vinco, victum	conquer	province, convict
Vir	man	triumvir, virtue
Vivo, victum	live	vivacious, vivisect
Voco, vocatum	call	revoke, avocation
*Volo	wish	malevolent, voluntary
Volvo, volutum	turn	revolver, evolution
Vox	voice	equivocal, vociferate

Latin Prefixes

Prefix	Meaning	English embodiments
*A, ab	from, away	avert, abnegation, abstract
*Ad	to	adduce, adjacent, affect, accede
*Ante	before	antediluvian, anteroom
*Bi	two	biped, bicycle
*Circum	around	circumambient, circumference
*Cum, com, con, co	with, together	combine, consort, coadjutor

INDIVIDUAL WORDS: OF VERBAL FAMILIES

Prefix	Meaning	English embodiments
*Contra	against	contradict, contrast
*De	from, down, negative, intensive	deplete, decry, demerit, declaim
*Di, dis	asunder, away from, negative	divert, disbelief
*E, ex	from, out of	evict, excavate
*Extra	beyond	extraordinary, extravagant
*In	in, into, not	innate, instil, insignificant
*Inter	among, between	intercollegiate, interchange
*Intro, intra	into, within	introduce, intramural
*Non	negative	nonage, nondescript
*Ob	against, before (facing), toward	obloquy, obstacle, offer
*Per	through, extremely	persecute, perfervid, pursue, pilgrim, pellucid
*Post	after	postpone, postscript
*Pre	before	prepay, preoccupy
*Pro	before	proceed, proffer
*Re	back, again	return, resound
*Retro	back, backward	retroactive, retrospective
*Se	apart, aside	seclude, secession
*Semi	half	semiannual, semicivilized
*Sub	under, less than, inferior	subscribe, suffer, subnormal, subcommittee
*Super	above, extremely	superfluous, supercritical, soprano
*Trans	across, through	transfer, transparent
*Ultra	beyond, extremely	ultramundane, ultraconservative

Greek Ancestors of English Words

(Scientific terms in English are largely derived from the Greek)

Greek word	Meaning	English representatives
*Aner, andros, anthropos	man, stamen	androgynous, philander, philanthropy
*Archos	chief, primitive	archaic, architect
*Astron	star	asterisk, disaster
Autos	self	autograph, automatic, authentic
*Barys	heavy	baritone, barites

Greek word	Meaning	English representatives
*Biblos	book	Bible, bibliomania
*Bios	life	biology, autobiography, amphibious
*Cheir	hand	chiropody, chirurgical, surgeon
*Chilioi	a thousand	kilogram, kilowatt
*Chroma	color	chromo, achromatic
Chronos	time	chronic, anachronism
*Cosmos	world, order	cosmopolitan, microcosm
*Crypto	hide	cryptogam, cryptology
*Cyclos	wheel, circle	encyclopedia, cyclone
*Deca	ten	decasyllable, decalogue
*Demos	people	democracy, epidemic
*Derma	skin	epidermis, taxidermist
*Dis, di	twice, doubly	dichromatic, digraph
*Didonai, dosis	give	dose, apodosis, anecdote
*Dynamis	power	dynamite, dynasty
*Eidos	form, thing seen	idol, kaleidoscope, anthropoid
*Ethnos	race, nation	ethnic, ethnology
Eu	well	euphemism, eulogy
*Gamos	marriage	cryptogam, bigamy
*Ge	earth	geography, geometry
Genos	family, race	gentle, engender
Gramma	writing	monogram, grammar
Grapho	write	telegraph, lithograph
*Haima	blood	hematite, hemorrhage, anemia
*Heteros	other	heterodox, heterogeneous
*Homos	same	homonym, homeopathy
*Hydor	water	hydraulics, hydrophobia, hydrant
*Isos	equal	isosceles, isotherm
*Lithos	stone	monolith, chrysolite
Logos	word, study	theology, dialogue
Metron	measure	barometer, diameter
*Micros	small	microscope, microbe
Monos	one, alone	monoplane, monotone
*Morphe	form	metamorphosis, amorphous
*Neos	new, young	neolithic, neophyte
*Neuron	nerve	neuralgia, neurotic
Nomos	law, science, management	astronomy, gastronomy, economy

INDIVIDUAL WORDS: OF VERBAL FAMILIES

Greek word	Meaning	English representatives
*Onoma	name	anonymous, patronymic
*Opsis	view, sight	synopsis, thanatopsis, optician
*Orthos	right	orthopedic, orthodox
*Osteon	bone	osteopathy, periosteum
*Pais, paidos	child	paideutics, pedagogue, encyclopedia
Pas, pan	all	diapason, panacea, pantheism
Pathos	suffering	allopathy, pathology
Petros	rock	petroleum, saltpeter
*Phaino	show, be visible	diaphanous, phenomenon, epiphany, fantastic
Philos	loving	bibliophile, Philadelphia
*Phobos	fear	hydrophobia, Anglophobe
Phone	sound	telephone, symphony
*Phos	light	phosphorous, photograph
*Physis	nature	physiognomy, physiology
*Plasma	form	cataplasm, protoplasm
*Pneuma	air, breath	pneumatic, pneumonia
Polis	city	policy, metropolitan
*Polys	many	polyandry, polychrome, polysyllable
Pous, podos	foot	octopus, chiropodist
*Protos	first	protoplasm, prototype
*Pseudes	false	pseudonym, pseudo-classic
*Psyche	breath, soul, mind	psychology, psychopathy
*Pyr	fire	pyrography, pyrotechnics
*Scopos	watcher	scope, microscope
*Sophia	wisdom	philosophy, sophomore
*Techne	art	technicality, architect
*Tele	far, far off	telepathy, telescope
*Temno / *Tomos	cut / that which is cut off	epitome, anatomy, tome
*Theos	god	theosophy, pantheism
*Therme	heat	isotherm, thermodynamics
Tithenai / Thesis	place / a placing, arrangement	epithet, hypothesis, anathema
*Treis	three	trichord, trigonometry
*Zoon	animal	zoology, protozoa, zodiac

Greek Prefixes

Prefix	Meaning	English embodiments
*A, an	no, not	aseptic, anarchy
*Amphi (Latin ambi)	about, around, both	ambidextrous, amphitheater
*Ana	up, again	anatomy, Anabaptist
*Anti	against, opposite	antidote, antiphonal, antagonist
*Cata	down	catalepsy, cataclysm
*Dia	through, across	diameter, dialogue
*Epi	upon	epidemic, epithet, epode, ephemeral
*Hyper	over, extremely	hypercritical, hyperbola
*Hypo	under, in smaller measure	hypodermic, hypophosphate
*Meta	after, over	metaphysics, metaphor
*Para	beside	paraphrase, paraphernalia
*Peri	around, about	periscope, peristyle
*Pro	before	proboscis, prophet
*Syn	together, with	synthesis, synopsis, sympathy

VI

WORDS IN PAIRS

OUR first task in this volume was the study of words in combination. Our second was the study of individual words in two of their aspects—first, as they are seen in isolation, next as they are seen in verbal families. Now our third task confronts us. It is the study of words as they are associated, not in actual blood kinship, but in meaning.

Such an association in meaning may involve only two words (pairs) or larger groups. In this chapter we shall confine ourselves to the study of pairs.

Of the relationship between pairs there are three types. In the first the words are hostile to each other. In the second they may easily be confused with each other. In the third they are parallel with each other. We shall examine the three types successively.

But we must make an explanation first. Although we shall, in this and the following chapters, have frequent occasion to give the meanings of individual words, we shall give them without regard to dictionary methods. We shall not attempt formal, water-tight, or exhaustive definitions; our purpose is to convey, in the simplest and most human manner possible, brief general explanations of what the words stand for.

Opposites

Pairs of the first type are made up of words by nature opposite to each other, or else thought of as opposite because they are so often contrasted. Here is a familiar, everyday list:

east, west	straight, crooked	myself, others
large, small	pretty, ugly	major, minor
laugh, cry	walk, ride	light, darkness
top, bottom	hard, soft	friend, enemy
sweet, sour	clean, dirty	temporal, spiritual
meat, drink	merry, sad	means, extremes
land, water	private, public	Jew, Gentile
man, woman	noisy, quiet	independent, dependent
old, new	general, particular	sublime, ridiculous
age, youth	wholesale, retail	give, receive
sick, well	savage, civilized	pride, humility
brain, brawn	wealth, poverty	constructive, destructive
soul, body	positive, negative	

None of these words needs explaining. If you think of one of them, you will think of its opposite; at least its opposite will be lurking in the back of your mind. As proof of this fact you have only to glance at the following list, from which the second member of each pair is omitted:

hot ——	hope ——
black ——	least ——
boy ——	asleep ——
in ——	buy ——
off ——	left ——
over ——	alive ——
love ——	winter ——
wrong ——	war ——
strong ——	succeed ——
wet ——	creditor ——
first ——	fat ——
day ——	internal ——
long ——	wise ——
fast ——	drunk ——
good ——	

Many words of a more difficult kind are thus pitted against each other, and we learn them, not singly, but in pairs. At least we should. As good verbal hunters we should be alert to the chance of killing two birds with one stone.

Allopath and *homeopath,* for example, are difficult opposites. We know of the existence of the two classes of medical practitioners; we know that they use different methods; but beyond this our knowledge is likely to be hazy. Let us set out, then, to *learn* the two words. The best way is to learn them together. *Allopathy* means other suffering, *homeopathy* like suffering. An allopath uses remedies which create within the patient a condition that squarely conflicts with the further progress of the disease. A homeopath prescribes medicines (in small doses) which produce within the patient the same condition that the disease would produce; he "beats the disease to it," so to speak—takes the job himself and leaves the disease nothing to do. The allopath travels around a race-track in the opposite direction from the disease, and thwarts it through a head-on collision. The homeopath travels around the race-track in the same direction as the disease, and thwarts it by pulling at the reins. If we consider the two words together and get these ideas in mind, we shall have no further trouble with allopaths and homeopaths—except, perhaps, when they have rendered their services and presented their bills.

Objective and *subjective* are also a troublesome pair. A thing is objective if it is an actual object or being, if it exists in itself rather than in our surmises. A thing is subjective if it is the creature of a state of mind, if it has its existence in the thought or imagination of some person or other. Thus if I meet a bear in the wilds, that bear is objective; whatever may be the state of my thoughts, *he is there*—and it would be to my advantage to reckon with this fact. But if a child who is sent off to bed alone says there is a bear in the room, the bear is subjective; it is not a living monster that will devour anybody, but a creature called into the mind of the child through dread.

Exercise

Study the following words in pairs. Consult the dictionary for actual meanings. Then test your knowledge by embodying each word of each pair in a sentence, or in an illustration like those of the race-track and the bear in the preceding paragraphs.

superior, inferior
concord, discord
export, import
domestic, foreign
fact, fiction
prose, poetry
verbal, oral
literal, figurative
predecessor, successor
genuine, artificial
postive, negative
practical, theoretical
optimism, pessimism
finite, infinite
longitude, latitude
evolution, revolution
oriental, occidental
pathos, bathos
sacred, profane
military, civil
clergy, laity
capital, labor
ingress, egress
element, compound
horizontal, perpendicular
competition, coöperation
predestination, freewill

universal, particular
extrinsic, intrinsic
inflation, deflation
dorsal, ventral
acid, alkali
synonym, antonym
prologue, epilogue
nadir, zenith
amateur, connoisseur
anterior, posterior
stoic, epicure
ordinal, cardinal
centripetal, centrifugal
stalagmite, stalactite
orthodox, heterodox
homogeneous, heterogeneous
monogamy, polygamy
induction, deduction
egoism, altruism
Unitarian, Trinitarian
concentric, eccentric
herbivorous, carnivorous
deciduous, perennial
esoteric, exoteric
endogen, exogen
vertebrate, invertebrate
catalectic, acatalectic

Words Often Confused

Pairs of the second type are made up of words which are often confused by careless writers and speakers, and which should be accurately discriminated.

Sometimes the words are actually akin to each other. *Continuous-continual* and *enormity-enormousness* are examples. Sometimes they merely look or sound much alike. *Mean-demean* and *affect-effect* are examples. Sometimes the things they designate are more or less related, so that the ideas behind the words rather than the words themselves are responsible for the confusion. *Contagious-infectious* and *knowledge-wisdom* are examples. Let us distinguish between the two members of each of the pairs named.

A thing is *continuous* if it suffers no interruption whatever, *continual* if it is broken at regular intervals but as regularly renewed. Thus "a continuous stretch of forest"; "the continual drip of water from the eaves."

Enormity pertains to the moral and sometimes the social, *enormousness* to the physical. Thus "the enormity of the crime," "the enormity of this social offense"; "the enormousness of prehistoric animals."

Demean is often used reproachfully because of its supposed relation to *mean*. But it has nothing to do with *mean*. The word with which to connect it is *demeanor* (conduct). Thus "We observed how he demeaned himself" implies no adverse criticism of either the man or his deportment. Both may be debased to be sure, but they may be exemplary.

To *affect* means to feign or to have an influence upon, to *effect* to bring to pass. Thus "He affects a fondness for classical music," "The little orphan's story affected those who heard it"; "We effected a compromise." *Affect* is never properly used as a noun. *Effect* as a noun means result, consequence, or practical operation. Thus "The shot took instant effect"; "He put this idea into effect."

A disease is *contagious* when the only way to catch it is through direct contact with a person already having it, or through contact with articles such a person has used. A disease is *infectious* when it is presumably caused, not by contact with a person, but through widespread general conditions, as of climate or sanitation.

Our *knowledge* is our acquaintance with a fact, or the sum total of our information. Our *wisdom* is our intellectual and spiritual discernment, to which our knowledge is one of the contributors. *Knowledge* comprises the materials; *wisdom* the ability to use them to practical advantage and to worthy or noble purpose. *Knowledge* is mental possession; *wisdom* is mental and moral power.

Exercise

1. Consult the dictionary for the distinction between the members of each of the following pairs. In each blank of the illustrative sentences insert the word appropriate in meaning.

Ability, capacity. ——— to receive knowledge. ——— to impart knowledge.
Abstain, refrain. He ——— from laughter. He steadfastly ——— from evil courses.
Abstinence, temperance. Though he always displayed ———, he did not carry it to the point of ———.
Accept, except. I shall ——— most of the suggestions, but must ——— the one made by Mr. Wheeler.

WORDS IN PAIRS

Accept, receive. When the package was ——— at the local post office, Bayard refused to ——— it.
Ache, pain. The dull ——— of his head. A sharp ——— below the shoulder-blade. I have known the ——— of cold hands. "My heart ———, and a drowsy numbness ——— My sense, as though of hemlock I had drunk."
Address, tact. With firmness and ——— he set about reconciling the factions. Her ——— enabled her to perceive that something was amiss.
Adhere, cohere. The magnetized iron filings ———. The cold iron ——— to the boy's tongue.
Adherence, adhesion. The ——— of the heated particles to each other was instantaneous. Amid these trials their ——— to the cause was unshaken.
Admission, admittance. His ——— to the room was forced. He obtained ——— into a fraternal order.
Admit, confess. When he ——— that he had a weapon, he practically ——— that he had slain the man.
Adverse, averse. He was ——— to going. Their answer was ———.
Advice, counsel. In this emergency he sought ———. He asked my ——— as to the best place to hang the picture.
Aggravate, irritate. To let these mishaps ——— you is to ——— your suffering.
Allusion, illusion. It is an ——— to suppose that I made any ——— to you.
Allusion, reference. It was more than a possible ———; it was an unmistakable ———.
Amateur, novice. Though we call him a(n) ———, he is in skill by no means the ——— you might think him.
Ambiguous, equivocal. You are unintentionally ———. These words are deliberately ———.
Anticipate, expect. Since we ——— the enemy to advance, would it not be wise to ——— him?
Appearance, aspect. He was handsome in ———. The ——— of the sky was ominous.
Apprehend, comprehend. "Lovers and madmen have such seething brains, Such shaping fantasies, that ——— More than cool reason ever ———."
Ardor, fervor. The ——— of the worshipers. The ——— of the soldiers.
Artist, artisan. The ——— who was decorating the walls called to an ——— who was mixing mortar.
Ascent, ascension. We easily made the ——— of the slope, and from the summit witnessed the balloon ———

CENTURY VOCABULARY BUILDER

Ascent, assent. He gave his ——— when I proposed that we wait for the others to complete the ——— to this point.

Ascribe, impute. I ——— it to you as a fault rather than ——— it to you as an honor.

Assembly, assemblage. It was an informal ———. The ——— considered the matters it had been called to discuss.

Assent, consent. When told that the measure would advance his interests, he ———; but he would not ——— to it.

Avenge, revenge. The injury was slight, but he ——— it with unsparing malice. "———, O Lord, thy slaughtered saints."

Avocation, vocation. The lawyer, besides his regular ———, had the collecting of birds' eggs as his ———.

Aware, conscious. Though not ——— of the seriousness of his malady, he was ——— of the pain it caused him.

Balance, remainder. Darrell added the ——— of the coins, but not even they brought about the ——— he sought between assets and obligations.

Bashful, modest. Though ——— socially, he was not what you would term a ——— man.

Behavior, conduct. His ——— in this time of trial was exemplary. She praised the ——— of the children at the party.

Belief, faith. He possibly had ———, but not an active ———.

Benignant, benign. Her social manner was ———. The ——— influence of sunlight.

Beside, besides. ——— his personal friends, many people he had not even met stood ——— his sickbed.

Blanch, whiten. At this threat the face of the heroine ———. With a pail of cheap paint he ——— the dingy wall.

Blessing, benediction. After telling his parishioners to be mindful of their ———, the clergyman pronounced the ———.

Blockade, siege. Daily attacks on exposed redoubts marked the progress of the ———. The fleet lay there in silent ——— of the port.

Bravery, bravado. The incident proved that his ——— was not founded in real ———.

Bring, fetch. When you come, ——— the official documents with you. ——— me the scales you will find in the granary yonder.

Broad, wide. A man with ——— shoulders stood in the ———, open doorway.

Bury, inter. After they had solemnly ——— their comrade, they ——— the treasure. They also ——— their comrade's dog.

2. Consult the dictionary for the distinction between the members of each of the following pairs. Determine whether the

WORDS IN PAIRS

words are correctly used in the illustrative sentences. (Some are; some are not.)

Can, may. Can I stay at home this afternoon, papa? Because of the floods, the train beyond doubt may not get through.

Character, reputation. His character among them was very good. A man's reputation can never be taken from him.

Childish, childlike. Your conduct is peevish; it is childishly so. Her innocence was childlike.

Cite, quote. He was always citing snatches of Tennyson. We might quote Hamlet's soliloquy on suicide as an example of Shakespeare's ability to go to the heart of deep questions.

Claim, assert. He claimed that Jefferson was our third President. He asserted that bears sleep through the winter.

Clothing, costume. At the masquerade ball we each wore special clothing. The mariner who had swum from the wreck to the desert shore had not a shred of costume.

Comfort, ease. Comfort after labor. The ease of owning a home.

Commercial, mercantile. Petty commercial transactions. A mercantile treaty.

Common, mutual. This pavilion was the common playhouse for the children of the neighborhood. Ward and Aker held this property as their mutual possession.

Complement, compliment. This addition is the complement of our quota. He paid his dancing partner a compliment.

Complement, supplement. His downrightness is the complement of his uprightness. As a supplement to his wages he received an occasional bonus.

Complete, finish. He put in the completing touches. He had finished the task.

Composure, equanimity. His composure was not to be shaken. After this inner tumult came equanimity.

Comprehensible, comprehensive. Numbers of such magnitude are scarcely comprehensible. That men by the million should die for a cause is a thing not really comprehensive.

Compulsion, obligation. Who does not feel within him a compulsion to help the weak? It was through obligation, through having slave-drivers stand over them, that these wretched folk built the pyramids.

Congratulate, felicitate. I congratulated my friend on his appointment to the commission. I also felicitated the stranger on his appointment.

Consecutive, successive. Three consecutive convictions

proved the ability of the prosecuting attorney. The quiet passing of successive summer days.

Contemptible, contemptuous. Its size was insignificant, even contemptible. He won the prize by a contemptuous trick.

Continuation, continuance. The investigator was surprised to find the tradition of such long continuation. We waited impatiently for the continuance of the story in the next issue.

Corporal, corporeal. I am more and more amazed at the perfection of man's corporal frame. His corporeal vigor was unusual.

Correct, rectify. A man may correct many of his false judgments on current affairs by studying history. The mistake is ours; it shall be rectified.

Cozy, snug. The cozy fit of a garment. A snug place by the fire.

Crawl, creep. We crawled forward at dawn to surprise their outposts. In his humility he fairly crept on the earth.

Credible, creditable. I do not doubt it; it is entirely credible. The success of the antidote seemed scarcely creditable.

Credit, accredit. Though he is the official and credited ambassador, his assertions are not accredited.

Cure, heal. I cured the dog's wounds. The physician declared he could heal leprosy.

Custom, habit. "A custom more honor'd in the breach than the observance." Is it your custom to watch the clock while you eat? The habit in that region was to rise at cockcrow.

Decided, decisive. A decided battle. A decisive fault in manners.

Definite, definitive. We still await a definite edition of this author's works. His answer was so definitive that we no longer doubted what he meant.

Demesne, domain. Clive added India to the British demesne. The king went riding through his personal domain.

Deprecate, depreciate. The German mark has deprecated in value. He depreciated the praise they were lavishing upon him.

Descent, dissent. They tied themselves together with a rope in order to make their dissent safer. The dissent to a lower plane of conversation was what he most desired.

Discovery, invention. The discovery of the wireless telegraph is Marconi's chief claim to remembrance. The invention of a water passage between Tierra del Fuego and the mainland was the work of Magellan.

Discriminate, distinguish. He could not discriminate in-

WORDS IN PAIRS

dividuals at that distance. Any man can distinguish right from wrong.

Disinterested, uninterested. His course was entirely generous and disinterested. Most visitors to art galleries have an uninterested manner.

Disposal, disposition. This disposal of the matter is authoritative, final. His disposition of his forces was well-considered.

Dissatisfied, discontented. Though the colonists were dissatisfied for the moment, they could hardly be called discontented.

Distinct, distinctive. The distinct quality of his character was aggressiveness. There were four separate and distinctive calls.

Dramatic, theatrical. An affected, dramatic manner. A truly theatrical situation.

Dry, arid. A dry plain. An arid place to sleep in.

Dumb, mute. The man stood dumb with surprise. Always be kind to mute animals.

Durable, lasting. Our joy is durable. Oak is a lasting wood.

3. Consult the dictionary for the distinction between the members of each of the following pairs. Frame sentences to illustrate the correct use of the words. (Some of the words in this list, as well as some in other parts of the chapter, are considered in larger groups in the chapters following.)

earth, world
efficiency, efficacy
egoism, egotism
eldest, oldest
elemental, elementary
elude, evade
emigrate, immigrate
enough, sufficient
envy, jealousy
equable, equitable
equal, equivalent
essential, necessary
esteem, respect
euphemism, euphuism
evidence, proof
exact, precise
exchange, interchange
excuse, pardon
exempt, immune

expect, suppose
expedite, facilitate

facsimile, copy
familiar, intimate
fancy, imagination
farther, further
feeling, sentiment
feminine, effeminate
fervent, fervid
fewer, less
first (or last) two, two first (or last)
fluid, liquid
food, feed
foreign, alien
force, strength
forgive, pardon

gayety, cheerfulness
genius, talent
gentle, tame
genuine, authentic
glance, glimpse
grateful, thankful
grieve, mourn

hanged, hung
happen, transpire
happiness, pleasure
healthy, healthful
hear, listen
heathen, pagan
honorable, honorary
horrible, horrid
human, humane

illegible, unreadable
image, effigy
imaginary, imaginative
impending, approaching
imperious, imperial
imply, infer
in, into
inability, disability
ingenious, ingenuous
intelligent, intellectual
insinuation, innuendo
instinct, intuition
involve, implicate
irony, sarcasm
irretrievable, irreparable

judicious, judicial
just, equitable
justify, warrant

lack, want
languor, lassitude
later, latter
lawful, legal
lax, slack
leave, let
lend, loan

liable, likely
libel, slander
lie, lay
like, love
linger, loiter
look, see
loose, lose
luxurious, luxuriant

majority, plurality
marine, maritime
martial, military
moderate, temperate
mood, humor
moral, ethical
moral, religious
mutual, reciprocal
myth, legend

natal, native
nautical, naval
near, close
necessaries, necessities
needy, needful
noted, notorious
novice, tyro

observance, observation
observe, perceive
obsolete, archaic
omnipresent, ubiquitous
on, upon
oppose, resist
opposite, contrary
oppress, depress

palliate, extenuate
passionate, impassioned
pathos, pity
patron, customer
peculiar, unusual
perspicuity, perspicacity
permeate, pervade
permit, allow
perseverance, persistence

WORDS IN PAIRS

pertain, appertain
pictorial, picturesque
pitiable, pitiful
pity, sympathy
pleasant, pleasing
politician, statesman
practicable, practical
precipitous, precipitate
precision, preciseness
prejudice, bias
prelude, overture
pride, vanity
principal, principle
process, procedure
procure, secure
professor, teacher
progress, progression
propitious, auspicious
proposal, proposition

quiet, quiescent

raise, rear
raise, rise
ransom, redeem
rare, scarce
reason, understanding
reasonable, rational
recollect, remember
regal, royal
reliable, trustworthy
requirement, requisite
restive, restless
reverse, inverse
ride, drive
rime (or rhyme), rhythm

sacred, holy
salutation, salute
scanty, sparse
scholar, student
science, art
scrupulous, conscientious

serf, slave
shift, expedient
sick, ill
silent, taciturn
sit, set
skilled, skilful
slender, slim
smart, clever
sociable, social
solicitude, anxiety
stay, stop
stimulus, stimulation
strut, swagger
suppress, repress

termination, terminus
theory, hypothesis
tolerate, permit
torment, torture
tradition, legend
truth, veracity

unbelief, disbelief
unique, unusual

varied, various
variety, diversity
venal, venial
vengeance, revenge
verse, stanza
vindictive, revengeful
visit, visitation
visitant, visitor

wander, stray
warn, caution
will, volition
wit, humor
witness, see
womanish, womanlike
worth, value

Parallels

Pairs of the third type are made up of words parallel in meaning. This class somewhat overlaps the second; many terms that are frequently confused are parallels, and parallelism is of course a cause of confusion.

Parallels are words that show likeness in meaning. Likeness, not sameness. Yet at one time actual sameness may have existed, and in many instances did. Nowadays this sameness has been lost, and the words have become differentiated. As a rule they still are closely related in thought; sometimes, however, the divergence between them is wide.

Why did words having the same meaning find lodgment in the language in the first place? The law of linguistic economy forbids any such happening, and only through sheer good fortune did English come to possess duplications. The original Anglo-Saxon did not contain them. But the Roman Catholic clergy brought to England the language of religion and of scholarship, Latin. Later the Normans, whose speech as a branch of French was an offshoot of Latin, came to the island as conquerors. For a time, therefore, three languages existed side by side in the country—Anglo-Saxon among the common folk, Latin among the clergy, and Norman-French at the court and among the nobility. The coalescing of the three (or of the two if we count Latin in its direct and indirect contributions as one) was inevitable. But other (mostly cognate) languages also had a part in the speech that was ultimately evolved. The Anglo-Saxon element was augmented by words from Dutch, Scandinavian, and the

Germanic tongues in general; and Latin was reinforced by Greek. Thus to imply, as is sometimes done, that modern English is simply a blend of Anglo-Saxon and Latin elements is misleading. *Native* and *classic* are the better terms to use, provided both are used broadly. *Native* must include not only Anglo-Saxon but the other Germanic elements as well, and *classic* must include French and Greek as well as Latin.

The welding of these languages made available two—in some instances more than two—words for a single object or idea. What became of these duplicates? Sometimes one of the words was dropped as needless. Oftentimes, however, both were retained—with such modifications in meaning that thereafter they designated, not the same object or idea, but different forms or aspects of it. Thus they became parallels, and the new language waxed rich with discriminations which neither of the component tongues had possessed.

Scott in *Ivanhoe* gives the basis upon which the unification of the languages proceeded. The jester Wamba in conversation with the swineherd Gurth explains how the Anglo-Saxon term took on the homelier, rougher, more workaday uses and left the more refined and fastidious uses for the Norman-French. A domestic animal, says Wamba, was cared for by the conquered people, and in consequence bore while living a "good Saxon" name—swine, ox, or calf; but it was served at the tables of the conquerors, and therefore when ready for consumption bore a "good Norman-French" name—pork, beef, or veal. "When the brute [a sow] lives, and is in charge of a Saxon slave, she goes by her Saxon name; but becomes Norman and is called pork, when she is carried into the castle hall to feast among the nobles. . . . He [a calf] is Saxon when he requires tendance, and takes a Norman name [Monsieur de Veau] when he becomes matter of enjoyment."

Let us see how Scott's contention fares if we extend his list of terms relative to animal life. As throughout the rest of this chapter, with the single and necessary exception of List B, the first word in each pair is native, the second classic:

List A

sheep, mutton
deer, venison
horse, equine
cow, bovine
bull, taurine
sheep, ovine
wolf, lupine
hog, porcine
bear, ursine
fox, vulpine

cat, feline
dog, canine
fish, piscatorial
mouse, vermin
rat, rodent
mankind, humanity
man, masculine
woman, feminine
childish, infantile
boyish, puerile

A glance at this list will show that, at least as regards animal life, the native word is likely to be the more familiar and unpretentious. But we must not leap to the conclusion that, taking the language as a whole, the simple, easy word is sure to be native, the abstruse word classic. In the following list one word in each pair is simpler, oftentimes much simpler, than the other; yet both are of classic origin. (In some instances the two are doublets; that is, they spring from the same stem.)

List B

boil, effervesce
plenty, abundance
force, coerce

clear, transparent
sound, reverberate
echo, reverberate

WORDS IN PAIRS

toil, labor
false, perfidious
prove, verify
join, unite
join, annex
try, endeavor
carry, convey
save, preserve
save, rescue
safe, secure
poor, pauper
poor, penurious
poor, impecunious
native, indigenous
strange, extraneous
excuse, palliate
excusable, venial
cannon, ordnance
corpse, cadaverous
parish, parochial
fool, stultify
fool, idiot
rule, govern
governor, gubernatorial
wages, salary
nice, exquisite
haughty, arrogant
letter, epistle
pursue, prosecute
use, utility
use, utilize
rival, competitor
male, masculine
female, feminine
beauty, esthetics
beauty, pulchritude
beautify, embellish
poison, venom
vote, franchise
vote, suffrage
taste, gusto
tasteful, gustatory
tasteless, insipid
flower, floral
count, compute

cowardly, pusillanimous
tent, pavilion
money, finance
monetary, pecuniary
trace, vestige
face, countenance
turn, revolve
bottle, vial
grease, lubricant
oily, unctuous
revive, resuscitate
faultless, impeccable
scourge, flagellate
power, puissance
barber, tonsorial
bishop, episcopal
carry, portable
fruitful, prolific
punish, punitive
scar, cicatrix
hostile, inimical
choice, option
cry, vociferate
ease, facility
peaceful, pacific
beast, animal
chasten, castigate
round, rotunda
imprison, incarcerate
bowels, viscera
boil, ebullient
city, municipal
color, chromatics
nervous, neurotic
pleasing, delectable
accidental, fortuitous
change, mutation
lazy, indolent
fragrance, aroma
pay, compensate
face, physiognomy
joy, rapture
charitable, eleemosynary
blame, blaspheme
priest, presbyter

coy, quiet
prudent, provident
pupil, disciple
story, narrative
pause, interval
despise, abhor
doctor, physician
fate, destiny
country, rustic
aged, senile
increase, increment
gentle, genteel
clear, apparent

eagle, aquiline
motion, momentum
nourishment, nutrition
pure, unadulterated
closeness, proximity
number, notation
ancestors, progenitors
confirm, corroborate
convert, proselyte
benediction, benison
treasury, thesaurus
egotism, megalomania

Sometimes the native word is less familiar than the classic:

List C

seethe, boil
loam, soil
fare, travel
abide, remain
bestow, present
bestow, deposit
din, noise
quern, mill
learner, scholar
shamefaced, modest
hue, color
tarnish, stain
ween, expect
leech, physician
shield, protect
straightway, immediately

steadfast, firm
withstand, resist
dwelling, residence
heft, gravity
delve, excavate
forthright, direct
tidings, report
bower, chamber
rune, letter
borough, city
baleful, destructive
gainsay, contradict
cleave, divide
hearten, encourage
hoard, treasure

Again, the native word is sometimes less emphatic than the classic:

List D

fly, soar
old, venerable
flood, cataclysm
steep, precipitous
wonder, astonishment

speed, velocity
sparkle, scintillate
stir, commotion
stir, agitate
strike, collide

WORDS IN PAIRS

learned, erudite
small, diminutive
scare, terrify
burn, combustion
fire, conflagration
fall, collapse
uproot, eradicate
skin, excoriate
hate, abominate

work, labor
bright, brilliant
hungry, famished
eat, devour
twisted, contorted
thin, emaciated
sad, lugubrious
mirth, hilarity

Despite these exceptions, the native word is in general better known and more crudely powerful than the classic. Thus of the pair *sweat-perspiration, sweat* is the plainspoken, everyday member, *perspiration* the polite, even learned member. The man of limited vocabulary says *sweat;* even the sophisticated person, unless there is occasion to soften effects, finds *sweat* the more natural term. No one would say that a horse perspires. No one would say that human beings must eat their bread in the perspiration of their faces. But *sweat* is a word of connotation too vigorous (though honest withal) for us to use the term in the drawing room. A questionable woman in *The Vicar of Wakefield* betrays her lack of breeding by the remark that she is in a muck of sweat.

The native word, besides being in itself simpler and starker than the classic, makes stronger appeal to our feelings and affections. In nearly every instance the objects and relationships that have woven themselves into the very texture of our lives are designated by native terms. Even if they are not so designated solely, they are so designated in their more cherished aspects. We warm more to the native *fatherly* than to the classic *paternal*. We have a deeper sentiment for the native *home* than for the classic *residence*.

That the native is the more downright term may be seen from the following words. (These pairs are of course merely illustrative. With them might be grouped a few special pairs, like *devilish-diabolical* and *church-ecclesiastical,* of which the first members are classic in origin but of such early naturalization into English that they may be regarded as native.)

List E

belly, stomach
belly, abdomen
navel, umbilicus
suck, nurse
naked, nude
murder, homicide
dead, deceased
dead, defunct
dying, moribund
lust, salacity
lewd, libidinous
read, peruse
lie, prevaricate
following, subsequent
hearty, cordial
crowd, multitude
chew, masticate
food, pabulum
eat, regale
meal, repast
meal, refection
thrift, economy
sleepy, soporific
slumberous, somnolent
live, reside
swelling, protuberant
soak, saturate
soak, absorb
stinking, malodorous
spit, saliva
spit, expectorate
rot, putrefy
thievishness, kleptomania
belch, eructate
sticky, adhesive
house, domicile
eye, optic
walker, pedestrian
talkative, loquacious
talkative, garrulous
wisdom, sapience
bodily, corporeal
name, appellation
finger, digit
show, ostentation
nearness, propinquity
handwriting, chirography
waves, undulations
shady, umbrageous
fat, corpulent
wash, lave
muddy, turbid
horseback, equestrian
weight, avoirdupois
widow, relict
blush, erubescence

The word of classic origin in many instances survives only or mainly in the form of an adjective; as a noun (or other part of speech) it has completely or largely disappeared. This fact may be observed in lists already given, particularly List A. It may also be observed in the following words:

List F

moon, lunar
star, stellar
star, sidereal
sun, solar
earth, terrestrial
world, mundane
heaven, celestial
hell, infernal
earthquake, seismic
ear, aural
head, capital
hand, manual
foot, pedal
breast, pectoral
heart, cardial
hip, sciatic
tail, caudal
throat, guttural
lung, pulmonary
bone, osseous
hair, hirsute
tearful, lachrymose
early, primitive
sweet, dulcet
sweet, saccharine
young, juvenile
bloody, sanguinary
deadly, mortal
red, florid
bank, riparian
hard, arduous
wound, vulnerable
written, graphic
spotless, immaculate

sell, mercenary
son, filial
salt, saline
meal, farinaceous
wood, ligneous
wood, sylvan
cloud, nebulous
glass, vitreous
milk, lacteal
water, aquatic
stone, lapidary
gold, aureous
silver, argent
iron, ferric
honey, mellifluous
loving, amatory
loving, erotic
loving, amiable
wedded, hymeneal
plow, arable
priestly, sacerdotal
wholesome, salubrious
warlike, bellicose
arrow, sagittal
timely, temporary
fiery, igneous
ring, annular
soap, saponaceous
nestling, nidulant
snore, stertorous
window, fenestral
twilight, crepuscular
soot, fuliginous
hunter, venatorial

The fact that English is a double-barreled language, and that of parallel terms one is likely to be native and the other classic, is interesting in itself. Our lists of parallels, however, though (with the exception of List B) they are arranged to bring out this duality of origin, have other and more vital uses as material for exercises. For after all it matters little whether we know where a word comes from, provided we know thoroughly the meaning and implications of the word itself. The lists already given and those to follow show the more important words actually yoked as parallels. Your task must be to ascertain the differences in import between the words thus joined.

Exercise

List G

Study the discriminations between the members of the following pairs. At each blank in the illustrative sentences insert the appropriate word.

Brotherly, fraternal. *Brotherly* is used of actual blood kinship, or indicates close feeling, deep affection, or religious love. *Fraternal* is used less personally and intimately; it normally betokens that the relations are at least in part formal (as relations within societies). "The sight of the button on the stranger's lapel caused Wilkes to give him the cabalistic sign and ask his —— assistance." "Though the children of different parents, we bear for each other a true —— devotion." "Because we both are newspaper men I feel a —— interest in him."

Daily, diurnal. *Daily,* the popular word, is often used loosely. We may say that we eat three meals daily without implying that we have never gone dinnerless. *Diurnal,* the scientific term, is used exactly, whether applying to the period of daylight or to the whole twenty-four hours. A diurnal flower closes at night; a diurnal motion is precisely coincident with the astronomical day. In poetry, however, *diurnal* is often used for *daily*. "Give us this day our —— bread." "The —— rotation of the earth on its axis is the cause of our day and night." "Fred and I went for our —— ramble through the hills."

Cold, frigid. Which is the more popular word? Let us see. Would the man in the street be more likely to use one than the other? Which one? Does this answer our question? Another question: Which word is the more inclusive in meaning? Again, let us see. A blacksmith is beating iron; does the iron grow cold or frigid? Which term, then, approaches the closer in meaning to the idea of mere coolness? On the other hand, may that same term represent a temperature far beyond mere coolness? Would you speak of a morning as bitterly cold or bitterly frigid? Now think of the term you have not been using. *Can* it convey as wide meanings, or is it limited in range? Does the word *frigid* carry for you a geographical suggestion (to the frigid zone)? Do you yourself use the term? If so, do you use it chiefly (perhaps entirely) in connection with human temperament or demeanor? Is *cold* used thus figuratively also? Which is the more often thus used? "I suffer from —— hands and feet." "The slopes of Mont Blanc are —— with eternal snow." "He did not warm to the idea at all. His inclinations are absolutely ——."

Manly, virile. *Manly* implies possession of traits or qualities a man should possess; it may be used of immature persons. *Virile* implies maturity and robust masculinity; it is also used of the power to procreate. "A —— lad." "A —— reply." "—— energy." "—— and aggressive." "—— forbearance."

Inner, internal. *Inner* is somewhat within, or more within than something else is; it is also used in figurative and spiritual senses. *Internal* is entirely within. "The —— organs of the human body." "The —— layer of the rind." "The injury was ——." "The —— nature of man." "The —— meaning of the occurrence."

Height, altitude. "He was five feet, eleven inches in height." Can you substitute *altitude?* Is *altitude* used of persons? "At an altitude of eleven feet from the ground." Would *height* be more natural? Does *altitude* betoken great height? If so, does Hamlet speak jestingly when he greets the player, "Your ladyship is nearer heaven than when I saw you last, by the altitude of a chopine?" What of the sentence: "The altitude of Galveston was not sufficient to protect it from the tidal wave"? Does the magnitude or importance of the object (Galveston) compensate for its lack of elevation and thus justify *altitude?* Could *height* be substituted? If so, would the words *above sea-level* have to follow it? Does this fact give you a further clue as to the distinction between the two words? You are comparing the elevation of two peaks, both plainly visible; you measure them merely by your eye. Do you say "This exceeds the other in height" or "This exceeds the other in altitude"? Suppose the peaks are so distant from each other that the two are not visible simultaneously, and suppose you are speaking from a knowledge of the scientific measurements. Do you say "This exceeds the other in height" or "This exceeds the other in altitude"?

Talk, conversation. *Talk* may be one-sided and empty. *Conversation* requires that at least two shall participate, and it is not spoken of as empty, though it may be trivial. "Our —— was somewhat desultory." "Thought is less general than ——." "His —— was so lively that I had no chance to interrupt." "That is meaningless ——."

Homesickness, nostalgia. All of us have heard physicians call commonplace ailments by extraordinary names. When homesickness reaches the stage where a physician is or might be called in, it becomes nostalgia. The latter term suggests morbid or chronic suffering. A healthy boy away from home for the first time is homesick. An exile who has wasted himself with pining for his native land is nostalgic. "His —— was more than ——; it had so preyed upon his thoughts that it had grown into ——."

Rise, ascend. *Rise* is the more general term, but it expresses less than *ascend* in degree or stateliness. "He had foretold to them that he would —— into heaven." "Do not —— from your seat." "The diver slowly —— to the surface." "The travelers —— the mountain."

Sell, vend. *Sell* is the more dignified word socially, but may express greater moral degradation. *Vend* is used of the petty (as that which can be carried about in a wagon), and may suggest the pettily dishonest. "That man would —— his country." "We shall —— a million dollars' worth of goods." "The hucksters —— their wares."

List H

Study the discriminations between the members of the following pairs. Determine whether the words are correctly used in the illustrative sentences. (Some are; some are not.)

Friendly, amicable. *Friendly* denotes goodwill positive in quality though perhaps limited in degree; we may be friendly to friends, enemies, or strangers. *Amicable* is negative, denoting absence of open discord; it is used of those persons between whom some connection already exists. "The newcomer has an amicable manner." "Both sides were cautious, but at last they reached a friendly settlement." "I have only amicable feelings for an enemy who is thus merciful." "The two met, if not in a friendly, at least in an amicable way."

Willing, voluntary. Both words imply an act of the will; but *willing* adds positive good-nature, desire, or enthusiasm, whereas *voluntary* conveys little or nothing of the emotional attitude. *Voluntary* is often thought of in contrast with *mechanical*. "They made willing submission." "They rendered wholehearted and voluntary service." "Though torn by desire to return to his mother, he willingly continued his journey away from her." "The sneeze was unwilling."

Greedy, voracious. *Greedy* denotes excessiveness (usually habitual) of appetite or, in its figurative uses, of desire; it nearly always carries the idea of selfishness. *Voracious* denotes intense hunger or the hasty and prolonged consumption of great quantities of food; it may indicate, not habitual selfishness, but the stress of circumstances. "Nobody else I know is so greedy as he." "The young poet was voracious of praise." "Trench, though a capital fellow, was so hungry that he ate voraciously."

Offspring, progeny. *Offspring* is likely to be used when our thought is chiefly on the children, *progeny* when our thought is chiefly on the parents. *Offspring* may be used of one or many; *progeny* is used in collective reference to many. "He was third among the progeny who won distinction." "They are the progeny of very rich parents." "Clayton left his offspring well provided for."

Ghost, spirit. *Ghost* is the narrower term. It never expresses, as *spirit* does, the idea of soul or of animating mood or purpose. With reference to incorporeal beings, it denotes (except in the phrase "the Holy Ghost") the reappearance of the dead in disembodied form. *Spirit* may denote a variety of incorporeal beings—among them angels, fairies (devoid of moral nature), and personalities returned from the grave and manifested—seldom visibly—through spiritualistic tappings and the like. "The superstitious natives thought the spirit of their chief walked in the graveyard." "The ghost of the ancestors survives in the descendants." "I can call spirits from the vasty deep."

Foe, enemy. Nowadays the chief difference between the two terms is that *foe* is the more used in poetry, *enemy* in prose. But *foe* tends to express the more personal and implacable hostility. We do not think of foes as bearing any friendship for each other; enemies may, or they may be enemies in public affairs but downright friends in their private relations. A man is hardly spoken of as being his own foe, but he may be his own enemy. "For the moment we found ourselves foes." "Suspicion is an enemy to content." "I paid a tribute to my friend, who was the dominant personality among the enemy."

Truth, veracity. *Truth* has to do with the accuracy of the statement, of the facts; *veracity* with the intention of the person to say nothing false. "I cannot vouch for the veracity of the story, but I can for the truth of the teller." "Though he is not a man of veracity, I believe he is now speaking the truth." "Veracity, crushed to earth, will rise again."

Break, fracture. *Break* is the broader term. It need not refer clearly to the operation or result of external force, nor need it embody the idea that this force is brought against a hard substance. In these respects it differs from *fracture*, as also in the fact that it may designate a mere interruption. Furthermore it has figurative uses, whereas *fracture* is narrowly literal. "There was a fracture in the chain of mountains." "The break in his voice was distinct." "The fracture of the bones of his wrist incapacitated him." "The fracture of the rope."

Hug, embrace. To *hug* is to clasp violently or enthusiastically, and perhaps ludicrously. To *embrace* is to clasp in a more dignified, perhaps even in a formal, way; the term also means to include, to comprise. "This topic embraces the other." "Did you see that ardent bumpkin embracing his sweetheart?" "Her sister gave her a graceful but none too cordial hug." "The wounded bear hugged the hunter ferociously."

Shorten, abridge. The two terms overlap; but there is a fairly strong tendency to use *shorten* for reduction in length, and *abridge* for reduction in quantity or mass. Both words are used figuratively as well as literally. "The tyrant shortened the privileges of his subjects." "We shortened the rope." "The teacher abridged the recitation." "The report of the committee appears in abridged form in Volume 2 of our records."

List I

With the help of the dictionary discriminate between the members of the following pairs. Determine whether the words are correctly used in the illustrative sentences. (Some are; some are not.)

Fiery, inflammable. "He delivered a fiery address." "The underbrush was dry and fiery." "Your disposition is too inflammable."

Lean, attenuated. "The fat man had grown attenuated." "Yon Cassius has a lean and hungry look." "The hot metal was then drawn into an attenuated wire." "Only a lean line of our soldiers faced the dense masses of the enemy."

Home-like, domestic. "The scene was quiet and domestic." "It is home-like, inexpressibly dear." "To Waltham, heartsick from his wanderings, the room in all its arrangements was thoroughly domestic."

WORDS IN PAIRS

Vigilant, watchful. "We must be vigilant if we would maintain our liberty." "He was wakeful, even watchful, though not from set purpose." "He was vigilant for evidences of friendship."

Building, edifice. "It is a big, barn-like building." "Spare yonder sacred edifice." "This is the most imposing building I ever saw."

Hole, aperture. "I poked a stick into the aperture which the crawfish had made." "Through the aperture of the partly open door I gazed out on the street." "The hole of the hornet's nest was black with the emerging and angry insects."

Farming, agriculture. "Two hundred students graduated this year from the college of farming." "For long years he had devoted himself to the homely, grinding tasks of agriculture." "I have looked rather carefully into the theories of farming."

Rest, repose. "He obtained some repose even while standing." "We wished for a moment's rest from our exertions." "Worn out, he was compelled to seek repose." "Lincoln's face in repose was very melancholy."

Help, aid. "The man was so injured he could do nothing for himself; I had to aid him." "Help, help!" "Aid us, O God, in our sore distress." "The little fellow could not quite get the bundle to his shoulder; a passerby helped him."

Hide, conceal. "By refraining from comment he hid his connection with the affair." "Wild creatures hide themselves by means of their protective coloring." "The frost on the panes conceals the landscape from you." "Do not hide your misdeeds from your mother."

List J

In the following list only the native member of each pair is given. Determine what the classic member is, and frame sentences to illustrate the correct use of the two words. (Make a conscientious effort to find the classic member by means of its parallelism with the native. If, and after, you definitely fail in any instance to find it, obtain a clue to it through study of the words in List G. Every pair in that list is clearly suggestive of one or more pairs in this list.)

nightly, ——
breadth, ——
hot, ——
thought, ——
fatherly, ——
outer, ——
womanly. ——

motherly, ——
buy, ——
fall, ——
sleeplessness, ——
yearly, ——
depth, ——
speech, ——

List K

Discriminate between the members of each of the following pairs, and frame sentences to illustrate the correct use of the two words.

freedom, liberty
freedom, independence
free, acquit
door, portal
begin, commence
behead, decapitate
belief, credence
belief, credulity
swear, vow
curse, imprecate
curse, anathema
die, expire
die, perish
die, succumb
lively, vivacious
walk, ambulate
leave, depart
leave, abandon
go with, accompany
go before, precede
hasten, accelerate
quicken, accelerate
speed, celerity
hatred, animadversion
fearful, timorous

well, cistern
give, donate
happen, occur
lessen, abate
lessen, diminish
forefathers, ancestors
friend, acquaintance
lead, conduct
end, finish
end, complete
end, terminate
warn, admonish
warn, caution
rich, affluent
wealthy, opulent
help, assistance
help, succor
answer, reply
find out, ascertain
take, appropriate
shrewd, astute
breathe, respire
busy, industrious
growing, crescent
grow, increase

List L

Cover with a piece of paper the classic (right-hand) members of the following pairs, and if possible ascertain what they are by studying the native members. Frame sentences to illustrate the correct use of both words in each pair.

neighborhood, vicinity
hang, impend
hang, suspend
rash, impetuous
flood, inundation
drunk, intoxicated
harmful, injurious

tool, instrument
mind, intellect
mad, insane
birth, nativity
sail, navigate
sailor, mariner
ship, vessel

lying,	mendacious	upright,	erect
early,	premature	upright,	vertical
first,	primary	shake,	vibrate
raise,	elevate	swing,	oscillate
lift,	elevate	leaves,	foliage
greet,	salute	beg,	importune
choose,	select	beggar,	mendicant
choose,	elect	smell,	odor
same,	identical	sink,	submerge
name,	nominate	dip,	immerse
follow,	pursue	room,	apartment
follow,	succeed	see,	perceive
teach,	instruct	see,	inspect
teach,	inculcate	sight,	visibility
teacher,	pedagogue	sight,	vision
tiresome,	tedious	sight,	spectacle
empty,	vacant	glasses,	spectacles
farewell,	valediction		

List M

Cover with a piece of paper the native (left-hand) members of the following pairs, and if possible ascertain what they are by studying the classic members. Frame sentences to illustrate the correct use of both words in each pair.

skin,	cuticle	thunder,	fulminate
skin,	integument	sleep-walking,	somnambulism
hide,	epidermis	bird,	ornithology
fleshly,	carnal	bird,	aviary
hearer,	auditor	bee,	apiary
snake,	serpent	bending,	flexible
heap,	aggregation	wrinkle,	corrugation
laugh,	cachinnation	slow,	dilatory
laughable,	risible	lime,	calcimine
fear,	trepidation	coal,	lignite
live,	exist	man,	anthropology
bridal,	nuptial	winter,	hibernate
wed,	marry	gap,	hiatus
husband		right,	ethical
(or wife),	spouse	showy,	ostentatious
forswear,	perjure	spelling,	orthography
steal,	peculate	time,	chronology
steal,	embezzle	handbook,	manual
lockjaw,	tetanus	hole,	cavity
mistake,	error	dig,	excavate
mistake,	erratum	boil,	tumor

CENTURY VOCABULARY BUILDER

shore,	littoral	fiddle,	violin
wink,	nictation	sky,	firmament
tickle,	titillate	sky,	empyrean
blessing,	benediction	**flatter,**	compliment
dry,	desiccated	flee,	abscond
wet,	humid	flight,	fugitive
warm,	tepid	forbid,	prohibit
flirt,	coquet	hinder,	impede
forgetfulness,	oblivion	hold,	contain

List N

For each of the following pairs frame a sentence which shall contain one of the members. Can the other member be substituted without affecting the meaning of the sentence? Read the discrimination of *height-altitude* on page 167. Ask yourself similar questions to bring out the distinction between the two words you are considering.

threat, menace
call, summon
talk, commune
cleanse, purify
short, terse
short, concise
better, ameliorate
lie, recline
new, novel
straight, parallel
lawful, legitimate
law, litigation
law, jurisprudence
flash, coruscate
late, tardy
watch, chronometer
foretell, prognosticate
king, emperor
winding, sinuous
hint, insinuate
burn, incinerate
fire, incendiarism
bind, constrict
crab, crustacean
fowls, poultry
lean, incline

flat, level
flat, vapid
sharpness, acerbity
sharpness, acrimony
shepherd, pastor
word, vocable
choke, suffocate
stifle, suffocate
clothes, raiment
witness, spectator
beat, pulsate
mournful, melancholy
beginning, incipient
drink, imbibe
light, illuminate
hall, corridor
stair, escalator
anger, indignation
fight, combat
sleight-of-hand, prestidigitation
build, construct
tree, arbor
ask, interrogate
wench, virgin
frisk, caper

WORDS IN PAIRS

water, irrigate
coming, advent
old, antiquated
sew, embroider
grave, sepulcher
tell, narrate
nose, proboscis
green, verdant
grass, verdure
drive, propel
book, volume
warrior, belligerent
owner, proprietor
bow, obeisance
kneel, genuflection
work, occupation
shut, close
fill, replenish

silly, foolish
feeling, sentiment
forerunner, precursor
unload, exonerate
readable, legible
kiss, osculate
striking, percussion
stroke, concussion
bowman, archer
greed, avarice
stingy, parsimonious
bath, ablution
wrong, incorrect
top, summit
food, nutrition
seize, apprehend
field, agrarian

Turn back to Lists A, B, C, D, E, and F. Discriminate between the members of each pair contained in these lists. Frame sentences to illustrate the correct use of the words.

VII

SYNONYMS IN LARGER GROUPS (1)

IN considering pairs we have, without using the word, been studying synonyms. For most pairs are synonyms (or in some instances antonyms) that hunt in couples. We must now deal with synonyms, and incidentally antonyms, as they associate themselves in larger groups.

A vocabulary is impoverished. Why? Nine times in ten, because of a disregard of synonyms. Listen to the talk of the average person. Whatever is pleasing is *fine* or *nice* or *all to the good;* whatever is displeasing is *bum* or *awful* or *a fright*. Life is reflected, not as noble and complex, but as mean and meager. Out of such stereotyped utterance only the general idea emerges. The precise meaning is lazily or incompetently left to the hearer to imagine. The precise meaning? There is none. A person who does not take the trouble to speak clearly has not taken the trouble to think clearly.

But the master of synonyms expresses, instead of general, hazy, commonplace conceptions, the subtlest shadings of thought and feeling. He has so trained himself that he selects, it may be unconsciously, from a throng of possible words. One word may be strong, another weak. One may be broad, another narrow. One may present an alternative in meanings, another permit no liberty of choice. One may be suggestive, another literal or colorless. One may penetrate to the core of the idea, another strike only in the environs. With these possibilities the master of synonyms reckons. He must have the right word. He chooses it, not at haphazard, but in conformity with a definite purpose.

For synonyms are not words that have the same meaning. They are words that have similar meanings. They may be compared to circles that overlap but do not coincide. Each embraces a common area, but each embraces also an area peculiar to itself. Though many words cluster about a given idea, rarely if ever are even two of these words entirely equivalent to each other. In scope, in suggestion, in emotional nuance, in special usage, or what not, is sure to lurk some denial of perfect correspondence. And of synonyms, so of antonyms. Antonyms are words opposite in meaning; but the opposition, for the same reasons as the likeness, is seldom or never absolute.

In your study of synonyms you will find most of the dictionaries previously named (see page 70) of great help. You may also profitably consult the following books of synonyms (heavy, scholastic works not suited for ordinary use are omitted):

Books of Plain Synonyms and Antonyms

Edith B. Ordway: *Synonyms and Antonyms*. A compact, practical volume, with antonyms (in italics for contrast) immediately following synonyms.
Louis A. Flemming: *Putnam's Word Book*. A book of the ordinarily used synonyms of words, with antonyms after some

of them, and with lists of associated words wherever these are likely to be useful.

Samuel Fallows: *100,000 Synonyms and Antonyms.* A handy little volume, with useful lists of various kinds in appendices.

Richard Soule: *Dictionary of English Synonyms* [revised and enlarged by George H. Howison]. A much larger and more expensive book than the others, and less practical for ordinary use, but fuller in treatment of material, with words of more than one meaning carefully divided into their various senses.

Synonyms with Word Discriminations

George Crabb: *English Synonyms.* A standard volume for over 100 years. Has close distinctions, but is somewhat scholarly for ordinary use. Revised edition of 1917, omitting illustrative quotations from literature, not so good as editions before that date.

James C. Fernald: *English Synonyms, Antonyms, and Prepositions.* A pleasing book to read, with much information about the use of words and their shades of meaning (with exercises), also with proper prepositions to follow words. Material taken from the *Standard Dictionary*.

Peter Mark Roget: *Thesaurus of English Words and Phrases.* Issued in many editions and revisions. Words grouped under general ideas. An excellent book for serious and laborious study, but not for quick use.

How to Acquire Synonyms

The best principle for the extension of one's mastery of synonyms is the principle already used over and over in this book—that of proceeding from the known to the unknown. It is the fundamental principle, indeed, of any kind of successful learning. We should build on what we have, fit each new piece of material into the structure already erected. But normally it is our ill fortune to learn through chance rather than through system. We perceive elucidation here, draw an inference there. These isolated fragments of knowledge may mislead rather than inform us.

SYNONYMS IN LARGER GROUPS (1)

The principle of proceeding from the known to the unknown may be applied to synonyms in various ways. Two of these—the two of most importance—we must consider here.

First, you should reckon with your personal, demonstrated needs. Just as you have already (see page 62 and following) analyzed your working vocabulary for its general limits and shortcomings, so should you analyze it with particular reference to your poverty in synonyms. Watch your actual speech; make a list of the words—nouns, verbs, and adjectives particularly—that you employ again and again. Make each of these words the starting-point for a linguistic exploring expedition. First, write the word down. Then under it write all the synonyms that come forthwith to your mind. These constitute your present available stock; in speaking or writing you could, if you kept yourself mentally alert, summon them on the moment. But the list, as you know, is not exhaustive. Draw a line under it and subjoin such synonyms as come to you after reflection. These constitute a second stock, not instantaneously available, yet to be tagged as among your resources. Next add a list of the synonyms you find through research, through a ransacking of dictionaries and books of synonyms. This third stock, but dimly familiar if familiar at all, is in no practical sense yours. And indeed some of the words are too abstruse, learned, or technical for you to burden your memory with them. But many—most—are worth acquiring. By writing down the words of these three classes you have done something to stamp them upon your memory as associates. You must now make it your business to bring them into use. Never call upon them for volunteers, but like a wise commander summon the individual that can rightly perform a particular service. Thus will your speech, perhaps vague and indolent now, become exact, discriminating, competent, vital.

In the second place, you should obtain specific and detailed command of general ideas. Not of out-of-the-way ideas. But of the great basic ideas that are the common possession of all mankind. For through these basic ideas is the most natural and profitable approach to the study of synonyms. Each of them is represented by a generic word. So elementary are idea and word alike that a person cannot have the one in mind without having the other ready and a-quiver on his tongue. Every person is master of both. But it is unsafe to predicate the person's acquaintance with the shades and phases of the idea, or with the corresponding discriminations in language. He may not know them at all, he may know them partially, he may know them through and through. Let us suppose him ignorant of them but determined to learn. His progress, both in the thought and in the language, will be from the general to the specific. His acquaintance with the idea in the large he will gradually extend to an acquaintance with it in detail, and his command of the broad term for it he will little by little supplement with definite terms for its phases. An illustration will make this clear.

We are aware that the world is made up of various classes and conditions of men. How did we learn this? Let us go back to the time when our minds were a blank, when we were babes and sucklings, when we had not perceived that men exist, much less that mankind is infinitely complex. A baby comes slowly to understand that all objects in the universe are divisible into two classes, human and non-human, and that a member of the former may be separated from the others and regarded as an individual. It has reached the initial stage of its knowledge on the subject; it has the basic idea, that of the individual human being. As soon as it can speak, it acquires a designating term—not of course the sophisticated *human being,* but the simpler *man.* It uses this word in the generic sense, to indicate *any* member of the human race; for as yet it knows nothing and cares nothing about differences in species. With increasing enlightenment, however, it discerns five species, and distinguishes among them by swelling this branch of its vocabulary to five words: man (in the sense of adult male), woman, boy, girl, baby. (To be sure, it may chance to have acquired a specific term, as *boy* or *baby,* before the generic term *man;* but if so, it has attached this term to some particular individual, as the grocer's boy or itself, rather than to the individuals of a species. Its understanding of the species as a species comes after its understanding of the genus.) As time passes, it divides mankind into yet further species by sundry other methods: according to occupation, for example, as doctors, chauffeurs, gardeners; to race or color, as white men, negroes, Malays, Chinese; to disposition, as heroes, gift-givers, teasers, talkers; and so on. It perceives moreover that species are made up of sub-species. Thus instead of lumping all boys together it begins to distinguish them as big boys, little boys, middle-sized boys, boys in long trousers, boys in short trousers, barefoot boys, schoolboys, poor boys, rich boys, sick boys, well boys, friends, enemies, bullies, and what not. It even divides the sub-species. Thus it classifies schoolboys as bright boys, dullards, workers, shirkers, teachers' favorites, scapegoats, athletes, note-throwers, truant-players, and the like. And of these classes it may make yet further sub-divisions, or at least it may separate them into the individuals that compose them. In fine, with its growing powers and experience, it abandons its old conception that all persons are practically alike, and follows human nature through the countless ramifications of man's status, temperament, activities, or fate. And it augments its vocabulary to keep pace, roughly at least, with its expanding ideas. In thought and terminology alike its growth is from genus to species.

So it is with all our ideas and with all our words to cap them. We radiate from an ascertained center into new areas of knowledge; we proceed from the broad, fundamental, generic to the precise, discriminatory, specific. Upon this natural law are based the exercises in this chapter and the two to follow. The starting-point is always a word representative of an elementary idea— a word and an idea which everybody knows; the advance is into the unknown or the unused, at any rate into the particular. Now fundamental ideas are not very numerous, and these exercises include the commoner ones. Such a method of studying synonyms must therefore yield large and tangible results.

One matter, however, should be explained. Most books of synonyms start with a word and list all the terms

SYNONYMS IN LARGER GROUPS (1)

in any way related to it. The idea of the compilers is that the more they give the student the more they help him. But oftentimes by giving more than is strictly pertinent they actually hinder and confuse him. They may do this in various ways, of which two must be mentioned. First, they follow an idea too far afield. Thus in listing the synonyms of *love* they include such terms as *kindness* and *lenity*, words only through stretched usage connected with *love*. Secondly, they trace, not one meaning of a word, but two or more unrelated meanings when the word chances to possess them. Thus in listing the synonyms of *cry* they include both the idea of weeping and the idea of calling or screaming. What are the results of these methods? The student finds a clutter where he expects rationalized order; he finds he must exclude many words which lie in the borders and fringes of the meaning. Moreover he finds mere chance associations mingled with marked kinships. In both cases he finds dulled distinctions.

This book offers synonyms that are apropos and definite rather than comprehensive. Starting with a basic idea, it finds the generic term; it then disregards dim and distant relationships, confines itself rigorously to one of perhaps two or three legitimate senses, and refuses to consider the peculiar twists and devious ways of subsidiary words when they wander from the idea it is tracing. It thus deliberately blinds itself to much that is interesting. But this partial blindness enables it to concentrate attention upon the matter actually under study, to give sharper distinctions and surer guidance.

Exercise

A

After three introductory groups (dealing with thoroughly concrete ideas and words) the synonyms in this exercise are arranged alphabetically according to the first word in each group.

This first word is generic. It is immediately followed by a list of its synonyms. These are then informally discriminated or else (in a few instances) questions are asked about them. Perhaps a few less closely related synonyms are then listed for you to discriminate in a similar way. Finally, illustrative sentences are given. Each blank in these you are to fill with the word that conveys the meaning exactly. (To prevent monotony and inattention, the number of illustrative sentences varies. You may have to use a particular word more than once, and another word not at all.)

Walk, plod, trudge, tread, stride, stalk, strut, tramp, march, pace, toddle, waddle, shuffle, mince, stroll, saunter, ramble, meander, promenade, prowl, hobble, limp, perambulate.

Any one may be said to *walk* who moves along on foot with moderate speed. He *plods* if he walks slowly and heavily, and perhaps monotonously or spiritlessly as well. He *trudges* if he walks toilsomely and wearily, as though his feet were heavy. He *treads* if his walk is suggestive of a certain lightness and caution—if, for instance, he seems half-uncertain whether to proceed and sets one foot down carefully before the other. He *strides* if he takes long steps, especially in a firm, pompous, or lofty manner. He *stalks* if there is a certain stiffness or haughtiness in his walking. He *struts* if he walks with a proud or affectedly dignified gait, especially if he also raises his feet high. He *tramps* if he goes for a long walk, as for pleasure or enjoyment out-of-doors. He

SYNONYMS IN LARGER GROUPS (1)

marches if he walks in a measured, ordered way, especially in company with others. He *paces* if he engages in a measured, continuous walk, as from nervousness, impatience, or anger. He *toddles* if his steps are short, uneven, and unsteady, like those of a child. He *waddles* if his movement is ungainly, with a duck-like swaying from side to side. He *shuffles* if he drags his feet with a scraping noise. He *minces* if he takes short steps in a prim, precise, or affectedly nice manner. He *strolls* or *saunters* if he goes along in an easy, aimless, or idle fashion. He *rambles* if he wanders about, with no definite aim or toward no definite goal. He *meanders* if he proceeds slowly and perhaps listlessly in an ever-changing course, as if he were following the windings of the crooked Phrygian river, Meander. He *promenades* if he walks in a public place, as for pleasure or display. He *prowls* if he moves about softly and stealthily, as in search of prey or booty. He *hobbles* if he jerks along unevenly, as from a stiff or crippled condition of body. He *limps* if he walks lamely. He *perambulates* when he walks through, perhaps for observation or inspection. (*Perambulates* is of course a learned word.)

Assignment for further discrimination: **sneak, shamble, amble, wander, stamp, slouch, gad, gallivant, glide, hike.**

Sentences: They —— down the lane in the moonlight. Rip Van Winkle loved to —— about the mountains. "The plowman homeward —— his weary way." The old man —— down the street with his cane. The excavators —— about the ruins in search of relics. He —— about the room, almost bursting with importance. The nervous man —— up and down the station platform. They —— along the beach at the sea resort. The baby learned to —— when it was eleven months old. The two of them —— about the field all day hunting rabbits. A ghost, so they tell me, —— about the haunted house at midnight. He carefully —— the plank that spans the abyss. The baby —— toward us with outstretched arms. The Chinaman —— out of the back room of the laundry in his carpet slippers. They caught glimpses of gaunt wolves —— about their campfire. He was terrified when the giant —— into the room. The fat lady —— down the aisle of the street car. The sick man will —— a few steps each day until he is stronger. A turkey cock —— about the barnyard. A boy with a rag tied around his toe —— painfully down the street. They reported to the police that a man had been —— about the place. She held her skirts daintily and —— along as if she were walking on eggs. The lovers —— along the banks of the stream. He —— through the hall like a conqueror. The children wore themselves out by —— through the snow to school. We —— through the meadows, often stooping to pick flowers as we went. The soldiers —— into camp at nightfall.

Laugh, giggle, snicker, titter, chuckle, guffaw, cachinnate.

What differences in human nature, conditions, and disposition are revealed by laughter! If a person gives audible expression to mirth, **gayety,** or good-humor, the simplest word to apply to what he does is *laugh*. But suppose a girl, with slight or insufficient provocation, engages in silly or foolish though perhaps involuntary laughter. We should say she *giggles*. Suppose a youngster is amused at an inappropriate moment and but partly suppresses his laughter; or suppose he wilfully permits the breaking forth of just enough laughter to indicate disrespect. He *snickers*. Suppose a person gives a little, light laugh; or more especially, suppose a crowd gives such an one as the result of slight, simultaneous amusement. Our word now is *titters*. Suppose

SYNONYMS IN LARGER GROUPS (1)

we laugh low or gently or to ourselves. We *chuckle*. Suppose some one laughs loudly, boisterously, even coarsely, in a manner befitting a lumber camp rather than a drawing room. That person *guffaws*. Suppose a man engages in explosive and immoderate laughter. He *cachinnates*.

Assignment for further discrimination: **chortle, roar.**
Second assignment: Name all the words you can that designate inaudible laughter (for example, **smile, smirk, grin**).

Sentences: The rough fellow —— in the lecturer's face. "If you prick us, do we not bleed? if you tickle us, do we not ——?" He kept —— at the thought of the surprise he would give them. "The swain mistrustless of his smutted face, While secret laughter —— round the place." The ill-bred fellow was —— with strident, violent, irritating sounds. "The little dog —— to see such sport." The audience —— when the speaker's glasses began to slip from his nose. The girl kept —— in a way that embarrassed us both. The small boy —— when the preacher's notes fluttered out of the Bible to the floor. The rude fellows —— at this evidence of my discomfiture. He —— very kindly and told me not to feel any regrets. The little maids tried to be polite, but —— irrepressibly.

Look, glance, gaze, stare, peer, scan, scrutinize, gloat, glare, glower, lower, peek, peep, gape, con, pore, ogle.

A person simply directs his eyes to see. He *looks*. But eyes may speak, we are told, and since this person undergoes many changes of mood and purpose, we shall let his eyes tell us all they will about his different manners of looking. At first he but looks momentarily (as from lack of time) or casually (as from lack of interest). He *glances*. Soon he makes a business of looking, and fastens his eyes for a long time on something he admires or wonders at. He *gazes*. Presently he looks with a blank, perhaps a rude, expression and with eyes opened widely; he may be for the moment overcome with incomprehension, surprise, or fright, or perhaps he wishes to be insolent. He *stares*. Now he is looking narrowly or closely at something that he sees with difficulty. He *peers*. The next moment he looks over something with care or with an encompassing sweep of vision. He *scans* it. His interest thoroughly enlisted, he looks at it carefully point by point to see that it is right in each detail. He *scrutinizes* it He then alters his mood, and looks with scornful or malignant satisfaction upon something he has conquered or has power over. He *gloats*. Anger, perhaps fierceness, takes possession of him, and he looks with piercing eyes. He *glares*. Threat mingles with anger, and in all likelihood he looks scowlingly or frowningly. He *glowers*. An added expression of sullenness or gloom comes into his look. He *lowers*. He throws off his dark spirit and looks slyly and playfully, let us say through a small opening. He *peeks*. Playfulness gives place to curiosity; he looks quickly and furtively, perhaps through some tiny aperture, and probably at something he has no business to see. He *peeps*. The while he looks his mouth falls open, as from stupidity or wonder. He *gapes*. He looks at something a long time to study it. He *cons* or *pores*. His study is not of the thing itself; it is meditation or reverie. He *pores*. A member of the opposite sex is present; he looks at her with the effort of a flirt to attract attention to himself.

or less scrupulous, he directs toward her amorous or inviting glances. He *ogles*.

Assignment for further discrimination: **leer, view, survey, inspect, regard, watch, contemplate.**

Sentences: The inspecting officer —— the men's equipment. The student —— his lessons carefully. At this unexpected proposal Dobbett merely ——. Jimmie —— at the fellow who had kicked the pup. The inquisitive maid —— into all the closets. He —— over his fallen adversary. The bookkeeper —— over his ledger. In the darkened hallway he —— at the notices on the bulletin board. "The poet's eye, in a fine frenzy rolling, Doth —— from heaven to earth, from earth to heaven." From the way her father —— the foolish young man should have known it was time to go. He —— long and lovingly upon the scenes he was leaving. The newcomer —— insolently at his host and —— the young ladies.

Abandon, desert, forsake.

Abandon denotes absolute giving up, as from force of circumstances or shirking of responsibility. *Desert* refers to leaving or quitting in violation of obligation, duty, or oath. *Forsake*, which may involve no culpability, usually implies a breaking off of intimate association or attachment.

Sentences: The sailor —— his ship. Necessity compelled him to —— his friends in a time of sore trouble. They hated to —— their old haunts. A brave man never —— hope. An unscrupulous man will —— his principles when it is to his advantage. "When my father and my mother —— me, then the Lord will take me up." We —— our attempt to save the ship.

Abase, debase, degrade, humble, humiliate, disgrace.

To *abase* is to bring down so that the victim feels himself lowered in estate or external condition. To *debase* is to produce a marked decline in actual worth or in moral quality. To *degrade* is to lower in rank or status. To *humble* is to lower in dignity or self-esteem, or as used reflexively, to restrain one's own pride; the word often implies that the person has been over-proud or arrogant. To *humiliate* is to deprive of self-esteem or to bring into ignominy. To *disgrace* is to bring actual shame upon.

> *Sentences:* They —— the guilty officer from captain to lieutenant. A man should —— himself before God. He had so —— himself that I no longer expected good of him. His detection at cheating had —— him before the students. By successive overlords they had been —— into a condition of serfdom. The aristocratic old lady was —— by her loss of social position. The conversion of so much bullion into money had —— the coinage.

Answer, reply, response, rejoinder, retort, repartee.

An interesting thing about the *answer* group is that the generic term has a somewhat strong rival in *reply,* itself fairly inclusive. We must therefore discriminate rather fully between *answer* and *reply*. The former is a return in words to a question, a communication, or an argument. The latter suggests a more or less formal answer, as one carefully prepared or intelligently thought out. We might give an *answer* offhand, but are less likely to give a *reply* so. We may give any kind of *answer* to a question, but if we give a *reply,* the implication is that we have answered it definitely, perhaps satisfactorily. On the other hand, in controversial matters we may, though we by no means always do, imply a more conclusive meeting of objections through *answer* than through *reply*. A *response* is an expected answer, one in

SYNONYMS IN LARGER GROUPS (1)

harmony with the question or assertion, or in some way carrying the thought farther. A *rejoinder* is a quick reply to something controversial or calling forth opposition. A *retort* is a short, sharp reply, such as turns back censure or derision, or as springs from anger. A *repartee* is an immediate and witty reply, perhaps to a remark of similar character which it is intended to surpass in cleverness.

Sentences: The detailed —— to our letter should reach us within a week. The plays of Oscar Wilde abound in brilliant ——. The speaker's —— to the heckler was incisive and scathing. My —— to that third question in the examination in history was incorrect. The congregation read the —— in unison. You have enumerated objections to my course; here is their ——. "This is no ——, thou unfeeling man, To excuse the current of thy cruelty." There was silence throughout the chamber as the old statesman rose to make his ——. To the tenderfoot's remark the guide mumbled an indifferent ——. Our appeal for the sufferers elicited but a poor ——.

Ask, inquire, question, interrogate, interpellate, query, quiz, catechize, request, beg, solicit, entreat, beseech, crave, implore, supplicate, importune, petition.

From the general tree of asking grow many branches, different in size, in the direction they take, in the shades of meaning they cast. What can we learn from a rapid scrutiny of each? That to *inquire* is to ask for specific information. That to *question* is to keep asking in order to obtain detailed or reluctantly given information. That to *interrogate* is to question formally, systematically, or thoroughly. That to *interpellate* is to question as of unchallenged right, as in a deliberative body. That to *query* is to bring a thing into question because of doubt as to its correctness or truth. That to *quiz* is to question closely and persistently, as from meddlesomeness, opposition, or curiosity. That to *catechize* is to question in a minute, perhaps impertinent, manner in order to ascertain one's secrets or the amount of his knowledge or information. That to *request* is to ask formally and politely. That to *beg* is to ask for deferentially or humbly, especially on the ground of pity. That to *solicit* is to ask with urgency. That to *entreat* is to ask with strong desire and moving appeal. That to *beseech* is to ask earnestly as a boon or favor. That to *crave* is to ask humbly and abjectly, as though unworthy of receiving. That to *implore* is to ask with fervor and intense earnestness. That to *supplicate* is to ask with urgent or even desperate appeal. (Both *implore* and *supplicate* imply humility, as of a prayer to a superior being.) That to *importune* is to ask for persistently, even wearyingly. That to *petition* is to ask a superior, usually in writing, for some favor, grant, or right.

Assignment for further discrimination: **plead, pray.**

Sentences: The leader of the minority —— the upholders of the measure sharply as to a secret understanding. I —— you to keep your promise. I shall —— that solution for the present. The colonists —— Great Britain for a redress of grievances. She —— the governor to grant her husband a pardon. A child is naturally inquisitive and —— many questions. I —— you to show mercy. On bended knees he —— God's forgiveness. "I'm stopp'd by all the fools I meet And —— in every street." The policeman —— the suspect closely. The prosecuting attorney —— the witness. We are —— funds to aid the famine-stricken people of India. He —— me about your health. You should —— at the office about the lost package. She —— your presence at the party. Every one resents being ——. I —— you to care for the child after

SYNONYMS IN LARGER GROUPS (1)

I am gone. A fool can —— questions a wise man can't answer. She annoyed them by constantly —— them for favors. The reporter —— into the causes of the riot. "——, and it shall be given you." I —— your pardon, though I well know I do not deserve it. The man —— me to give him some money for food.

Burn, scorch, singe, sear, parch, char, incinerate, cremate, cauterize.

If you consume or injure something by bringing it in contact with fire or heat, you *burn* it. If you do not consume it but burn it superficially so as to change the texture or color of its surface, you *scorch* it. If you burn off ends or projections of it, you *singe* it. If you burn its surface to dryness or hardness, you *sear* it. If you dry or shrivel it with heat, you *parch* it. If through heat you reduce it to a state of charcoal or cinders, you *char* it. If you burn it to ashes, you *incinerate* it. (This word is learned and but little used in ordinary discourse.) If you burn a dead body to ashes, you *cremate* it. If you burn or sear anything with a hot iron or a corrosive substance, you *cauterize* it.

Sentences: The hired girl —— the cloth in ironing it. By getting too close to the fire he —— the nap of his flannels. The doctor at once —— the wound. The cook had picked the chicken and now —— its down over the coals. I used to —— grains of field corn on the cookstove while my mother prepared dinner. Shelley's body was —— on a funeral pyre. The lecturer spoke of the time when the whole earth might be ——. The earth was —— and all growing things were —— by the intense summer heat.

Busy, industrious, diligent, assiduous, sedulous.

From much of the talk that we hear nowadays it might be supposed that the earnest devotion of one's self to a task is a thing that has disappeared from the earth. But a good many people are exhibiting this very devotion. Let us see in what different degrees. The man who actively applies himself to something, whether temporarily or habitually, is *busy*. The man who makes continued application to work a principle or habit of life, is *industrious*. The man who applies himself aggressively to the accomplishment of some specific undertaking or pursuit, is *diligent*. The man who quietly and determinedly sticks to a task until it is accomplished, no matter what its difficulties or length, is *assiduous*. The man who makes steady and painstaking application to whatever he is about, is *sedulous*.

> *Sentences:* Early in life he acquired —— habits. By patient and —— study you may overcome those defects of your early education. "How doth the —— little bee Improve each shining hour." The manager gave such —— attention to details that he made few mistakes. He is —— at present. Oh, yes, he is always ——. "Nowhere so —— a man as he ther nas, And yet he semed —— than he was."

Concise, terse, succinct, compendious, compact, sententious, pithy, laconic, curt.

Words descriptive of brief utterance are, in nearly every instance, in their origin figurative. The brevity is brought out by comparison with something that is noticeably short or small. Let us examine the words of our list for their figurative qualities. A *concise* statement is one that is *cut down* until a great deal is said in a few words. A *terse* statement is *rubbed off,* rid of unessentials. A *succinct* statement has its important thoughts *bound* into small compass, as by a girdle. A *compendious* statement *weighs together* the various thoughts and aspects of a subject; it shows by means of a few effective words just what these amount to, gives a summary of them. A *compact* statement has its units of thought *fastened together* into firmness of structure; its brevity is well-knit. A *sententious* statement gives *feelings or opinions* in a strikingly pointed or axiomatic way, so that they can be easily grasped and remembered; if *sententious* is unfavorably used, the statement may be filled with paraded platitudes. A *pithy* statement gives the very *pith,* the heart of a matter; it is sometimes slightly quaint, always effective and arresting. A *laconic* statement is made in the manner of *the Spartans,* who hated talk and used as few words as possible. A *curt* statement is *made short;* its abruptness is oftentimes more or less rude.

Sentences: "A tale should be judicious, clear, ———, The language plain, and incidents well link'd." "Charles Lamb made the most ——— criticism of Spenser when he called him the poet's poet." With a ———, disdainful answer she turned away. The sermon was filled with ——— sayings. By omitting all irrelevant details, he made his statement of the case ———. It requires great skill to give a ——— statement of what such a treatise contains. A proverb is a ——— statement of a truth.

Death, decease, demise.

Men are as mindful of rank and pretension in their terms for the cessation of life as in their choice of tombstones for the departed. *Death* is the great, democratic, unspoilable word. It is not too good for a clown or too poor for an emperor. *Decease* is a more formal word. Its employment is often legal—the death proves to be of sufficient importance for the law (and the lawyers) to take notice. *Demise,* however, is outwardly the most resplendent term of all. It implies that the victim cut a wide swath even in death. It is used of an illustrious person, as a king, who transmits his title to an heir. Ordinary people cannot afford a *demise.* If the term is applied to their shuffling off of this mortal coil, the use is euphemistic and likely to be stilted.

> *Sentences:* "The crown at the moment of —— must descend to the next heir." "—— is a fearful thing." "In their —— they were not divided." At the —— of his father he inherited the estate. "Each shall take His chamber in the silent halls of ——." "Many a time I have been half in love with easeful ——."

Early, primitive, primeval, primordial, primal, pristine.

Early is the simple word for that which was in, or toward, the beginning. That is *primitive* which has the old-fashioned or simple qualities characteristic of the beginning. That is *primeval* which is of the first or earliest ages. That is *primordial* which is first in origin, formation, or development. That is *primal* which is first or original. (The word is poetic.) That is *pristine* which has not been corrupted from its original state.

Assignment for further discrimination: **aboriginal, prehistoric.**

> *Sentences:* It was a hardy mountain folk that preserved the —— virtues. The —— history of mankind is shrouded in uncertainty. "This is the forest ——." "It hath the —— eldest curse upon 't, A brother's murder." "A —— leaf is that which is immediately developed from the cotyledon." As the explorers penetrated farther into the country, they beheld all the —— beauties of nature. Some countries still use the —— method of plowing with a stick.

SYNONYMS IN LARGER GROUPS (1)

Face, countenance, features, visage, physiognomy.

We hear some one say that he reads faces. How? Through long study of them and what they indicate. The human race as a whole has been reading faces through the centuries. It has felt such need to label certain recurring aspects of them that it has invented the designating terms. Of these terms the simple, inclusive one is of course *face* itself. If, however, we are thinking of the face as its look or expression reveals thoughts, emotions, or state of mind, our term is *countenance*. If we are thinking of it as distinguished or individualized by the contour, lines, etc., we speak of the *features*. If we are thinking of its external appearance or aspect, we call it the *visage*. If, finally, we are thinking of it as indicative of mind, disposition, or fundamental character, we say *physiognomy*.

Assignment for further discrimination: **lineaments.**

Sentences: His grotesque —— reminded one of a gargoyle. It is said that the —— of persons living constantly together tend to become alike. "Behind a frowning providence He hides a smiling ——." The teacher told the students to wash their —— every morning. "A —— more in sorrow than in anger." The firm but kind —— of the old statesman shone happily at this ovation. "For now we see through a glass, darkly; but then —— to ——." She turned an eager —— up to me as she spoke. One's —— is moulded by one's thoughts. Cosmetics injure the ——. His clear-cut —— impressed his employer.

Financial, monetary, pecuniary, fiscal.

Financial is usually applied to money matters of considerable size or moment. *Monetary* applies to money.

coin, or currency as such. *Pecuniary* refers to practical matters in which money is involved, though not usually in large amounts. *Fiscal* refers especially to the time when money, receipts, and accounts are balanced or reckoned.

> *Sentences:* A —— reward has been offered. We gave the unfortunate man —— assistance. The —— system of the country was sound. It was Hamilton who more than any one else shaped the —— policies of the new government. Experts audit the company's accounts at the end of the —— year. The —— interests of the country were behind the bill.

Flee, abscond, decamp.

To *flee* is to run away from what one would avoid, as danger, arrest, or the like. To *abscond* is to steal off secretly and hide one's self, as from some disgraceful reason or to avoid arrest. To *decamp* is to leave suddenly in great haste to get away; the word is often used humorously.

> *Sentences:* They went to have their money refunded, but the swindler had ——. The bank teller —— after having squandered most of the deposits. Yes, we were in proximity to a polecat, and without further parley we ——. "Resist the devil, and he will —— from you." William Wallace, when pursued by the English, —— into the Highlands.

Foretell, predict, prophesy, forecast, presage, forebode, portend, augur, prognosticate.

Foretell is the general word for stating or perceiving beforehand that which will happen. *Predict* implies foretelling based on well-founded or precise knowledge. *Prophesy* often implies supernatural inspiration to foretell correctly. The word is especially so used in connection with the Scriptures; but in the Scriptures themselves it frequently expresses insight and admonition without the element of foretelling. *Forecast* involves a marked degree of conjecture. *Presage* usually means to give as a presentiment or warning. *Forebode* expresses an uncertain foreknowledge of vague impending evil. *Portend* indicates the likelihood that something will befall which is threatening or evil in its consequences. *Augur* means foretelling from omens. *Prognosticate* means foretelling through the study of signs or symptoms.

> *Sentences:* "For we know in part, and we —— in part." (Insert in the blank, successively, the terms just distinguished. In each instance how is the meaning affected? Do any of the terms fail to make sense at all? Which term do you think the right one? Bearing in mind the distinctions we have made, frame sentences of your own to embody the terms.)

Get, acquire, obtain, procure, attain, gain, win, earn.

Get, the general term, may be used of whatever one comes by whatsoever means to possess, experience, or realize. To *acquire* is to get into more or less permanent possession, either by some gradual process or by one's determined efforts. To *obtain* is to get something desired by means of deliberate effort or request. To *procure* is to get by definitely planned effort something which, in most instances, is of a temporary nature or the possession of which is temporary. To *attain* is to get through striving that which one has set as a goal or end of his desire or ambition. To *gain* is to get that which is advantageous. To *win* is to get as the result of successful competition or the overcoming of opposition. To *earn* is to get as a deserved reward for one's efforts or exertions.

Sentences: With such wages as those, he can barely —— a living. He —— a pardon by appealing to the governor. The speaker —— his point by forcing his opponent to admit that the figures were misleading. By buying in June I can —— a good overcoat at half price. Did you —— only seven thousand dollars for your house? Walpole believed in —— one's ends in the surest and easiest way possible. It is illegal to —— money through false pretences. A junior —— the prize in the oratorical contest. Kirk —— his advancement by taking a personal interest in the firm's welfare. The painter —— a foreign accent while he was studying in Paris. He —— their gratitude by loyally serving them. It was through sacrifices that he —— an education.

Give, bestow, grant, confer, present.

We *give* that which we transfer from our own to another's possession or ownership, usually without compensation. We *bestow* that which we give gratuitously, or of which the recipient stands in especial need. We *grant* that which has been requested by one dependent upon us or inferior to us, and which we give with some formality. From a position of superiority we *confer* as a favor or honor that which we might withhold or deny. We *present* that which is of importance or value and which we give ceremoniously.

Assignment for further discrimination: **furnish, supply, impart.**

Sentences: William the Conqueror —— English estates upon his followers. The rich man —— his wonderful art collection to the museum. My application for a leave of absence has been ——. The ticket agent —— us complete information. Every year he —— alms upon the poor in that neighborhood. The school board may —— an increase in the salaries of teachers. Many merchants —— premiums with the articles they sell. The college —— an honorary degree upon the distinguished visitor. The Pilgrims —— thanks to God for their preservation. "Not what we ——, but what we share."

Haste, celerity, speed, hurry, expedition, despatch.

What did John Wesley mean by saying, "Though I am always in haste, I am never in a *hurry*"? Does Lord Chesterfield's saying "Whoever is in a *hurry* shows that the thing he is about is too big for him" help explain the distinction? Explain the distinction (taking *speed* in the modern sense) in the saying "The more *haste*, ever the worse *speed*." "The tidings were borne with the usual *celerity* of evil news." Give the well-known saying in four simple words that express the same idea. Which of the two statements is the more forceful? Which is the more literary? Why did Prescott use the former in his *Ferdinand and Isabella*? "*Despatch*," says Lord Chesterfield, "is the soul of business." What does *despatch* suggest about getting work done that *haste* or *speed* does not? In which way would you prefer for your employee to go about his task—with *haste*, with *speed*, or with *despatch*? "With wingéd *expedition*, Swift as the lightning glance, he executes His errand on the wicked." Why is it that this use of *expedition* in Milton's lines is apt? Would *despatch* have served as well? If not, why not?

Hate, detest, abhor, loathe, abominate, despise.

To *hate* involves deep or passionate dislike, sometimes bred of ill-will. To *detest* involves an intense, vehement, or deep-seated antipathy. To *abhor* involves utter repugnance or aversion, with an impulse to recoil. To *loathe* involves disgust because of physical or moral offensiveness. To *abominate* involves strong moral aversion, as of that which is odious or wicked. To *despise* is to dislike and look down upon as inferior.

> *Sentences:* When he had explained his fell purpose, I could only —— him. Who would not —— a slimy creature like Uriah Heep? It is natural for us to —— our enemies. She —— greasy food. There suddenly in my pathway was the venomous reptile, darting out its tongue; oh, I —— snakes! A wholesome nature must —— such principles as these. A child —— to kiss and make up. The pampered young millionaire —— those who are simply honest and kind. These daily practices of her associates she ——.

Healthful, wholesome, salutary, salubrious, sanitary, hygienic. (With this group contrast the *disease* group on page 226.)

The words of this group are assuredly blessed. Every one of them has to do with the giving, promotion, or preservation of health. But health is of various kinds, and therefore the words apply differently. *Healthful* is the most inclusive of them; it means that the thing it refers to is full of health for us. *Wholesome* also is a very broad term; what is wholesome is good for us physically, mentally, or morally. *Salutary* is confined to that which affects for good our moral (including civic and social) welfare, especially if it counteracts evil influences or propensities. *Salubrious* is confined to the physical; it is used almost solely of healthful air or climate. *Sanitary* and *hygienic* apply to physical well-being as promoted by the eradication of the causes for sickness, disease, or the like; *sanitary,* however, is used of measures and conditions affecting people in general, whereas *hygienic* connects itself with personal habits.

Assignment for further discrimination: The word *healthy* is often confused with *healthful*. You have already discriminated between these two terms (page 156), but you should renew your knowledge of the distinction between them.

Sentences: Colorado is noted for its —— air. He offered the young people some —— advice. A person should brush his teeth every day for —— reasons. In spite of its horrors, the French Revolution has had a —— effect upon civilization. Damp, low places do not have a —— climate. Cities in the middle ages were not ——. His is a very —— way of life. My doctor recommends buttermilk as ——.

Heavy, weighty, burdensome, onerous.

He knew that it was a —— responsibility. (Insert the four words in the blank space in turn, and analyze the differences in meaning thus produced.)

Liberal, generous, bountiful, munificent.

He made a —— donation to the endowment fund. (Insert the four words in the blank space in turn, and analyze the differences in meaning.)

Masculine, male, manly, manlike, manful, mannish, virile.

"A man's a man for a' that," sang the poet. So he is, but not all the adjectives allusive to his state are equally complimentary. *Masculine* betokens the qualities and characteristics belonging to men. *Male* designates sex and is used of animals as well as human beings. *Manly* (used of boys as well as men) implies the possession of qualities worthy of a man, as strength, courage, sincerity, honesty, independence, or even tenderness. *Manlike* refers to qualities, attributes, or foibles characteristically masculine. *Manful* suggests the valor, prowess, or resolution properly belonging to men. *Mannish* (a derogatory word) indicates superficial or affected qualities of manhood, especially when inappropriately possessed by a woman. *Virile* applies to the sturdy and intrepid qualities of mature manhood.

> *Sentences:* The Chinese especially prize —— children. He was a —— little fellow. She walked with a —— stride. With —— courage he faced the crisis. It was a —— defense of an unpopular cause. —— strength is the complement of female grace. The old sailor still retained the rugged and —— strength of a man much younger. With —— bluntness he told her what he thought. Such gentleness is not weak; it is ——. He made a —— struggle against odds. "His —— brow Consents to death, but conquers agony." Now isn't that assumption of omniscience ——?

Name, appellation, designation, denomination, title, alias.

A *name* is the word or words by which a person or thing is called or known. If the name be descriptive or characterizing, even though in a fanciful way, it is an *appellation*. If it particularizes an individual through reference to distinctive quality or nature, perhaps without employing any word the individual is usually known by, it is a *designation*. If it specifies a class, especially a religious sect or a kind of coin, it is a *denomination*. If it is an official or honorary description of rank, office, place within a profession, or the like, it is a *title*. If it is assumed, as to conceal identity, it is an *alias*.

> *Assignment for further discrimination:* **cognomen, patronymic, nom de plume, pseudonym.**

> *Sentences:* Yes, it is a five-dollar gold piece, though one does n't often see a coin of that —— nowadays. The Little Cor-

SYNONYMS IN LARGER GROUPS (1)

poral is the —— applied to Napoleon by his soldiers. The eldest son of the king of England bears the —— of the Prince of Wales. The government issues stamps in various ——. "That loafer" was his contemptuous —— of the man who could not find work. "Duke" is the highest —— of nobility in England. The crook was known to the police under many ——. At the battle of Bull Run Jackson received the —— "Stonewall." "What's in a[n] ——? that which we call a rose By any other —— would smell as sweet." The head of the American government bears the —— of President. The Mist of Spring was the little Indian maiden's ——. His —— was Thornberg.

Old, ancient, olden, antique, antiquated, archaic, obsolete, immemorial, elderly, aged, hoary, venerable, decrepit, senile, superannuated.

We reserve the right to judge for ourselves when told that something—especially a joke—is "the very latest." So may we likewise discriminate among degrees of age. *Old* is applied to a person or thing that has existed for a long time or that existed in the distant past. The word may suggest a familiarity or sentiment not found in *ancient,* which is used of that which lived or happened in the remote past, or has come down from it. *Olden* applies almost wholly to time long past. *Antique* is the term for that which has come down from ancient times or is made in imitation of the style of ancient times, whereas *antiquated* is the term for that which has gone out of style or fashion. *Archaic* and *obsolete* refer to words, customs, or the like, the former to such as savor of an earlier period though they are not yet completely out of use, the latter to such as have passed out of use altogether. *Immemorial* implies that a thing is so old that it is beyond the time of memory or record. *Elderly* is applied to persons who are between middle age and old age. *Aged* is used of one who has lived for an unusually long time. *Hoary* refers to age as revealed by white hair. *Venerable* suggests the reverence to be paid to the dignity, goodness, or wisdom of old age. *Decrepit* conveys a sense of the physical infirmities and weakness which attend old age; *senile* of the lessening powers of both body and mind that result from old age. *Superannuated* is applied to a person who on account of old age has been declared incapable of continuing his activities.

> *Sentences:* He liked to read romances of the —— days. Dana records that he once saw a man so —— that he had to raise his eyelids with his fingers. Many writers use —— words to give quaintness to their work. He liked to sit around in his —— clothes. "The moping owl does to the moon complain Of such as, wandering near her secret bower, Molest her —— solitary reign." Some of these —— sequoia trees were old before the white man discovered this continent. They are building the church in the —— Roman style of architecture. "Be not . . . the last to lay the —— aside." Many of Chaucer's words, being ——, cannot possibly be understood without a glossary. Most churches now have funds for —— ministers. A man is as —— as he feels; a woman is as —— as she looks. The —— old man could scarcely hobble across the room. What better proof that he is —— do you ask than that he babbles constantly about what happened when he was young? "I am a very foolish fond —— man, Fourscore and upward." They revered the —— locks of the old hero. At sixty a man is considered a[n] —— person. That the earth is flat is a[n] —— idea. The young warriors listened respectfully to the —— chief's advice. They unearthed a[n] —— vase. "—— wood best to burn, —— wine to drink, —— friends to trust, and ——. authors to read." His favorite study was —— history. "Grow —— along with me." "The most —— heavens, through thee, are fresh and strong."

Pay, compensate, recompense, remunerate, requite, reimburse, indemnify.

SYNONYMS IN LARGER GROUPS (1)

Most men are willing to receive what is due them. They might even be persuaded to receive a bit more. Why should they not be as scrupulous to receive what they are entitled to in the medium of language as of money? Sometimes they are. Offering to *pay* some people instead of to *compensate* them is like offering a tip to the wrong person. Why? Because there is a social implication in *compensate* which is not contained in *pay*. To *pay* is simply to give what is due, as in wages (or even salary), price, or the like. To *compensate* is to make suitable return for service rendered. Does *compensate* not sound the more soothing? But save in exceptional circumstances the downrightness of *pay* has no hint of vulgarity. To *recompense* is to make a return, especially if it is not monetary, for work, pains, trouble, losses, or suffering; or some quality or blessing (as affection or happiness) may be said to recompense one. To *remunerate* is to disburse a large amount to a person, or to give it to him as a reward, or otherwise to make him a return in a matter of importance. To *requite* is to put a just value upon one's work, deeds, or merit and to make payment strictly in accordance with his deserts. To *reimburse* is to make good what some one has spent for you. To *indemnify* is to secure some one against loss or to make restitution for damages he has sustained.

Assignment for further discrimination: **disburse, reward.**

Sentences: Let us —— him for his efforts in our behalf. Let us —— their kindness with kindness, their cruelty with cruelty. To —— them adequately for such patriotic sacrifices is of course impossible. The government demanded

that it be —— for the injury to its citizens. I shall ——
you for all sums expended. He —— the bill by a check.
The success of her children —— a mother for her sacrifices
for them. Wages are —— to laborers; salaries are —— to
judges.

Proud, arrogant, presumptuous, haughty, supercilious, insolent, insulting.

Most persons feel in their hearts that their claims and
merits are superior to those of other people. But they
do not like for you, in describing them, to imply that
their self-appraisal is too high. "Comparisons are
odious," and therefore in comparing their fancied with
their real selves you must choose your terms carefully.
Of the words that suggest an exaggerated estimate of
one's merits or privileges the broadest, as well as the
least offensive, is *proud*. In fact this word need not
carry the idea of exaggeration. A proud man may but
hold himself in justifiable esteem, or wish to measure up
to the demands of his station or to the expectations of
others. On the other hand, he may overvalue his attainments, possessions, connections, etc. To say that the man
is *arrogant* means that he combines with pride a contempt
for others, that he claims for himself greater attention,
consideration, or respect than he is entitled to. To say
that he is *presumptuous* makes him an inferior (or at
least not a superior) who claims privileges or takes liberties improperly. To say that he is *haughty* means that
he assumes a disdainful superiority to others, especially
through fancied or actual advantage over them in birth
or social position. To say that he is *supercilious* means
that he maintains toward others an attitude of lofty

indifference or sneering contempt. To say that he is *insolent* means that he is purposely and perhaps coarsely disrespectful toward others, especially toward his superiors. To say that he is *insulting* means that he gives or offers personal affront, probably in scornful or disdainful speech.

Assignment for further discrimination: **scornful, imperious, contumelious, impudent, impertinent.**

Sentences: He was —— in replying to the questions. She paid no attention to his words, but kept looking at him with a[n] —— smile. He was —— in acting as if he were their equal. The hot-tempered fellow answered this —— remark with a blow. She resented his presuming to speak to her, and turned away in a[n] —— manner. The servant was —— to her mistress. Are you not very —— of your family connections? The old man was so —— that he expected people to raise their hats to him and not to sit down till he gave permission.

Punish, chastise, chasten.

To *punish* a person is to inflict pain or penalty upon him as a retribution for wrong-doing. There may be, usually is, no intention to improve the offender. To *chastise* him is to inflict deserved corporal punishment upon him for corrective purposes. To *chasten* him is to afflict him with trouble for his reformation or spiritual betterment. The word is normally employed in connection with such affliction from God.

Assignment for further discrimination: **castigate, scourge.**

Sentences: "Hearing oftentimes The still, sad music of humanity, Nor harsh nor grating, though of ample power

To —— and subdue." Ichabod Crane freely used his ferule in —— his pupils. "Whom the Lord loveth he ——." A naughty child should be ——.

Rich, wealthy, affluent, opulent.

"It is easier for a camel to go through the eye of a needle, than for a rich man to enter into the kingdom of God." Substitute *wealthy* for *rich*. Is the meaning exactly the same? Is Goldsmith's description of the village preacher—"passing rich with forty pounds a year" —as effective if *wealthy* is substituted? What is the difference between *riches* and *wealth?* Which implies the greater degree of possession, which the more permanence and stability? Which word suggests the more personal relationship with money? Which word the more definitely denotes money or its immediate equivalent? Why do we say "get-rich-quick schemes" rather than "get-wealthy-quick schemes"? What besides the possession of wealth does *affluent* suggest? Could we say that a rich miser lives in affluence? If not, why not? A poor clerk who has ten dollars to spend as he pleases may feel affluent. A rich banker may be a man of affluence in his town. What power does this suggest that he has besides the possession of a great deal of money? Explain all that Swift implies by the word *opulence* in the quotation "There in full opulence a banker dwelt, Who all the joys and pangs of riches felt." If you substitute *affluence,* what different impression do you get?

Rural, rustic, pastoral, bucolic.

"The *rural* inhabitants of a country." Are the people being spoken of favorably, unfavorably, or neutrally?

How would the meaning be affected if they were called *rustic* inhabitants? Would you ordinarily speak of the *rural* or the *rustic* population to distinguish it from the urban? Would you speak of *rural* or *rustic* activities? *rural* or *rustic* manners? When the two adjectives may be employed, is one of them unflattering? Is a *rustic* bridge something to be ashamed of? a *rustic* chair? a *rustic* gate? What, then, is the degree of reproach that attaches to each of the two adjectives? the degree of commendation? Wherein do *pastoral* scenes differ from *rural? pastoral* amusements from *rustic?* Can you trace a connection between the *pastor* of a church and a *pastoral* life? Do you often hear the word *bucolic?* In what mood is it oftenest uttered? Which of the four adjectives best fits into Goldsmith's dignified lament: "And ―― mirth and manners are no more"?

Silent, reserved, uncommunicative, reticent, taciturn. (This group may be contrasted with the *talkative* group, below.)

We pass through a crowded room and notice that some of its occupants are not adding their voices to the chatter. We resolve to study these unspeaking persons. Some of them merely have nothing to say, or are timid or preoccupied; or it may be they deliberately have set themselves not to talk. These are *silent*. Some plainly desire not to talk, it may be in general or it may be upon some particular topic; they may (but need not) regard themselves as superior to their associates, or for some other reason let aloofness or coldness creep into their manner. These are *reserved*. Others withhold information that persons about them are, or would be, interested in. These are *uncommunicative*. Others maintain their own counsel; they neglect opportunities to reveal their thoughts, plans, and the like. These are *reticent*. Others are disinclined—and habitually, we perceive—to talking. These are *taciturn*.

> *Sentences:* The —— prisoner evaded all questions. He was as —— as nature itself; he never gave his views upon any subject. He was —— about the firm's affairs, especially toward persons who seemed inquisitive. We knew there had been a love affair in his life, but he was —— on the subject. She sat —— throughout the discussion. If to be —— is golden, Lucas should have been a billionaire.

Sing, chant, carol, warble, troll, yodel, croon, hum, chirp, chirrup.

You hear a "concord of sweet sounds," not instrumental but vocal, and wish to tell me so. You say that some person *sings*. Then you recall that I am something of an expert in music, and you cast about for the word that shall state specifically the kind of singing that is being done. Does the person sing solemnly in a more or less uniform tone? You tell me that he *chants*. Does he sing gladly, spontaneously, high-spiritedly, as if his heart were pouring over with joy? You say that he *carols*. Does he sing with vibratory notes and little runs, as in bird-music? You say that he *warbles*. Does he sing loudly and freely? You say that he *trolls*. Does he sing with peculiar modulations from the regular into a falsetto voice? You say that he *yodels*. Does he sing a simple, perhaps tender, song in a low tone (as a lullaby to an infant)? You say that he *croons*. Does he sing

SYNONYMS IN LARGER GROUPS (1)

with his lips closed? You say that he *hums*. Does he utter the short, perhaps sharp, notes of certain birds and insects? You say that he *chirps* or *chirrups*.

Assignment for further discrimination: **trill, pipe, quaver, peep, cheep, twitter.**

> *Sentences:* A cricket —— in the grass outside the door. He abstractedly gazed out of the window and —— a few strains of an old song. Listen, they are —— the Te Deum. "And —— still dost soar, and soaring ever ——." A strange, uncanny blending of false and true notes it is when the Swiss mountaineers are ——. Negroes, as a race, love to ——. As she soothes the child to sleep she —— a "rock-a-bye-baby."

Suave, bland, unctuous, fulsome, smug.

Suave implies agreeable persuasiveness or smooth urbanity. *Bland* suggests a soothing or coaxing kindness of manner, one that is sometimes lacking in sincerity. *Unctuous* implies excessive smoothness, as though one's manner were oiled. The word carries a decided suggestion of hypocrisy. *Fulsome* suggests such gross flattery as to be annoying or cloying. *Smug* suggests an effeminate self-satisfaction, usually not justified by merit or achievement.

Assignment for further discrimination: **complaisant, elegant, trim, dapper, spruce, genteel, urbane, wellbred, gracious, affable, benign.**

> *Sentences:* He thought his answer exceedingly brilliant and settled back into his chair with —— complacency. "—— the smile that like a wrinkling wind On glassy water drove his cheek in lines." They were irritated by his —— praise. Although he disliked them, he greeted them with —— cordiality. "A bankrupt, a prodigal, ... that used to come so —— upon the mart; let him look to his bond." —— as a diplomat.

Talkative, loquacious, garrulous, fluent, voluble, glib. (This group may be contrasted with the *silent* group, above.)

A little while ago you were in a crowded room and made a study of the persons disposed to silence. But your study was carried on under difficulties, for many of those about you showed a tendency to copious or excessive speech. One woman entered readily into conversation with you and convinced you that her natural disposition was to converse a great deal. She was *talkative*. From her you escaped to a man who soon proved that he talked too much and could run on with an incessant flow of words, perhaps employing many of them where a few would have sufficed. He was *loquacious*. The two of you were joined by an old gentleman who forthwith began to talk wordily, tediously, continuously, with needless repetitions and in tiresome detail; you suspected that he had suffered a mental decline from age, and that he might be excessively fond, in season and out of season, of talking about himself and his opinions. He was *garrulous*. You broke away from these two and fell into the hands of a much more agreeable interlocutor. He talked with a ready, easy command of words, so that his discourse *flowed* smoothly. He was *fluent*. He introduced you to a lady whose speech possessed smoothness and ease in too great degree; it fairly *rolled* along, as a hoop does downhill. The lady was *voluble*. Into your triangular group broke a newcomer whose speech had in it a flippant, or at least a superficially clever, fluency. He was *glib*. Leaving these three to fight (or

SYNONYMS IN LARGER GROUPS (1)

talk) it out as best they might, you grabbed your hat and hurried outside for a fresh whiff of air.

Assignment for further discrimination: **chattering, long-winded, prolix, wordy, verbose.**

Sentences: The insurance agent was so —— a talker that I was soothed into sleepiness by his voice. The —— old man could talk forever about the happenings of his boyhood. Through —— descriptions of life in the city the dapper summer boarder entranced the simple country girl. I met a —— fellow on the train, and we had a long conversation. She was so —— that I spent half the afternoon with her and learned nothing.

Weak, debilitated, feeble, infirm, decrepit, impotent.

Weak is the general word for that which is deficient in strength. *Debilitated* is used of physical weakness, in most instances brought on by excesses and abuses. *Feeble* denotes decided or extreme weakness, which may excite pity or contempt. *Infirm* is applied to a person whose weakness or feebleness is due to age. *Decrepit* is used in reference to a person broken down or worn out by infirmities, age, or sickness. *Impotent* implies such loss or lack of strength or vitality as to render ineffective or helpless.

Assignment for further discrimination: **enervated, languid, frail.**

Sentences: "Here I stand, your slave, A poor, ——, weak, and despis'd old man." A[n] —— old man shuffled along with the aid of a cane. Though still in his youth, he was —— from intemperance and fast living. A fellow who does that has a[n] —— mind. He staggered about trying to strike his opponent, but rage and his wound rendered him for the time ——. The grasp of the old man was so —— that the cup trembled in his hand. "Like rich hangings in a homely house, So was his will in his old —— body." After his long illness he was as —— as a child. He made but a[n] —— attempt to defend himself.

Wise, learned, erudite, sagacious, sapient, sage, judicious, prudent, provident, discreet. (Compare the distinction between *knowledge* and *wisdom* on page 150.)

Wise implies sound and discriminating judgment, resulting from either learning or experience. *Learned* denotes the past acquisition of much information through study. *Erudite* means characterized by extensive or profound knowledge. *Sagacious* implies far-sighted judgment and intuitive discernment, especially in practical matters. *Sapient* is now of infrequent use except as applied ironically or playfully to one having or professing wisdom. *Sage* implies deep wisdom that comes from age or experience. *Judicious* denotes sound judgment or careful discretion in weighing a matter with reference to its merits or its consequences. *Prudent* conveys a sense of cautious foresight in judging the future and planning for it upon the basis of the circumstances at hand. *Provident* suggests practical foresight and careful economy in preparing for future needs. *Discreet* denotes care or painstakingness in doing or saying the right thing at the right time, and the avoidance thereby of errors or unpleasant results.

Sentences: Against the time when his children would be going to college he had been ——. "Most —— judge!" The —— old warrior could not be deceived by any such ruse. "Be ye therefore as —— as serpents, and harmless as doves." The —— advice of his elders was wasted on him. The course was ——, not rash. He was —— in avoiding all reference to the subject. "Type of the ——, who soar but never roam, True to the kindred points of heaven and home." Even by those scholars, those specialists, he was deemed ——. How —— the young man is! "Where ignorance is bliss, 'Tis folly to be ——." Is it —— to spend money thus lavishly? He considered the matter well and gave a most —— answer. To spend every cent of one's income is surely not to be ——.

Work, labor, toil, drudgery.

All of us, at times anyhow, get out of as much work as we can. We even use the word *work* and its synonyms loosely and indolently. Perhaps this is a literary aspect of the labor problem. If, however, we can shake off our sluggishness and exert ourselves in discriminating our terms, we shall use *work* as a general word for effort, physical or mental, to some purposive end; *labor* for hard, physical work; *toil* for wearying or exhaustive work; and *drudgery* for tedious, monotonous, or distasteful work, especially of a low or menial kind.

Sentences: It required the —— of thousands of men to complete the tunnel. To be condemned to the galleys meant a life of unending ——. The man who enjoys his —— will succeed. Twenty years of incessant —— had extinguished in him every spark of ambition. He was weary after the —— of the day. All —— and no play makes Jack a dull boy. Through the heart-breaking —— of thousands the pyramids were built to commemorate a few. He was sentenced to hard ——.

VIII

SYNONYMS IN LARGER GROUPS (2)

YOU have now seen enough of the method of discriminating synonyms to take more of the responsibility for such work upon yourself. In this chapter, therefore, the plan followed in Exercise A is abandoned and no discriminations are supplied you.

Exercise

B

For some of the generic words in Exercise A you will find antonyms in Exercise C. Here is a list:
    In Exercise A: walk, laugh, busy, hate, masculine, old
    In Exercise C: run, cry, idle, love, feminine, young.
Now each of the generic terms in C is followed by a list of its synonyms. But for the six generic terms just given let us see how many synonyms you can find for yourself. Simply study each word in turn, think of all the synonyms for it you can summon, strike out those you consider far-fetched. Then compare your list with the list under the antonym in Exercise A; if possible, improve your list by means of this comparison. Finally, compare your revised list with the list in Exercise C.

In Exercise C are two generic terms that carry the same idea (but not in the same part of speech) as generic terms in Exercise A. They are as follows:
    In Exercise A: sing, death
    In Exercise C: song, die.
Take *song* and *die*. First, find all the satisfactory synonyms you can for yourself. Then if possible improve your list by studying the list under the corresponding word in Exercise A. Finally, compare your revised list with the one in Exercise C.

SYNONYMS IN LARGER GROUPS (2)

C

After three introductory groups (dealing with thoroughly concrete ideas and words) the synonyms in this exercise are arranged alphabetically according to the first word in each group.

Discriminate the words in each group, and fill each blank in the illustrative sentences with the word that conveys the meaning exactly.

See, perceive, descry, distinguish, espy, discern, note, notice, watch, observe, witness, behold, view.

Sentences: The intruder he —— in the early dawn-light might have been man or beast; he could not have —— one from the other. After a long search I —— on the map the name of the town. The teacher —— the throwing of the paper wad, but thought best not to —— it. "He that hath eyes to ——, let him ——." I —— the encounter. "I hope to —— my Pilot face to face When I have crossed the bar." "When my eyes turn to —— for the last time the sun in heaven." I sat by the flower and —— the bee plunder it. The scrawl on the paper was meaningless, but at length by close attention he —— secret writing. "Your young men shall —— visions, and your old men shall dream dreams." He had —— human nature manifesting itself under various conditions.

Kill, slay, slaughter, massacre, butcher, murder, assassinate, execute, hang, electrocute, guillotine, lynch, despatch, decimate, crucify.

Sentences: With the jawbone of an ass Samson —— a thousand of his enemies. It was his duty as sheriff to —— the criminal, and the method decreed by the state was that he should —— him. Previously the method of carrying out a sentence of death had been to —— the criminal. On our left wing we lost one man in ten; thus our lines were literally ——. On our right wing, where we advanced to the attack in the open, our men were simply ——. After the garrison had laid down its arms the Indians —— men, women, and children. "I would not —— thy soul." During the French Revolution many of the nobility were ——. In the country late fall is the time to —— hogs. Thinking that his accomplice was no longer of use, he quietly —— him. The anarchist who had —— the governor was taken by a mob and ——.

Sleep, slumber, repose, nap, doze, drowze, lethargy, dormancy, coma, trance, siesta.

Sentences: Since he had not exerted himself beforehand, his state was one of —— rather than one of ——. The sultry heat of the day put him into a ——. "Not poppy, nor mandragora, Nor all the —— syrops of the world, Shall ever medicine thee to that sweet —— Which thou ow[n]edst yesterday." Light and pleasant be thy ——. "And still she slept an azure-lidded ——." From the —— induced by his injury the physicians were unable to arouse him. "Oh ——! it is a gentle thing, Beloved from pole to pole!" "The poppied warmth of —— oppress'd Her soothéd limbs, and soul fatigued away." In Spanish-speaking South American countries every one expects to take his ——. He lay down under the tree for a short —— and had just fallen into a preliminary —— when the picnic party arrived. "Macbeth does murder ——, the innocent ——, —— that knits up the ravel'd sleave of care."

Abolish, repeal, rescind, revoke, abrogate, annul, nullify, cancel, reverse.

Sentences: A declaration of war would of course —— the treaty. The legislature has the right to —— old laws as well as to enact new ones. Because they left his grounds littered with paper, he —— their privilege of holding picnics there. The king —— the decree that the conspirators should be exiled. Slavery was —— by the Emancipation Proclamation. The emperor —— many of the ancient rights of the people. They —— the mortgage when he paid the money. The violation of these provisions has —— the contract. It was an ill day for France when the Edict of Nantes was —— by Louis XIV. The Supreme Court —— the decision of the lower tribunal. The Mormons have officially —— polygamy. The codicil —— some of the earlier provisions in his will.

Acquit, exculpate, exonerate, absolve.

Sentences: He —— himself from all blame. The king —— them from their allegiance. The teacher —— the student who had been suspected of theft. The father confessor —— the penitent. The jury —— the man on the first ballot

SYNONYMS IN LARGER GROUPS (2)

Afraid, fearful, frightened, alarmed, scared, aghast, terrified, timid, timorous. (This group may be compared with the *fear* group, below.)

Sentences: One child was too —— to speak to the strangers; the other too —— to do anything but squall. "If Cæsar hide himself, shall they not whisper 'Lo, Cæsar is ——'?" Any one might have been —— by this noise in a room said to be haunted; and for my part, I stood ——.

Allay, alleviate, mitigate, assuage, mollify, relieve.

Sentences: The judge —— the severity of the punishment. They collected funds to —— the sufferings of the poor. He could not —— the wrath of the angry man. Shall we try to —— their fears by telling them the accident may have been less calamitous than they have heard? A mustard plaster —— the pain. The grief of the mother was —— by the presence of her child. This experience had by no means —— his temper.

Allow, permit, suffer, tolerate.

Sentences: Visitors are not —— to see the king. The overrunning of my yard by the neighbors' chickens is a nuisance I shall not ——. "—— little children to come unto me." The use of bicycles and velocipedes on the pavement, though not —— by the city, is good-naturedly —— by most of the citizens. She —— her children to play in the street.

Ascribe, attribute, impute.

Sentences: I —— my failure to poor judgment. He —— sinister motives for their actions. So many ideal characteristics have been —— to Washington that it is difficult to think of him as a man.

Awkward, clumsy, ungainly, gawky, lanky.

Sentences: An elephant is —— in its movements. Some —— countrymen hung around the circus entrance. He was tall and ——; he seemed to be a mere prop on which clothes were hung. Isn't that man —— in his carriage? The fingers of the ball-players might as well have been thumbs, so —— were they from the cold. Girls throw a ball in a[n] —— manner.

Bite, nibble, gnaw, chew, masticate, champ.

Sentences: Fletcher taught people to —— their food well. The mouse —— the cheese, but the trap did not spring. A horse —— his bits. When I —— into the apple, I found that it was sour. The rat —— a hole through the board.

Break, crack, fracture, sever, rend, burst, smash, shatter, shiver, splinter, sunder, rive, crush, batter, demolish, rupture. (After discriminating these terms for yourself, see the treatment of *break, fracture* on page 170.)

Sentences: "—— my timbers!" the old salt exclaimed. The anaconda is an immense serpent that wraps itself about its victim and —— it. The child blew the soap bubble wider and wider till it ——. "You may ——, you may ——, the vase if you will." Looking closely at the eggs, she perceived that one of them was ——. With a board the thoughtless child —— the anthill. During a violent fit of coughing he —— a blood vessel. The thick cloud was —— and the sunshine streamed through.

Careful, cautious, wary, circumspect, canny.

Sentences: A mouse must be —— lest it be caught in a trap. He had learned to be —— in advancing his radical opinions. The man was a Scot and therefore ——. With a —— movement I opened the door to investigate the strange noise. He was —— in checking up the accounts. Be extremely —— in your behavior, for they are watching to criticize you.

Condescend, deign, vouchsafe.

Sentences: The king —— them safe conduct through the country. He would not —— to touch the money that had been gained dishonestly. His —— manner irritated them. The master —— to hear the complaints of the servants.

Confirm, corroborate, substantiate, verify.

Sentences: He —— the charge with positive proof. The finding of Desdemona's handkerchief —— Othello's belief that she was guilty. The other witnesses —— his testimony. The doctor —— the appointment his assistant had made for him. He —— his results by repeating the experiment a number of times.

SYNONYMS IN LARGER GROUPS (2)

Courage, bravery, resolution, dauntlessness, gallantry, boldness, intrepidity, daring, valor, prowess, fortitude, heroism. (With this group contrast the *fear* group, below.)

Sentences: It seemed they must be driven from their works but they held to them with the utmost ——. He had the —— to fight an aggressive battle, but not the —— to stand for long days upon the defensive; less still did he have the —— to disregard unjust criticism. The silent —— of the women who bide at home surpasses the —— of the warriors who engage in battle. He had the dashing —— of a cavalry officer.

Cruel, brutal, ferocious, fierce, savage, barbarous, truculent, merciless, unmerciful, pitiless, ruthless, fell. (With this group contrast the *kind* group, below.)

Sentences: "But with the whiff and wind of his —— sword The unnerved father falls." "Poor naked wretches, wheresoe'er you are, That bide the pelting of this —— storm." The —— fellow could cause suffering to a child without the least tinge of remorse. Such conduct is unheard of in civilized communities; it is ——, it is ——. "I must be —— only to be kind."

Cry, weep, sob, snivel, whimper, blubber, bawl, squall, howl, wail.

Sentences: "—— no more, woeful shepherds; —— no more." The woman covered her face with her hands and ——, while the children ——. He —— a forced regret at the death of his uncle, and asked that the will be read. "Rachel —— for her children." "Rejoice with them that do rejoice, and —— with them that ——." "I could lie down like a tired child And —— away this life of care Which I have borne and yet must bear." "An infant —— in the night." "What's Hecuba to him or he to Hecuba That he should —— for her?" I was disgusted at the sight of that overgrown boy standing in the corner ——. "You think I'll ——; No, I'll not ——: I have full cause of ——, but this heart Shall break into a hundred thousand flaws Or ere I'll ——."

Cut, cleave, hack, haggle, notch, slash, gash, split, chop, hew, lop, prune, reap, mow, clip, shear, trim, dock, crop, shave, whittle, slice, slit, score, lance, carve, bisect, dissect, amputate, detruncate, syncopate.

Sentences: "I'll —— around your heart with my razor, And shoot you with my shotgun too." "O Hamlet! thou hast —— my heart in twain." By the pressure of his hands he could —— an apple. With his new hatchet George began —— at the cherry tree. He carelessly —— off a branch or two. The horses were —— the rank grass. An old form of punishment was to —— the nose of the offender. The nobleman ordered the groom to —— the tails of the carriage horses. You should —— your meadows in the summer and —— your grapevines in the late fall or early winter. "Do you," asked the barber, "wish your hair —— or ——?" —— to the line. It is painful to see Dodwell trying to —— a turkey. In geometry we learned to —— angles, in biology to —— cats. The bad man in the West —— his gunstock each time he shot a tenderfoot. Betty, will you —— this cucumber? " 'Mark's way,' said Mark, and —— him thro' the brain."

Deadly, mortal, fatal, lethal.

Sentences: He has a *fatal* disease. The spirit of Virgil guided Dante through the *mortal* shades. Cyanide of potassium is a *deadly* poison. He struck a *lethal* blow.

Defeat, subdue, conquer, overcome, vanquish, subjugate, suppress.

Sentences: Napoleon *conquered* his enemies in many battles, but he was not able to *subdue* them. The new governor general —— the uprising. He was —— in the election. Cæsar —— many countries and made them swear allegiance to Rome. "Who —— by force Hath —— but half his foe." The militia —— the rioters.

Deny, contravene, controvert, refute, confute.

Sentences: He produced evidence to —— the charge. They could not —— the facts we presented. It is difficult to —— those who are spreading these rumors, yet all right-minded people think the rumors false. "I put thee now to thy book-oath; —— it if thou canst." Either admit or —— the truth of this allegation. Such a law —— the first principles of justice.

Destroy, demolish, raze, annihilate, exterminate, eradicate, extirpate, obliterate.

Sentences: All the ferocious wild animals are gradually being ——. As weeds from a field, so is it difficult to —— all the faults from man's nature. But how shall we —— the cause of this disease? Fire —— the bank. The wrecking crew —— the building. She tried to —— the terrible scene from her memory. "—— all that's made To a green thought in a green shade." The cyclone —— the church. The Spanish Inquisition tried to —— heresy. "—— out the written troubles of the brain." The army was not only defeated; it was ——. "A bold peasantry, their country's pride, When once ——, can never be supplied."

Die, expire, perish, decease, succumb.

Sentences: All men are mortal and must ——. "As wax melteth before the fire, so let the wicked —— at the presence of God." "I still had hopes, my long vexations past, Here to return, and —— at home at last." The late —— Mr. Brown left all his property to his family. "Cowards —— many times before their deaths." "The poor beetle, that we tread upon, In corporal sufferance finds a pang as great As when a giant ——." "Government of the people, by the people, for the people, shall not —— from the earth." "Thus on Mæander's flowery margin lies Th' —— swan, and as he sings he dies." Over a thousand people —— in the fire at the theater. "To ——, to sleep; to sleep: perchance to dream." He —— to a lingering disease. "Aye, but to ——, and go we know not where; To lie in cold obstruction and to rot." "Wind my thread of life up higher, Up, through angels' hands of fire! I aspire while I ——."

Dip, douse, duck, plunge, immerge, immerse, submerge, sink, dive.

Sentences: He —— his head under the hydrant. The Baptists —— at baptism. She —— the cloth into the dye. The sophomores —— the freshmen into the icy water of the lake. Paul Jones could not —— the enemy's ship; he therefore resolved to board it. The wreck lay —— in forty fathoms of water. Uncle Tom —— overboard to rescue the child. When the gun is discharged, the loon does not rise from the water; it ——. Lewis became badly strangled when the other boys —— him.

Disease, sickness, illness, indisposition, ailment, affection, complaint, disorder, distemper, infirmity, malady. (With this group contrast the *healthful* group on page 202.)

Sentences: He was suffering the —— of age. Cancer is still in many instances an incurable ——. The —— of the lady ended as soon as the maid told her the callers had gone away. It was an old —— of the tonsils, but this time the child's —— was slight. "To help me through this long ——, my life."

Disloyal, false, unfaithful, faithless, traitorous, treasonable, treacherous, perfidious.

Sentences: The king discovered many —— schemes among those who pretended to be his loyal supporters. England's enemies have long called her "—— Albion." They were afraid the Indian guide would betray them by some —— action. "O you beast! O —— coward! O dishonest wretch!" He was —— to his adopted country. "Bloody, bawdy villain! Remorseless, ——, lecherous, kindless villain! O! vengeance!"

Do, perform, execute, accomplish, achieve, effect.

Sentences: An officer —— the orders with despatch. He —— a mighty name for himself. "If it were —— when 'tis ——, then 'twere well It were —— quickly." Constant efforts will —— miracles. The student —— the problems quickly. The doctor hopes his new treatment will —— a cure. "God moves in a mysterious way His wonders to ——." He persevered till he —— his purpose. He always —— more than was expected of him.

Dress, clothes, clothing, garments, apparel, raiment, habiliments, vestments, attire, garb, habit, costume, uniform.

SYNONYMS IN LARGER GROUPS (2)   227

Sentences: The spy concealed his identity by wearing the —— of a monk. The soldiers wore blue ——. She was an excellent horsewoman, and rode in a fashionable ——. "No man putteth a piece of new cloth unto an old ——." Millions of men left farms and factories and shops to don the —— of war. The invitation specified that the men should wear evening ——. The store specialized in women's wearing ——. A person should wear warm —— in winter. The king appeared in his royal ——. He always wore expensive ——. The bishop entered in his clerical ——. "The —— oft proclaims the man." The theatrical —— was full of spangles. One's —— should never be conspicuous.

Drink, imbibe, sip, sup, swallow, quaff, tipple, tope, guzzle, swig.

Sentences: "She who, as they voyaged, —— With Tristram that spiced magic draught." Plants —— moisture through their roots. "A little learning is a dang'rous thing; —— deep, or taste not the Pierian spring." He —— down the liquor in a couple of huge draughts. On the fan was a picture of Japanese maidens daintily —— tea. "—— to me only with thine eyes." His red nose betrayed the fact that he constantly ——.

Elicit, extract, exact, extort.

Sentences: They —— payment to the last cent. The police —— a confession from the prisoner by intimidating him. This terrible suffering —— our sympathy. His resolve to begin again after his failure —— their admiration. "But lend it rather to thine enemy; Who if he break, thou mayst with better face —— the penalty." They —— all the information they could by questioning the child.

Embarrass, disconcert, discompose, discomfit, confuse, confound, agitate, abash, mortify, chagrin, humiliate.

Sentences: The annoying little raids —— the enemy. Such conclusive proof of his lies completely —— him. His sudden proposal —— her. He stood —— in the presence of the king. The traveler was —— by the many turns in the road. She was —— by the delay in having dinner ready. She was —— by her husband's ill manners. The possibility that her daughter might have been in the accident —— her. I was —— at being so cleverly outwitted.

Excuse, pardon, forgive, condone.

Sentences: We should —— even those who do us wrong. "Father, —— them; for they know not what they do." I trust you will —— my being late. Ignorance —— no one before the law. The governor —— the convict. He thought it better to —— the offense than to try to punish it.

Explain, expound, interpret, elucidate.

Sentences: The minister —— the doctrine of predestination. The tribesman —— his chief's words for us. He —— his meaning by giving clear examples. Joseph was called upon to —— Pharaoh's dream. Can you —— the reason for your absence? Various scholars have —— the passage differently.

Fat, fleshy, stout, plump, buxom, corpulent, obese, portly, pursy, burly, pudgy, chubby.

Sentences: "There live not three good men unhanged in England, and one of them is —— and grows old." A[n] ——, rosy-faced child walking beside a girl just pleasantly —— came past the garden. The —— lady was talking with a[n] ——, ill-conditioned man. "So ——, blithe, and debonair." "He's ——, and scant of breath." The ruffian was a[n] —— fellow. They were —— in varying degrees: one was ——, one ——, and one downright ——.

Fear, dread, fright, apprehension, affright, alarm, dismay, consternation, panic, terror, horror, misgiving, anxiety, scare, timidity, trepidation, tremor. (With this group compare the *afraid* group, above, and contrast the *courage* group, also above.)

Sentences: "Like one, that on a lonesome road Doth walk in —— and ——." "His scepter shows the force of temporal power, The attribute to awe and majesty, Wherein doth sit the —— and —— of kings." —— changed to —— when we perceived the corpse. Washington felt some —— as to the

SYNONYMS IN LARGER GROUPS (2)

loyalty of Charles Lee, but was amazed to find his force retreating in ———, indeed almost in a[n] ———.

Feminine, female, womanly, womanlike, womanish, effeminate, ladylike.

Sentences: She possessed every ——— charm. He gave a[n] ——— start of curiosity. The pistil is considered the ——— organ of a flower. It was once not thought ——— for a woman to ride astride a horse. He inherited the throne through the ——— line. Patience is one of the greatest of ——— virtues. The hired girl in her finery minced along with a[n] ——— step. Some people consider it ——— to wear a wrist watch. Her ——— heart was touched at the sight. It is ——— to jump at the sight of a mouse.

Fight, combat, struggle, scuffle, fray, affray, attack, assault, onslaught, brawl, mêlée, tournament, battle, conflict, strife, clash, collision, contest, engagement, skirmish, encounter, brush, bout, set-to.

Sentences: "A darkling plain Swept with confused alarms of ——— and flight." The ——— upon Fort Sumter was the direct cause of the Civil War. The ——— between our forces and theirs was brief and trivial; it was only a cavalry ———. There is an excellent account of a knightly ——— in *Ivanhoe*. We repelled their general ———; then ourselves advanced; the ——— of our lines with theirs soon resulted in an inextricable ———. A chance ——— of small forces at Gettysburg brought on a terrible ———. There had long been ——— between the two factions within the party. Angered by what had begun as a playful ———, one of the men challenged the other to ———.

Fleeting, transient, transitory, ephemeral, evanescent.

Sentences: It is the lot of every one to endure many sorrows in this ——— life. They saw for a short while a[n] ——— comet. The ——— glories of dawn had merged into the sordid realities of daytime. The remark made but a[n] ——— impression upon him. The ——— moments sped away. "Art is long, and time is ———." Joy is ———. Much of the popular literature of the day is ——— in character.

Frank, candid, open, artless, guileless, ingenuous, unsophisticated, naïve.

Sentences: It was a[n] —— excuse. It was a pleasure to meet a person so simple and ——. He was —— to say that he did not like the arrangement. "Who, mindful of the unhonored dead, Dost in these lines their —— tale relate." "The Moor is of a free and —— nature." He gave them his —— opinion.

Frustrate, foil, thwart, counteract, circumvent, balk, baffle, outwit.

Sentences: The schemers were themselves ——. He was —— by the many contradictory clues. Circumstances —— all his plans to get rich. The parents —— the attempt of the couple to elope. The guard —— the prisoner's attempt to escape. He was —— at every turn. They put forth a statement to —— the influence of their opponents' propaganda. By slipping away during the night, Washington —— the enemy. The politician by his shrewdness —— the attempt to discredit him.

Glad, happy, cheerful, mirthful, joyful, joyous, blithe, gay, frolicsome, merry, jolly, sportive, jovial, jocular, jocose, jocund.

Sentences: "The milkmaid singeth ——." "And all went —— as a marriage bell." "How beautiful are the feet of them that preach the gospel of peace, and bring —— tidings of good things." A —— Lothario. "So buxom, ——, and debonair." As —— as a fawn. He kept smiling, for he was in —— mood. "You are sad Because you are not ——; and 'twere as easy For you to laugh and leap, and say you are ——, Because you are not sad." He longed for the —— life of a —— English squire.

Habit, custom, usage, practice, wont.

Sentences: —— makes perfect. The immigrants kept up many of the —— of their native land. "God fulfils himself in many ways, Lest one good —— should corrupt the world." It was his —— to walk among the ruins. An old —— permits a man to kiss a girl who is standing under mistletoe. —— establishes many peculiar idioms in a language. He acquired the

SYNONYMS IN LARGER GROUPS (2)

—— of smoking. "It is a —— More honor'd in the breach than the observance." De Quincey was a victim of the opium ——. "Age cannot wither her, nor —— stale Her infinite variety." "'Tis not his —— to be the hindmost man."

Harass, annoy, irritate, vex, fret, worry, plague, torment, molest, tease, tantalize.

Sentences: The merchant —— about his financial losses. "Life's but a walking shadow, a poor player That struts and —— his hour upon the stage, And then is heard no more." The children never lost an opportunity to —— the teacher. The other pupils —— him because he was the teacher's favorite. The newcomer was —— by their frequent questions. Don't —— the child by holding the grapes beyond its reach. "He was met even now As mad as the —— sea." Ah, but I am —— by doubts and fears. "The moping owl does to the moon complain Of such as, wand'ring near her secret bower, —— her ancient, solitary reign." The child —— because the rain kept it indoors. When the joke was discovered, they almost —— the life out of him. I was —— at their discovering my predicament. "You may as well forbid the mountain pines To wag their high tops, and to make no noise When they are —— with the gusts of heaven."

Hinder, restrain, obstruct, impede, hamper, retard, check, curb, clog, encumber, forestall, suppress, repress, prevent.

Sentences: Baggage —— the progress of an army. It is the purpose of modern medicine to —— disease. The accumulations of dust and grease —— the machine. "My tears must stop, for every drop —— needle and thread." By acknowledging his fault he hoped to —— criticism. Though before she had been unable to —— her tears, she could now scarcely —— a yawn. A fallen tree —— his further progress. The horse was —— with a heavy burden, and the unsure footing of the trail further —— the ascent. His jealous colleagues —— his plans in every way they could.

Hole, cavity, excavation, pit, cache, cave, cavern, hollow, perforation, puncture, rent, slit, crack, chink, crevice, cranny, breach, cleft, chasm, fissure, gap, open-

ing, interstice, burrow, crater, eyelet, pore, bore, aperture, orifice, vent, concavity, dent, indentation, depression.

Sentences: The explorers, having eaten all the provisions they had carried with them, hurried back to their ——. The battering-ram at last made a[n] —— in the walls. The —— in the log had been caused by the intense heat. He tore off the check along the line of the ——. The —— in the earth gradually deepened and narrowed into a[n] ——. Pyramus and Thisbe made love to each other through a[n] —— in a wall. "Once more unto the ——, dear friends, once more." The —— in the mountain ranges of Virginia influenced strategy during the Civil War. Several —— in the toe of one of his shoes apprised me that he had a sore foot. The supposed —— in the rock turned out to be a[n] —— that led into a dark but spacious ——. He suffered a[n] —— of one of his tires near the place where the laborers were making the ——. It was a gun of very large ——. The —— in the percolator was made by a flatiron aimed at Mr. Wiggins' head.

Idle, inert, lazy, indolent, sluggish, slothful.

Sentences: "He also that is —— in his work is brother to him that is a great waster." "The —— singer of an empty day." Mighty, —— forces lie locked up in nature, waiting for man to release them. He was a[n] ——, good-for-nothing fellow whose whole business in life was to keep out of work. "For Satan finds some mischief still For —— hands to do." He was too —— to do his work well. "The —— yawning drone." His steps were so —— one would almost think he was not moving. "As —— as a painted ship Upon a painted ocean." "I talk of dreams, Which are the children of an —— brain, Begot of nothing but vain fantasy."

Ignorant, illiterate, uninformed, uneducated, untutored, unlettered, unenlightened.

Sentences: Without public schools most children would be ——; without missionaries many barbarous tribes would remain ——. Andrew Jackson was —— that peace had been declared when he fought the battle of New Orleans. Even the wisest men are —— upon some subjects. "Lo, the poor Indian, whose

SYNONYMS IN LARGER GROUPS (2)

—— mind Sees God in clouds or hears Him in the wind!" The mountain whites, though often totally ——, are nevertheless a shrewd folk. "Their name, their years, spelt by th' —— muse, The place of fame and elegy supply." The percentage of —— persons is constantly decreasing in America.

Incline, tip, lean, cant, slant, slope, tilt, list, careen, dip.

Sentences: He —— the bucket of water over. The vessel —— to the stern and began to sink. The ship —— to larboard. He —— the top of the picture away from the wall. The sprinter —— forward and touched the tips of his fingers against the ground. The gable —— sharply. The hill —— gently. The cowboy had —— his hat fetchingly.

Journey, voyage, tour, pilgrimage, trip, jaunt, excursion, junket, outing, expedition.

Sentences: The people protested the expenditure of money for a Congressional —— to investigate the Philippine Islands. Each Sunday there is a[n] —— at half fare between the two cities. He conducted a party on a summer —— through Europe. Last summer I took a[n] —— to the Yellowstone National Park. It was a long —— from Philadelphia to Boston by stage coach. They hurriedly arranged for a[n] —— to the woods. Magellan was the first man to make a[n] —— around the globe. The scientific body organized a[n] —— to explore the polar regions. Thousands of Mohammedans make an annual —— to Mecca.

Kind, compassionate, merciful, lenient, benignant, benign, clement, benevolent, charitable, gracious, humane, sympathetic. (With this group compare the *cruel* group, above.)

Sentences: The weather was ——. She was as —— as a queen. "Thou dost wear The Godhead's most —— grace." Cowper was too —— to tread upon a worm needlessly. A judge in sentencing a convicted man may be as —— as circumstances and the law allow. —— neutrality. "Blessed are the ——." "She was so —— and so pitous She wolde wepe if that she sawe a mous Caught in a trappe." "—— hearts are more than coronets."

234 CENTURY VOCABULARY BUILDER

Love, affection, attachment, fondness, infatuation, devotion, predilection, liking.

Sentences: Between the two young people had grown a[n] —— which now ripened into ——. "The course of true —— never did run smooth." The mad —— of Mark Antony for Cleopatra was the cause of his downfall. She had only a[n] —— for him, but he an unqualified —— for her. "Man's —— is of his life a thing apart; 'Tis woman's whole existence." He shows a marked —— for the companionship of women. My —— for the tart was enhanced by my —— for the girl who baked it. That boy shows a[n] —— for horses, and a positive —— for dogs.

Margin, edge, limit, border, boundary, bound, bourn, brim, rim, brink, verge, skirt, confine.

Sentences: He had reached the —— of endurance. In writing, leave a wide —— on the left side of the page. "Borrowing dulls the —— of husbandry." "The extravagant and erring spirit hies To his ——." Within the —— of reason. He stood on the —— of ruin. The rock at the —— of the cañon is called the —— rock. I was on the —— of doing a very indiscreet thing. "The undiscover'd country from whose —— No traveler returns." Fill your glasses to the ——.

Matrimonial, conjugal, connubial, nuptial, marital.

Sentences: "However old a —— union, it still garners some sweetness." A court of —— relations. "Contented toil, and hospitable care, And kind —— tenderness are there." "To the —— bower I led her, blushing like the morn." She finally decided that he had no —— intentions. "And hears the unexpressive —— song In the blest kingdoms meek of joy and love."

Occupation, employment, calling, pursuit, vocation, avocation, profession, business, trade, craft.

Sentences: He gave his life to literary ——. My brother found —— as a tutor in a rich family. Colleges are trying to direct their students into the —— they are best fitted for. Andrew Johnson was a tailor by ——. Medicine is a very ancient ——. The shoemaker was very skilled at his ——.

SYNONYMS IN LARGER GROUPS (2)

After losing his hand he could no longer engage in his —— as telegrapher. The grocer carries on only a wholesale ——. He considered his —— to the ministry a sacred duty. "Sir, 'tis my —— to be plain." Do you find collecting coins a pleasant ——?

Pacify, appease, placate, propitiate, conciliate, mollify.

Sentences: We —— our hunger when we reached the inn. In olden times men tried to —— the offended gods by offering human sacrifices. They —— the angry man by promising to hear his grievances immediately. The premier thought he could —— this particular faction by offering its leader a seat in the cabinet. "Chiron —— his cruel mind With art, and taught his warlike hands to wind The silver strings of his melodious lyre." A friendly word will usually —— one's enemies.

Part, piece, portion, section, subdivision, fraction, instalment, element, component, constituent, ingredient, share, lot, allotment.

Sentences: One —— in his success was his courage. She was studying the —— of the pie; he the chances of getting another ——. Is it —— and —— alike? "I live not in myself, but I become —— of that around me." "Act well your ——; there all the honor lies." He owned a[n] —— of land near the city limits; a speculator bought a[n] —— of this and divided it into city lots. "I am a[n] —— of all that I have met." The purchaser, having only a[n] —— of this sum in ready money, offered to pay in ——.

Pay, hire, salary, wages, fee, stipend, honorarium.

Sentences: Give the manager his ——, the workmen their ——. "The laborer is worthy of his ——." He received his weekly —— from the parsimonious old man. The —— for enrolment is ten dollars. "This is —— and ——, not revenge."

Polite, civil, obliging, courteous, courtly, urbane, affable, complaisant, gracious.

Sentences: He was —— enough, but not definitely ——. "So —— that he ne'er ——." Though he had never lived in a city,

much less in the circle of royalty, his manners were ——, even
——. Your desire to please is shown in your —— greeting.
"Damn with faint praise, assent with —— leer, And without
sneering teach the rest to sneer."

Quarrel, altercation, disagreement, contention, controversy, breach, rupture, dispute, dissension, bickering, wrangle, broil, squabble, row, rumpus, ruction, spat, tiff, fuss, jar, feud.

Sentences: It was only a little —— between lovers. The ——
between the partners was over the right of the senior to make
contracts for the firm; it grew into an angry ——. It was a
long-drawn political ——. At the meeting of our committee
the chairman and one of the members had a sharp —— over a
point of order. A[n] —— in some minor matters led to a[n] ——
in their friendship. "Thrice is he armed that hath his —— just."
Those chattering, choleric fellows are always engaged in ——;
last night they on meeting had a[n] —— which brought on a
long-drawn ——, and when their friends joined in, there was a
noisy ——. I have seen all sorts of ——, from a trivial childish
—— to a grim —— of mountaineers.

Raise, lift, heave, hoist, erect, rear, elevate, exalt, enhance.

Sentences: Let the Lord be ——. "As some tall cliff that ——
its awful form." Because of this success his reputation was
——. The horse —— when the machine began to —— the huge
block of stone by means of a crane. "I will —— up mine eyes
unto the hills, from whence cometh my help." The load was
too heavy for him to carry; in fact he just managed to ——
it into the wagon.

Relinquish, waive, renounce, surrender, forego, resign, abdicate.

Sentences: The defense —— objection to the first of these
points. The refugee was willing to —— his right to resist
extradition. The teacher —— her position at the end of the
year. The king —— when the people rose in revolt. He ——
his command of the army. Do you —— your claim in this
mine? The bankrupt —— his property to the receiver to help
pay his debts.

SYNONYMS IN LARGER GROUPS (2)

Renounce, abjure, forswear, recant, retract, repudiate.

Sentences: He —— the statement. Thereupon Henry Esmond —— his allegiance to the House of Stuart. It is a serious matter for a government to —— its debts. Did the heretic ——? Do you —— the devil and all his works? "The wounded gladiator —— all fighting, but soon forgetting his former wounds resumes his arms." He had broken his solemn oath; he was ——.

Reprove, rebuke, reprimand, admonish, chide, upbraid, reproach, scold, rate, berate.

Sentences: "He —— their wanderings but relieved their pain." "Many a time and oft In the Rialto you have —— me About my moneys and my usances." They —— the man who had taken the savings of the poor, and —— him against such schemes thereafter. The general —— his subordinate.

Robber, bandit, brigand, ladrone, desperado, buccaneer, freebooter, pirate, corsair, raider, burglar, footpad, highwayman, depredator, spoiler, despoiler, forager, pillager, plunderer, marauder, myrmidon. (With this group compare the *steal* group, below.)

Sentences: Every boy has his period of wanting to be a ——. *Treasure Island* is one of the best —— stories ever written. The —— lurks in dark passageways and steals upon his victim. The fierce followers of Achilles were called ——. The men sent out by the army as —— seemed to the people of the countryside more like ——. The fearless —— had soon gathered about him a band of ——. Robin Hood was no —— of poor folk. The outcast became a —— among the mountaineers of northern Italy. Every boy likes to read of the bold —— who sailed the Spanish Main. Union plans were often upset by daring Confederate ——, such as Stuart, Morgan, and Forrest.

Run, scamper, scurry, scuttle, scud, scour, pace, gallop, trot, lope, sprint, sweep.

Sentences: Swift horsemen —— the country in search of the fugitive. Wherever they came, the inhabitants —— for shelter. "The dish —— away with the spoon." For his horse to —— made difficult riding, to —— made comfortable riding, to —— made exhilarating riding. "He may —— that readeth it." The old sailing-boat —— before the wind. "Haste me to know't, that I, with wings as swift As meditation or the thoughts of love, May —— to my revenge." The rats —— across the floor. "He who fights and —— away May live to fight another day."

Say, utter, pronounce, announce, state, declare, affirm, aver, asseverate, allege, assert, avouch, avow, maintain, claim, depose, predicate, swear, suggest, insinuate, testify. (With this group compare the *speak* and *talk* groups, below.)

Sentences: It was something I merely —— in passing; I would not —— to it. I could not —— in court, and therefore had to —— before a notary. The scientist —— that a seismograph will infallibly record earthquakes. He solemnly —— that he would not —— exemption from the draft.

Shine, beam, gleam, glisten, glister, glitter, glare, flare, flash, sparkle, twinkle, dazzle, glimmer, glow, radiate, scintillate, coruscate.

Sentences: The gorgeous parade —— the boy. "——, ——, little star." He was witty that night; he fairly ——. At this compliment the old lady ——. "Now fades the —— landscape on the sight." A rocket —— in the darkness. She —— her elderly wooer a look of defiance; then her eyes softened and —— with amusement. "All that —— is not gold." "How far that little candle throws his beams! So —— a good deed in a naughty world." The old man —— into sudden anger.

Slander, defame, asperse, calumniate, traduce, vilify, malign, backbite, libel.

Sentences: A newspaper must be careful not to —— any one. Too many supposedly religious people —— their fellow believers. I do not —— your motives. He —— the character of everybody who chances to possess one.

SYNONYMS IN LARGER GROUPS (2)

Smell, odor, savor, scent, fragrance, aroma, perfume, redolence, stench, tang.

Sentences: The —— of the flowers in the vase mingled with the —— of boiling cabbage in the kitchen. The —— of spring is on the meadows. So keen was the hound's sense of —— that he quickly picked up the —— again. Any smoker likes the —— of a good cigar. The —— of the handkerchief was delicate. Though it was a disagreeable ——, I should hardly call it a[n] ——. The —— of spices told him that his mother was baking his favorite cake, and he also detected the —— of coffee. The —— of the ocean was in the air. He sniffed the —— of frying bacon.

Song, ballad, ditty, lullaby, hymn, anthem, dirge, chant, pæan, lay, carol, lilt.

Sentences: "They learn in suffering what they teach in ——." The mother crooned a[n] —— to her babe. The Highland girl sang a moving old ——. The worshipers sang a[n] —— of praise. Charles Wesley wrote many ——. As I approached the cathedral, I could hear the —— of larks outside and the —— of the choir within. "Our sweetest —— are those that tell of saddest thought." "A[n] —— for her the doubly dead in that she died so young."

Speak, discourse, expatiate, descant, comment, argue, persuade, plead, lecture, preach, harangue, rant, roar, spout, thunder, declaim, harp. (With this group compare the *say* group, above, and the *talk* group, below.)

Sentences: "His virtues Will —— like angels trumpet-tongu'd against The deep damnation of his taking-off." "Here, under leave of Brutus and the rest, ... Come I to —— in Cæsar's funeral." "Ay me! what act, That —— so loud and —— in the index?" "Hadst thou thy wits and didst —— revenge, It could not move thus." "Thou canst not —— of that thou dost not feel." "Nay, if thou'lt mouth, I'll —— as well as thou." While the politician —— in the senate chamber upon theoretical ills, the agitator outside —— the mob about actual ones. "For murder, though it have no tongue, will —— With most miraculous organ."

240   CENTURY VOCABULARY BUILDER

Spend, expend, disburse, squander, waste, lavish.

Sentences: Large sums were —— in rebuilding the devastated regions of France. —— your money, but do not —— it. One should not —— more than one earns. The king —— great sums upon his favorites. The political boss —— the money among his henchmen. "The younger son . . . —— his substance with riotous living."

Spot, speck, speckle, fleck, dapple, mark, brand, blot, stain, discoloration, blotch, smutch, smudge, smear, flaw, blemish, defect, defacement.

Sentences: A —— in the crystal. The —— of Cain. A life free from ——. "Thou turn'st mine eyes into my very soul; And there I see such black and grained —— As will not leave their tinct." From the standpoint of theatrical effectiveness *A —— in the 'Scutcheon* is one of the best of Browning's plays. An eruption of the skin made a yellow —— on his right hand. Dragging my sleeve across the fresh ink had made a —— upon the page. The —— of foam by the roadside proved that his horse had been going fast. The —— at the end of his fingers told me he was a cigarette-smoker. On the left foreleg of the horse was a slight ——.

Stay, tarry, linger, stop, sojourn, remain, abide, live, reside, dwell, lodge.

Sentences: The Israelites —— in Egypt. He —— to chat with us, but could not —— overnight. I —— in a wretched tavern. "I can ——, I can —— but a night." "I did love the Moor to —— with him." "He that shall come will come, and will not ——." "I will —— in the house of the Lord forever." "If ye —— in me, and my words —— in you, ye shall ask what ye will, and it shall be done unto you." "I would rather be a doorkeeper in the house of my God, than to —— in the tents of wickedness." The guests —— in the cheerful drawing-room.

Steal, abstract, pilfer, filch, purloin, peculate, swindle, plagiarize, poach. (With this group, which excludes the idea of violence, compare the *robber* group, above.)

SYNONYMS IN LARGER GROUPS (2)

Sentences: I am afraid that our son —— the purse from the gentleman. No one knows how long the cashier has been —— the funds of the bank. To take our money on such unsound security is to —— us. He slyly —— a handkerchief or two. This paragraph is clearly ——. "Thou shalt not ——." Many government employees seem to think that to —— is their privilege and prerogative. The crown jewels have been ——. She —— a number of petty articles. A well-known detective story by Poe is called *The* —— *Letter*. "Who —— my purse —— trash.... But he that —— from me my good name Robs me of that which not enriches him, And makes me poor indeed." "A cut-purse of the empire and the rule, That from a shelf the precious diadem ——, And put it in his pocket!"

Strike, hit, smite, thump, beat, cuff, buffet, knock, whack, belabor, pommel, pound, cudgel, slap, rap, tap, box.

Sentences: —— him into the middle of next week. He —— and —— the poor beast unmercifully. "As of some one gently ——, —— at my chamber door." "Unto him that —— thee on the one cheek offer also the other." "Bid them come forth and hear me, Or at their chamber door I'll —— the drum Till it cry sleep to death." "One whom I will —— into clamorous whining." "—— for your altars and your fires!" By means of heavy stones the squaws —— the corn into meal.

Sullen, surly, sulky, crabbed, cross, gruff, grum, glum, morose, dour, crusty, cynical, misanthropic, saturnine, splenetic.

Sentences: "Between us and our hame [home], Where sits our ——, —— dame, Gathering her brows like gathering storm, Nursing her wrath to keep it warm." A —— old bachelor. A —— Scotchman. He hated all men; he was truly ——. He sat —— and silent all day; by nightfall he was truly ——.

Talk, chat, chatter, prate, prattle, babble, gabble, jabber, tattle, twaddle, blab, gossip, palaver, parley, converse, mumble, mutter, stammer, stutter. (With this group compare the *say* and *speak* groups, above.)

Sentences: It was a queer assembly, and from it arose a queer medley of sounds: the baby was ——, the old crone ——, the gossip ——, the embarrassed young man ——, the child ——, the tale-bearer ——, the hostess —— with the most distinguished guest, and the trickster —— with his intended victim. "Blest with each talent and each art to please, And born to write, ——, and live with ease." "I wonder that you will still be ——, Signor Benedick; nobody marks you."

Tear, rend, rip, lacerate, mangle.

Sentences: The explosion of the shell —— his flesh. The tailor —— the garment along the seam. I'll —— this paper into bits. Those savages would —— you limb from limb. She —— her dress on a nail. The cogs caught his hand and —— it. How could such reproaches fail to —— my feelings?

Throw, pitch, hurl, dash, fling, cast, toss, flip, chuck, sling, heave, launch, dart, propel, project.

Sentences: Suddenly he —— the glittering coins away. Goliath learned to his cost that David could —— a stone. The explosion of the gunpowder —— the bullet from the gun. "—— down your cups of Samian wine!" The children amused themselves by —— the ball back and forth. He —— himself dejectedly into a seat. The thief —— a glance beside him. The mischievous boy —— a stone through the window. They —— some of the cargo overboard to lighten the boat. The eager fisherman —— the fly for the trout. The untidy fellow —— the towel in a corner.

Whip, chastise, castigate, flagellate, scourge, lash, trounce, thrash, flog, maul, drub, switch, spank, bastinado. (This group limits the field of the *punish* group in Exercise A, and extends the list of synonyms.)

Sentences: The drunken driver —— the excited horses. The zealot was accustomed to —— himself. The ruler bade that the Christians be ——. The teacher —— the small children gently, but he unsparingly —— the big ones. "My father hath —— you with whips, but I will —— you with scorpions." The bully was always —— men smaller than himself till one of them turned on him and —— him thoroughly.

SYNONYMS IN LARGER GROUPS (2)

Wicked, sinful, felonious, illegal, immoral, heinous, flagitious, iniquitous, criminal, vicious, vile.

Sentences: "I am fled From this —— world, with —— worms to dwell." A[n] —— assault. "The —— prize itself Buys out the law." It was, though not a[n] —— act, a most —— one. "There the —— cease from troubling; and there the weary be at rest."

Young, youthful, boyish, girlish, juvenile, puerile, immature, adolescent, callow.

Sentences: The plan had all the faults of —— judgment. Many great authors have written books of —— fiction. The bird, which was still ——, was of course unable to fly. "Such sights as —— poets dream On summer eves by haunted stream." He was in that —— stage of development when one is neither a boy nor a man. "I was so ——, I loved him so, I had No mother, God forgot me, and I fell." He made a[n] —— attempt to impress them with his importance. "Bacchus ever fair, and ever ——." A red necktie gave him a more —— appearance. The self-satisfied air of a[n] —— youth is often trying to his elders.

D

In this exercise each group of synonyms is followed by quotations from authoritative writers in which the words are discriminatingly employed. Find the meaning of each italicized word in these quotations, and differentiate the word accurately from the others in that group. Substitute for it other words from the group, and observe precisely how the meaning is affected.

(So many of the quotations are from poetry that these will be printed as verse rather than, as in the preceding exercises, in continuous lines like prose.)

Affront, insult, indignity.

> A moral, sensible, and well-bred man
> Will not *affront* me,—and no other can.

> An old *affront* will stir the heart
> Through years of rankling pain.

The way to procure *insults* is to submit to them. A man meets with no more respect than he exacts.

It is often better not to see an *insult* than to avenge it.

Even a hare, the weakest of animals, may *insult* a dead lion.

To a native of rank, arrest was not merely a restraint, but a foul personal *indignity*.

Dishonor, disgrace, ignominy, infamy, obloquy, opprobrium.

His honor rooted in *dishonor* stood,
And faith unfaithful kept him falsely true.

It is hard to say which of the two we ought most to lament,—the unhappy man who sinks under the sense of his *dishonor*, or him who survives it.

Could he with reason murmur at his case
Himself sole author of his own *disgrace?*

Whatever *disgrace* we may have deserved, it is almost always in our power to re-establish our character.

When in *disgrace* with fortune and men's eyes
I all alone beweep my outcast state.

Their generals have been received with honor after their defeat; yours with *ignominy* after conquest.

Wilful perpetuations of unworthy actions brand with most indelible characters of *infamy* the name and memory to posterity.

And when his long public life, so singularly chequered with good and evil, with glory and *obloquy*, had at length closed forever, it was to Daylesford that he retired to die.

Great *opprobrium* has been thrown on her name.

Fame, honor, renown, glory, distinction, reputation, repute, celebrity, eminence, notoriety.

Let *fame*, that all hunt after in their lives,
Live register'd upon our brazen tombs.

Men have a solicitude about *fame;* and the greater share they have of it, the more afraid they are of losing it.

Fame is no plant that grows on mortal soil,

. . . .

But lives and spreads aloft by those pure eyes
And perfect witness of all-judging Jove;

SYNONYMS IN LARGER GROUPS (2)

> As he pronounces lastly on each deed,
> Of so much *fame* in heaven expect thy meed.

> When faith is lost, when *honor* dies,
> The man is dead.

> Act well your part; there all the *honor* lies.

The Athenians erected a large statue of Æsop, and placed him, though a slave, on a lasting pedestal, to show that the way to *honor* lies open indifferently to all.

> I could not love thee, dear, so much,
> Loved I not *honor* more.

That nation is worthless which does not joyfully stake everything on her *honor*.

> By heaven methinks it were an easy leap
> To pluck bright *honor* from the pale-fac'd moon.

That merit which gives greatness and *renown* diffuses its influence to a wide compass, but acts weakly on every single breast.

> Speak no more of his *renown*,
> Lay your earthly fancies down,
> And in the vast cathedral leave him,
> God accept him, Christ receive him.

The young warrior did not fly; but met death as he went forward in his strength. Happy are they who die in youth, when their *renown* is heard!

> The paths of *glory* lead but to the grave.

Glory long has made the sages smile; 'tis something, nothing, words, illusion, wind.

> Not once or twice in our rough island-story
> The path of duty was the way to *glory*.

He was a charming fellow, clever, urbane, free-handed, with all that fortunate quality in his appearance which is known as *distinction*.

Never get a *reputation* for a small perfection if you are trying for *fame* in a loftier area.

One may be better than his *reputation* or his conduct, but never better than his principles.

> I see my *reputation* is at stake:
> My *fame* is shrewdly gor'd.

CASSIO. *Reputation, reputation, reputation!* O! I have lost my reputation. I have lost the immortal part of myself, and what remains is bestial. My reputation, Iago, my reputation!

IAGO. As I am an honest man, I thought you had received some bodily wound.

You have a good *repute* for gentleness and wisdom.
Celebrity sells dearly what we think she gives.

          Kings climb to *eminence*
          Over men's graves.

Notoriety is short-lived; *fame* is lasting.

Hatred, hate, animosity, ill-will, enmity, hostility, bitterness, malice, malevolence, malignity, rancor, resentment, dudgeon, grudge, spite.

The *hatred* we bear our enemies injures their happiness less than our own.
Hate is like fire; it makes even light rubbish deadly.
He generously forgot all feeling of *animosity*, and determined to go in person to his succor.

          That thereby he may gather
The ground of your *ill-will*, and so remove it.

No place is so propitious to the formation either of close friendships or of deadly *enmities* as an Indiaman.
There need be no *hostility* between evolutionist and theologian.

      Shall we be thus afflicted in his wreaks,
      His fits, his frenzy, and his *bitterness?*

      Speak of me as I am; nothing extenuate,
      Nor set down aught in *malice*.

Every obstacle which partisan *malevolence* could create he has had to encounter.
His flight is occasioned rather by the *malignity* of his countrymen than by the enmity of the Egyptians.

      Where the soul sours, and gradual *rancor* grows,
      Imbitter'd more from peevish day to day.

Peace in their mouths, and all *rancor* and vengeance in their hartes [hearts].

      For them the gracious Duncan have I murder'd;
      Put *rancors* in the vessel of my peace
      Only for them.

Her *resentment* against the king seems not to have abated.
Mrs. W. was in high *dudgeon;* her heels clattered on the red-tiled floor, and she whisked about the house like a parched pea upon a drum-head.

If I can catch him once upon the hip,
I will feed fat the ancient *grudge* I bear him.

Men of this character pursue a *grudge* unceasingly, and never forget or forgive.

And since you ne'er provoked their *spite*,
Depend upon't their judgment's right.

Marriage, matrimony, wedlock. (With this group compare the *matrimonial* group in Exercise C, above.)

Marriages are made in heaven.
Hasty *marriage* seldom proveth well.
A man finds himself seven years older the day after his *marriage*.

Let me not to the *marriage* of true minds
Admit impediments.

Marriage is the best state for man in general; and every man is a worse man in proportion as he is unfit for the married state.
Matrimony—the high sea for which no compass has yet been invented.
Wedlock's a lane where there is no turning.

What is *wedlock* forced, but a hell,
An age of discord and continual strife?

Mercy, clemency, lenity, leniency, lenience, forbearance.

Teach me to feel another's woe,
To hide the fault I see;
That *mercy* I to others show,
That *mercy* show to me.

The quality of *mercy* is not strain'd,
It droppeth as the gentle rain from heaven
Upon the place beneath: it is twice bless'd;
It blesseth him that gives and him that takes;

. . . .

And earthly power doth then show likest God's
When *mercy* seasons justice.

Clemency is the surest proof of a true monarch.
Lenity will operate with greater force, in some instances, than vigor.

All the fellows tried to persuade the Master to greater *leniency*, but in vain.

It will be necessary that this acceptance should be followed up by measures of the utmost *lenience*.

There is however a limit at which *forbearance* ceases to be a virtue.

Pity, sympathy, compassion, commiseration, condolence.

>Careless their merits or their faults to scan,
>His *pity* gave ere charity began.

For *pity* melts the mind to love.

For *pitee* renneth [runneth] soon in gentle herte [heart].

Our *sympathy* is cold to the relation of distant misery.

Man may dismiss *compassion* from his heart, but God will never.

It is unworthy a religious man to view an irreligious one either with alarm or aversion; or with any other feeling than regret, and hope, and brotherly *commiseration*.

Their congratulations and their *condolences* are equally words of course.

Poverty, want, need, destitution, indigence, penury.

>Is there for honest *poverty*
>That hings [hangs] his head, and a' that?

Not to be able to bear *poverty* is a shameful thing, but not to know how to chase it away by work is a more shameful thing yet.

>Stitch! stitch! stitch!
>In *poverty*, hunger, and dirt,
>And still with a voice of dolorous pitch,
>Would that its tone could reach the Rich,
>She sang this "Song of the Shirt!"

Poverty is dishonorable, not in itself, but when it is a proof of laziness, intemperance, luxury, and carelessness; whereas in a person that is temperate, industrious, just and valiant, and who uses all his virtues for the public good, it shows a great and lofty mind.

>*Want* is a bitter and hateful good,
>Because its virtues are not understood;
>Yet many things, impossible to thought,
>Have been by *need* to full perfection brought.

Hundreds would never have known *want* if they had not first known waste.

> O! reason not the *need;* our basest beggars
> Are in the poorest thing superfluous:
> Allow not nature more than nature needs,
> Man's life is cheap as beast's.

The Christian inhabitants of Thessaly would be reduced to *destitution.*

It is the care of a very great part of mankind to conceal their *indigence* from the rest.

> Chill *penury* repress'd their noble rage,
> And froze the genial current of the soul.

Chill *penury* weighs down the heart itself; and though it sometimes be endured with calmness, it is but the calmness of despair.

> Where *penury* is felt the thought is chain'd,
> And sweet colloquial pleasures are but few.

Regret, compunction, remorse, contrition, penitence, repentance.

Regrets over the past should chasten the future.
He acknowledged his disloyalty to the king with expressions of great *compunction.*

> Through no disturbance of my soul,
> Or strong *compunction* in me wrought,
> I supplicate for thy control.

God speaks to our hearts through the voice of *remorse.*
To err is human; but *contrition* felt for the crime distinguishes the virtuous from the wicked.
Christian *penitence* is something more than a thought or an emotion or a tear; it is action.
Repentance must be something more than mere *remorse* for sins; it comprehends a change of nature befitting heaven.

Stubborn, obstinate, pertinacious, intractable, refractory, contumacious.

> For fools are *stubborn* in their way,
> As coins are harden'd by th' allay;
> And *obstinacy's* ne'er so stiff
> As when 'tis in a wrong belief.

They may also laugh at their *pertinacious* and incurable obstinacy.

He who is *intractable,* he whom nothing can persuade, may boast himself invincible.

> There is a law in each well-order'd nation
> To curb those raging appetites that are
> Most disobedient and *refractory.*

He then dissolved Parliament, and sent its most *refractory* members to the Tower.

If he were *contumacious,* he might be excommunicated, or, in other words, be deprived of all civil rights and imprisoned for life.

E

The following list of synonyms is given for the convenience of those who wish additional material with which to work. This is a selected list and makes no pretense to completeness. It is suggested that you discriminate the words within each of the following groups, and use each word accurately in a sentence of your own making.

Abettor, accessory, accomplice, confederate, conspirator.
Acknowledge, admit, confess, own, avow.
Active, agile, nimble, brisk, sprightly, spry, bustling.
Advise, counsel, admonish, caution, warn.
Affecting, moving, touching, pathetic.
Agnostic, skeptic, infidel, unbeliever, disbeliever.
Amuse, entertain, divert.
Announce, proclaim, promulgate, report, advertise, publish, bruit, blazon, trumpet, herald.
Antipathy, aversion, repugnance, disgust, loathing.
Artifice, ruse, trick, dodge, manœuver, wile, stratagem, subterfuge, finesse.
Ascend, mount, climb, scale.
Associate, colleague, partner, helper, collaborator, coadjutor, companion, helpmate, mate, team-mate, comrade, chum, crony, consort, accomplice, confederate.
Attach, affix, annex, append, subjoin.
Attack, assail, assault, invade, beset, besiege, bombard, cannonade, storm.
Begin, commence, inaugurate, initiate, institute, originate, start found.
Belief, faith, persuasion, conviction, tenet, creed.

SYNONYMS IN LARGER GROUPS (2)

Belittle, decry, depreciate, disparage.
Bind, secure, fetter, shackle, gyve.
Bit, jot, mite, particle, grain, atom, speck, mote, whit, iota, tittle, scintilla.
Bluff, blunt, outspoken, downright, brusk, curt, crusty.
Boast, brag, vaunt, vapor, gasconade.
Body, corpse, remains, relics, carcass, cadaver, corpus.
Bombastic, sophomoric, turgid, tumid, grandiose, grandiloquent, magniloquent.
Boorish, churlish, loutish, clownish, rustic, ill-bred.
Booty, plunder, loot, spoil.
Brittle, frangible, friable, fragile, crisp.
Building, edifice, structure, house.
Call, clamor, roar, scream, shout, shriek, vociferate, yell, halloo, whoop.
Calm, still, motionless, tranquil, serene, placid.
Care, concern, solicitude, anxiety.
Celebrate, commemorate, observe.
Charm, amulet, talisman.
Charm, enchant, fascinate, captivate, enrapture, bewitch, infatuate, enamor.
Cheat, defraud, swindle, dupe.
Choke, strangle, suffocate, stifle, throttle.
Choose, pick, select, cull, elect.
Coax, wheedle, cajole, tweedle, persuade, inveigle.
Color, hue, shade, tint, tinge, tincture.
Combine, unite, consolidate, merge, amalgamate, weld, incorporate, confederate.
Comfort, console, solace.
Complain, grumble, growl, murmur, repine, whine, croak.
Confirmed, habitual, inveterate, chronic.
Connect, join, link, couple, attach, unite.
Continual, continuous, unceasing, incessant, endless, uninterrupted, unremitting, constant, perpetual, perennial.
Contract, agreement, bargain, compact, covenant, stipulation.
Copy, duplicate, counterpart, likeness, reproduction, replica, facsimile.
Corrupt, depraved, perverted, vitiated.
Costly, expensive, dear.
Coterie, clique, cabal, circle, set, faction, party.
Critical, judicial, impartial, carping, caviling, captious, censorious.
Crooked, awry, askew.
Cross, fretful, peevish, petulant, pettish, irritable, irascible, angry.

Crowd, throng, horde, host, mass, multitude, press, jam, concourse.
Curious, inquisitive, prying, meddlesome.
Dainty, delicate, exquisite, choice, rare.
Danger, peril, jeopardy, hazard, risk.
Darken, obscure, bedim, obfuscate.
Dead, lifeless, inanimate, deceased, defunct, extinct.
Decay, decompose, putrefy, rot, spoil.
Deceit, deception, double-dealing, duplicity, chicanery, guile, treachery.
Deceptive, deceitful, misleading, fallacious, fraudulent.
Decorate, adorn, ornament, embellish, deck, bedeck, garnish, bedizen, beautify.
Decorous, demure, sedate, sober, staid, prim, proper.
Deface, disfigure, mar, mutilate.
Defect, fault, imperfection, disfigurement, blemish, flaw.
Delay, defer, postpone, procrastinate.
Demoralize, deprave, debase, corrupt, vitiate.
Deportment, demeanor, bearing, port, mien.
Deprive, divest, dispossess, strip, despoil.
Despise, contemn, scorn, disdain.
Despondency, despair, desperation.
Detach, separate, sunder, sever, disconnect, disjoin, disunite.
Determined, persistent, dogged.
Devout, religious, pious, godly, saintly.
Difficulty, hindrance, obstacle, impediment, encumbrance, handicap.
Difficulty, predicament, perplexity, plight, quandary, dilemma, strait.
Dirty, filthy, foul, nasty, squalid.
Discernment, perception, penetration, insight, acumen.
Disgraceful, dishonorable, shameful, disreputable, ignominious, opprobrious, scandalous, infamous.
Disgusting, sickening, repulsive, revolting, loathsome, repugnant, abhorrent, noisome, fulsome.
Dispel, disperse, dissipate, scatter.
Dissatisfied, discontented, displeased, malcontent, disgruntled.
Divide, distribute, apportion, allot, allocate, partition.
Doctrine, dogma, tenet, precept.
Dream, reverie, vision, fantasy.
Drip, dribble, trickle.
Drunk, drunken, intoxicated, inebriated.
Dry, arid, parched, desiccated.
Eat, bolt, gulp, gorge, devour.
Encroach, infringe, intrench, trench, intrude, invade, trespass.
End, conclude, terminate, finish, discontinue, close.

SYNONYMS IN LARGER GROUPS (2)

Enemy, foe, adversary, opponent, antagonist, rival.
Enough, adequate, sufficient.
Entice, inveigle, allure, lure, decoy, seduce.
Erase, expunge, cancel, efface, obliterate.
Error, mistake, blunder, slip.
Estimate, value, appreciate.
Eternal, everlasting, endless, deathless, imperishable, immortal.
Examination, inquiry, inquisition, investigation, inspection, scrutiny, research, review, audit, inquest, autopsy.
Example, sample, specimen, instance.
Exceed, excel, surpass, transcend, outdo.
Expand, dilate, distend, inflate.
Expel, banish, exile, proscribe, ostracize.
Experiment, trial, test.
Explicit, exact, precise, definite.
Faculty, gift, endowment, aptitude, attribute, talent, predilection, bent.
Failing, shortcoming, defect, fault, foible, infirmity.
Famous, renowned, celebrated, noted, distinguished, eminent, illustrious.
Fashion, mode, style, vogue, rage, fad.
Fast, rapid, swift, quick, fleet, speedy, hasty, celeritous, expeditious, instantaneous.
Fasten, tie, hitch, moor, tether.
Fate, destiny, lot, doom.
Fawn, truckle, cringe, crouch.
Feign, pretend, dissemble, simulate, counterfeit, affect, assume.
Fiendish, devilish, diabolical, demoniacal, demonic, satanic.
Fertile, fecund, fruitful, prolific.
Fit, suitable, appropriate, proper.
Flame, blaze, flare, glare, glow.
Flat, level, even, plane, smooth, horizontal.
Flatter, blandish, beguile, compliment, praise.
Flexible, pliable, pliant, supple, limber, lithe, lissom.
Flit, flutter, flicker, hover.
Flock, herd, bevy, covey, drove, pack, brood, litter, school.
Flow, pour, stream, gush, spout.
Follow, pursue, chase.
Follower, adherent, disciple, partisan, henchman.
Fond, loving, doting, devoted, amorous, enamored.
Force, strength, power, energy, vigor, might, potency, cogency, efficacy.
Force, compulsion, coercion, constraint, restraint.
Free, liberate, emancipate, manumit, release, disengage, disentangle, disembarrass, disencumber, extricate.
Freshen, refresh, revive, renovate, renew.

Friendly, amicable, companionable, hearty, cordial, neighborly, sociable, genial, complaisant, affable.
Frighten, affright, alarm, terrify, terrorize, dismay, appal, daunt, scare.
Frown, scowl, glower, lower.
Frugal, sparing, saving, economical, chary, thrifty, provident, prudent.
Game, play, amusement, pastime, diversion, fun, sport, entertainment.
Gather, accumulate, amass, collect, levy, muster, hoard.
Ghost, spirit, specter, phantom, apparition, shade, phantasm.
Gift, present, donation, grant, gratuity, bequest, boon, bounty, largess, fee, bribe.
Grand, magnificent, gorgeous, splendid, superb, sublime.
Greet, hail, salute, address, accost.
Grief, sorrow, distress, affliction, trouble, tribulation, woe.
Grieve, lament, mourn, bemoan, bewail, deplore, rue.
Guard, defend, protect, shield, shelter, screen, preserve.
Habitation, abode, dwelling, residence, domicile, home.
Harmful, injurious, detrimental, pernicious, deleterious, baneful, noxious.
Have, possess, own, hold.
Headstrong, wayward, wilful, perverse, froward.
Help (noun), aid, assistance, succor.
Help (verb), assist, aid, succor, abet, second, support, befriend.
Hesitate, falter, vacillate, waver.
Hide, conceal, secrete.
High, tall, lofty, elevated, towering.
Hint, intimate, insinuate.
Hopeful, expectant, sanguine, optimistic, confident.
Hopeless, despairing, disconsolate, desperate.
Holy, sacred, hallowed, sanctified, consecrated, godly, pious, saintly, blessed.
Impolite, discourteous, inurbane, uncivil, rude, disrespectful, pert, saucy, impertinent, impudent, insolent.
Importance, consequence, moment.
Impostor, pretender, charlatan, masquerader, mountebank, deceiver, humbug, cheat, quack, shyster, empiric.
Imprison, incarcerate, immure.
Improper, indecent, indecorous, unseemly, unbecoming, indelicate.
Impure, tainted, contaminated, polluted, defiled, vitiated.
Inborn, innate, inbred, congenital.
Incite, instigate, stimulate, impel, arouse, goad, spur, promote.
Inclose, surround, encircle, circumscribe, encompass.
Increase, grow, enlarge, magnify, amplify, swell, augment.

SYNONYMS IN LARGER GROUPS (2)

Indecent, indelicate, immodest, shameless, ribald, lewd, lustful, lascivious, libidinous, obscene.
Insane, demented, deranged, crazy, mad.
Insanity, dementia, derangement, craziness, madness, lunacy, mania, frenzy, hallucination.
Insipid, tasteless, flat, vapid.
Intention, intent, purpose, plan, design, aim, object, end.
Interpose, intervene, intercede, interfere, mediate.
Irreligious, ungodly, impious, godless, sacrilegious, blasphemous, profane.
Irritate, exasperate, nettle, incense.
Join, connect, unite, couple, combine, link, annex, append.
Kindle, ignite, inflame, rouse.
Lack, want, need, deficiency, dearth, paucity, scarcity, deficit.
Lame, crippled, halt, deformed, maimed, disabled.
Large, great, big, huge, immense, colossal, gigantic, extensive, vast, massive, unwieldy, bulky.
Laughable, comical, comic, farcical, ludicrous, ridiculous, funny, droll.
Lead, guide, conduct, escort, convoy.
Lengthen, prolong, protract, extend.
Lessen, decrease, diminish, reduce, abate, curtail, moderate, mitigate, palliate.
Lie (noun), untruth, falsehood, falsity, fiction, fabrication, mendacity, canard, fib, story.
Lie (verb), prevaricate, falsify, equivocate, quibble, shuffle, dodge, fence, fib.
Likeness, resemblance, similitude, similarity, semblance, analogy.
Limp, flaccid, flabby, flimsy.
List, roll, catalogue, register, roster, schedule, inventory.
Loud, resonant, clarion, stentorian, sonorous.
Low, base, abject, servile, slavish, menial.
Loyal, faithful, true, constant, staunch, unwavering, steadfast.
Lurk, skulk, slink, sneak, prowl.
Make, create, frame, fashion, mold, shape, form, forge, fabricate, invent, construct, manufacture, concoct.
Manifest, plain, obvious, clear, apparent, patent, evident, perceptible, noticeable, open, overt, palpable, tangible, indubitable, unmistakable.
Many, various, numerous, divers, manifold, multitudinous, myriad, countless, innumerable.
Meaning, significance, signification, import, purport.
Meet, encounter, collide, confront, converge.
Meeting, assembly, assemblage, congregation, convention, conference, concourse, gathering, mustering.

Melt, thaw, fuse, dissolve, liquefy.
Memory, remembrance, recollection, reminiscence, retrospection.
Misrepresent, misinterpret, falsify, distort, warp.
Mix, compound, amalgamate, weld, combine, blend, concoct.
Model, pattern, prototype, criterion, standard, exemplar, paragon, archetype, ideal.
Motive, incentive, inducement, desire, purpose.
Move, actuate, impel, prompt, incite.
Near, nigh, close, neighboring, adjacent, contiguous.
Neat, tidy, orderly, spruce, trim, prim.
Needful, necessary, requisite, essential, indispensable.
Negligence, neglect, inattention, inattentiveness, inadvertence, remissness, oversight.
New, novel, fresh, recent, modern, late, innovative, unprecedented.
Nice, fastidious, dainty, finical, squeamish.
Noisy, clamorous, boisterous, hilarious, turbulent, riotous, obstreperous, uproarious, vociferous, blatant, brawling.
Noticeable, prominent, conspicuous, salient, signal.
Order (noun), command, mandate, behest, injunction, decree.
Order (verb), command, enjoin, direct, instruct.
Oversight, supervision, direction, superintendence, surveillance.
Pale, pallid, wan, colorless, blanched, ghastly, ashen, cadaverous.
Patience, forbearance, resignation, longsuffering.
Penetrate, pierce, perforate.
Place, office, post, position, situation, appointment.
Plan, design, project, scheme, plot.
Playful, mischievous, roguish, prankish, sportive, arch.
Plentiful, plenteous, abundant, bounteous, copious, profuse, exuberant, luxuriant.
Plunder, rifle, loot, sack, pillage, devastate, despoil.
Pretty, beautiful, comely, handsome, fair.
Profitable, remunerative, lucrative, gainful.
Prompt, punctual, ready, expeditious.
Pull, draw, drag, haul, tug, tow.
Push, shove, thrust.
Puzzle, perplex, mystify, bewilder.
Queer, odd, curious, quaint, ridiculous, singular, unique, bizarre, fantastic, grotesque.
Rash, incautious, reckless, foolhardy, adventurous, venturous, venturesome.
Rebellion, insurrection, revolt, mutiny, riot, revolution, sedition.
Recover, regain, retrieve, recoup, rally, recuperate.
Reflect, deliberate, ponder, muse, meditate, ruminate.
Relate, recount, recite, narrate, tell.

SYNONYMS IN LARGER GROUPS (2)

Replace, supersede, supplant, succeed.
Repulsive, unsightly, loathsome, hideous, grewsome.
Requital, retaliation, reprisal, revenge, vengeance, retribution.
Responsible, answerable, accountable, amenable, liable.
Reveal, disclose, divulge, manifest, show, betray.
Reverence, veneration, awe, adoration, worship.
Ridicule, deride, mock, taunt, flout, twit, tease.
Ripe, mature, mellow.
Rise, arise, mount, ascend.
Rogue, knave, rascal, miscreant, scamp, sharper, villain.
Round, circular, rotund, spherical, globular, orbicular.
Rub, polish, burnish, furbish, scour.
Sad, grave, sober, moody, doleful, downcast, dreary, woeful, somber, unhappy, woebegone, mournful, depressed, despondent, gloomy, heavy-spirited, sorrowful, melancholy, dismal, dejected, disconsolate, miserable, lugubrious.
Satiate, sate, surfeit, cloy, glut, gorge.
Scoff, jeer, gibe, fleer, sneer, mock, taunt.
Secret, covert, surreptitious, furtive, clandestine, underhand, stealthy.
Seep, ooze, infiltrate, percolate, transude, exude.
Sell, barter, vend, trade.
Shape, form, figure, outline, conformation, configuration, contour, profile.
Share, partake, participate, divide.
Sharp, keen, acute, cutting, trenchant, incisive.
Shore, coast, littoral, beach, strand, bank.
Shorten, abridge, abbreviate, curtail, truncate, syncopate.
Show (noun), display, ostentation, parade, pomp, splurge.
Show, exhibit, display, expose, manifest, evince.
Shrink, flinch, wince, blench, quail.
Shun, avoid, eschew.
Shy, bashful, diffident, modest, coy, timid, shrinking.
Sign, omen, auspice, portent, prognostic, augury, foretoken, adumbration, presage, indication.
Simple, innocent, artless, unsophisticated, naïve.
Skilful, skilled, expert, adept, apt, proficient, adroit, dexterous, deft, clever, ingenious.
Skin, hide, pelt, fell.
Sleepy, drowsy, slumberous, somnolent, sluggish, torpid, dull, lethargic.
Slovenly, slatternly, dowdy, frowsy, blowzy.
Sly, crafty, cunning, subtle, wily, artful, politic, designing.
Smile, smirk, grin.
Solitary, lonely, lone, lonesome, desolate, deserted, uninhabited.

Sour, acid, tart, acrid, acidulous, acetose, acerbitous, astringent.
Speech, discourse, oration, address, sermon, declamation, dissertation, exhortation, disquisition, harangue, diatribe, tirade, screed, philippic, invective, rhapsody, plea.
Spruce, natty, dapper, smart, chic.
Stale, musty, frowzy, mildewed, fetid, rancid, rank.
Steep, precipitous, abrupt.
Stingy, close, miserly, niggardly, parsimonious, penurious, sordid.
Storm, tempest, whirlwind, hurricane, tornado, cyclone, typhoon
Straight, perpendicular, vertical, plumb, erect, upright.
Strange, singular, peculiar, odd, queer, quaint, outlandish.
Strong, stout, robust, sturdy, stalwart, powerful.
Stupid, dull, obtuse, stolid, doltish, sluggish, brainless, bovine.
Succeed, prosper, thrive, flourish, triumph.
Succession, sequence, series.
Supernatural, preternatural, superhuman, miraculous.
Suppose, surmise, conjecture, presume, imagine, fancy, guess, think, believe.
Surprise, astonish, amaze, astound.
Swearing, cursing, profanity, blasphemy, execration, imprecation.
Teach, instruct, educate, train, discipline, drill, inculcate, instil, indoctrinate.
Thoughtful, contemplative, meditative, reflective, pensive, wistful.
Tire, weary, fatigue, exhaust, jade, fag.
Tool, implement, instrument, utensil.
Trifle, dally, dawdle, potter.
Try, endeavor, essay, attempt.
Trust, confidence, reliance, assurance, faith.
Turn, revolve, rotate, spin, whirl, gyrate.
Ugly, homely, uncomely, hideous.
Unwilling, reluctant, disinclined, loath, averse.
Watchful, vigilant, alert.
Wave (noun), billow, breaker, swell, ripple, undulation.
Wave (verb), brandish, flourish, flaunt, wigwag.
Weariness, languor, lassitude, enervation, exhaustion.
Wearisome, tiresome, irksome, tedious, humdrum.
Wet (adjective), humid, moist, damp, dank, sodden, soggy.
Wet (verb), moisten, dampen, soak, imbrue, saturate, drench
Whim, caprice, vagary, fancy, freak, whimsey, crotchet.
Wind, breeze, gust, blast, flaw, gale, squall, flurry.
Wind, coil, twist, twine, wreathe.
Winding, tortuous, serpentine, sinuous, meandering.
Wonderful, marvelous, phenomenal, miraculous.
Workman, laborer, artisan, artificer, mechanic, craftsman.
Write, inscribe, scribble, scrawl, scratch.
Yearn, long, hanker, pine, crave.

SYNONYMS IN LARGER GROUPS (2)

F

Write three synonyms for each of the following words. Discriminate the three, and embody each of them in a sentence.

Accomplish	Conduct (noun)	Humble	Scream
Agree	Conspicuous	Indifferent	Shrewd
Anger	Cringe	Misfortune	Shudder
Attempt	Difficult	Obey	Skill
Big	Disconnect	Object (noun)	Soft
Brute	Erratic	Object (verb)	Splash
Business	Flash	Obligation	Success
Careless	Fragrant	Occupied	Sweet
Climb	Gain	Oppose	Trick
Collect	Generous	Persist	Wash
Commanding	Grim	Revise	Worship
Compel	Groan	Room	

G

Supply eight or ten intervening words between each of the following pairs. Arrange the intervening words in an ascending scale.

Dark, bright
Savage, civilized
Friend, enemy
Wise, foolish
Enormous, minute
Curse, bless

Wet, dry
Beautiful, ugly
Hope, despair
Love, hate
Admirable, abominable
Pride, humility

IX

MANY-SIDED WORDS

IN Chapter VII you made a study of printed distinctions between synonyms. In Chapter VIII you were given lists of synonyms and made the distinctions yourself. Near the close of Chapter VIII you were given words and discovered for yourself what their synonyms are. This third stage might seem to reveal to you the full joys and benefits of your researches in this subject. Certainly to find a new word for an old one is an exhilarating sort of mental travel. And to find a new word which expresses exactly what an old one expressed but approximately is a real acquisition in living. But you are not yet a perfectly trained hunter of synonyms. Some miscellaneous tasks remain; they will involve hard work and call your utmost powers into play.

Of these tasks the most important is connected with the hint already given (see page 183) that many words, especially if they be generic words, have two or more entirely different meanings. Let us first establish this fact, and afterwards see what bearing it has on our study of synonyms.

My friend says, "I hope you will have a good day." Does he mean an enjoyable one in general? a profitable or lucrative one, in case I have business in hand? a suc-

MANY-SIDED WORDS

cessful one, if I am selling stocks or buying a house? Possibly he means a sunshiny day if I intend to play golf, a snowy day if I plan to go hunting, a rainy day if my crops are drying up. The ideas here are varied, even contradictory, enough; yet *good* may be used of every one of them. *Good* is in truth so general a term that we must know the attendant circumstances if we are to attach to it a signification even approximately accurate. This does not at all imply that *good* is a term we may brand as useless. It implies merely that when our meaning is specific we must set *good* aside (unless circumstances make its sense unmistakable) in favor of a specific word.

Things is another very general term. In "Let us wash up the things" it likely means dishes or clothes. In "Hang your things in the closet" it likely means clothes. In "Put the things in the tool-box" it likely means tools. In "Put the things in the sewing-basket" it likely means thread, needles, and scissors. In "The trenches are swarming with these things" it likely means cooties. A more accurate word is usually desirable. Yet we may see the value of the generality in the saying "A place for everything, and everything in its place."

Good and *things* are not alone in having multitudinous meanings. There are in the language numerous many-sided words. These words should be studied carefully. True, they are not always employed in ambiguous ways. For example, *right* in the sense of correct is seldom likely to be mistaken for *right* in the sense of not-left, but a reader or hearer may frequently mistake it for *right* in the sense of just or of honorable. In the use of such words, therefore, we cannot become too discriminating.

EXERCISE

H

This exercise concerns itself with common words that have more than one meaning. Make your procedure as follows. First, look up the word itself. Under it you will find a number of defining words. Then look up each of these in turn, until you have the requisite number and kind of synonyms. (The word is sure to have more synonyms than are called for.) You will have to use your dictionary tirelessly.

Bare. Find three synonyms for *bare* as applied to the body; three for it as applied to a room.

Bear. Give three other words that might be used instead of *bear* in the sentence "The pillar bears a heavy weight"; three in the sentence "He bore a heavy load on his back"; three in the sentence "He bore the punishment that was unjustly meted out to him"; three in the sentence "He bore a grudge against his neighbor"; two in the sentence "The field did not bear a crop last year."

Bold. Give ten synonyms for *bold* as applied to a warrior; ten as applied to a young girl. Observe that the synonyms in the first list are favorable in import and suggest the idea of bravery, whereas those in the second list are unfavorable and suggest the idea of brazenness. How do you account for this fact? Can you think of circumstances in which a young girl might be so placed that the favorable synonyms might be applied to her?

Bright. Give as many words as you can, at least twelve, that can be used instead of *bright* as applied to a light, a diamond, a wet pavement, or a live coal. Give three words for *bright* as applied to a child of unusual intelligence; two as applied to an occasion that promises to turn out well; two as applied to a career that has been signally successful.

Clear. Give five synonyms for *clear* as applied to water; ten as applied to a fact or a statement; three as applied to

MANY-SIDED WORDS

the sky or atmosphere; three as applied to the voice; two as applied to a passageway or a view; three as applied to one's judgment or thinking.

Close. Give three words that could be substituted for *close* as applied to the atmosphere in a room; four as applied to a person who is uninclined to talk about a matter; three as applied to something not far off; four as applied to a friend; five as applied to a person who is reluctant to spend money; five as applied to a translation; five as applied to attention or endeavor.

Discharge. Substitute in turn four words for *discharge* in the sentence "The judge discharged the prisoner"; two in the sentence "The foreman discharged the workman"; two in the sentence "The hunter discharged the gun"; three in the sentence "The sore discharged pus"; two in the sentence "My neighbor discharged the debt"; two in the sentence "He discharged his duty."

Dull. Name three words besides *dull* that could be applied to a blade or a point; five to a person with slow intellect; three to indifference toward others; two to a color; three to a day that is not cheerful; five to talk or discourse that is not interesting.

Fair. Substitute five words for *fair* in the sentence "He gave a fair judgment in the case"; three in the sentence "The son made a fair showing in his studies"; four in the sentence "She had a fair face"; two in the sentence "Her complexion was fair"; three in the sentence "Let no shame ever fall upon your fair name."

False. Find two words that you can substitute for *false* as applied to a signature, to a report or a piece of news, to jewels or money, to a friend.

Fast. Name two words I might substitute for *fast* in the sentence "Drive the stake until it is fast in the ground"; three in the sentence "He made a fast trip for the doctor"; six in the sentence "By leading a fast life he soon squandered his inheritance."

Firm. Substitute four words for *firm* in the sentence "I made the board firm by nailing it to the wall"; three in the sentence "The water froze into a firm mass"; five in the sentence "He was firm in his determination to proceed."

CENTURY VOCABULARY BUILDER

Flat. Instead of *flat* use in turn four other words in the sentence "This is a flat piece of ground"; five in the sentence "It was as flat a story as ever wearied company"; three in the sentence "The cook having forgotten the salt, the soup was flat"; four in the sentence "I am surprised by your flat refusal."

Free. *Free* may be applied to a person not subject to a tax or a disease, to a person who has been released from confinement or restraint, to a person who is not reserved or formal in his relations to others, to a person who is willing to give. Out of your own resources substitute as many words as you can for *free* in each of these sentences. Now look up *free* in a dictionary or book of synonyms. What proportion of its synonyms were you able to think up unaided?

Great. Give three synonyms for *great* as applied to size, to number, to a man widely known for notable achievement, to an error or crime, to price.

Hard. Give six synonyms for *hard* as applied to a rock; six as applied to a task or burden; six as applied to a problem or situation; ten as applied to one's treatment of others.

Harsh. Give three words that can be applied instead of *harsh* to a sound; three that can be applied instead of *harsh* to the voice; five that can be applied to one's treatment of others; five that can be applied to one's disposition or nature.

Just. Substitute five words for *just* in the sentence "You are just in your dealings with others"; three in the sentence "A just punishment was meted out to him"; three in the sentence "They made a just division of the property"; two in the sentence "He had a just claim to the title."

Plain. Give six words that can be substituted for *plain* as applied to a fact or statement; four as applied to the decorations of a room; two as applied to the countenance; four as applied to a surface; three as applied to a statement or reply.

Poor. Give five words that can be used instead of *poor* as applied to a person who is without money or resources; ten as applied to a person lacking in flesh; three as applied to clothing that is worn out; five as applied to land that will bear only small crops or no crops at all; two as applied to an occasion that does not promise to turn out well.

MANY-SIDED WORDS

Quick. Give six words that could be used instead of *quick* as applied to a train or a horse in travel; six as applied to the movements of a person about a room or to his actions in the performance of his work; four to a disposition or temper that is easily irritated.

Serious. Give five synonyms for *serious* as applied to one's countenance or expression; three as applied to a problem or undertaking; two as applied to a disease or to sickness.

Sharp. Give two synonyms for *sharp* as applied to a blade or a point; six as applied to a pain or to grief; four as applied to a remark or reply; ten as applied to one's mind or intellect; three as applied to temper or disposition; three as applied to an embankment; three as applied to the seasoning of food; three as applied to a cry or scream.

Stiff. Give six synonyms for *stiff* as applied to an iron rod; three as applied to an adversary; six as applied to one's manner or bearing; two as applied to one's style of writing or speaking.

Strong. Give three synonyms for *strong* as applied to a person in regard to his health; ten as applied to him in regard to his muscularity of physique; four as applied to a fortress; three as applied to a plea or assertion; three as applied to an argument or reason; three as applied to determination; two as applied to liquor; three as applied to a light; two as applied to corrective measures; two as applied to an odor.

Vain. Give five synonyms for *vain* as applied to a man who overvalues himself or his accomplishments; six as applied to an attempt that comes to nothing; three as applied to hopes that have little chance of fulfilment.

Weak. Substitute five synonyms for *weak* in the sentence "I was very weak after my illness"; four in the sentence "The fortress was especially weak on the side toward the plain"; three in the sentence "He made a weak attempt to defend his actions"; three in the sentence "Many of these arguments are weak"; three in the sentence "Hamlet is usually interpreted as being weak of will"; three in the sentence "The liquor was so weak it had no taste"; three in the sentence "The lace was weak and soon tore."

Wild. Give two words instead of *wild* as applied to animals; two as applied to land; three as applied to people who have not been civilized; three as applied to a storm, an uncontrolled temper, or a mob; three as applied to a scheme that has no basis in reason or practicality.

I

In Exercise H you started with ideas and objects, and had to find words of a given meaning that could be applied to them. In this exercise you start with the words, and must find the ideas and objects.

Base. To what is *base* applied when inferior, cheap, worthless could be used as its synonyms? To what is it applied when debased, impure, spurious, alloyed, counterfeit could be used? When mean, despicable, contemptible, shameful, disgraceful, dishonorable, discreditable, scandalous, infamous, villainous, low-minded could be used? When ignoble, servile, slavish, groveling, menial could be used? When plebeian, obscure, untitled, vulgar, lowly, nameless, humble, unknown could be used?

Mortal. Can you properly contrast mortal with immortal existence? mortal with porcine existence? Is porcine existence also mortal? Is mortal existence also porcine? What adjective pertaining to mankind forms a true contrast to *porcine*? What is a synonym for *mortal* in its broad sense? in its narrow sense?

Severe. To what is *severe* applied when harsh, stern, rigorous, drastic, austere, hard could be substituted for it? When plain, unembellished, unadorned, chaste could be substituted? When acute, violent, extreme, intense, sharp, distressing, afflictive could be substituted? When keen, cutting, biting, stinging, caustic, critical, trenchant could be substituted?

J

Reread the discussion of *good* and *things* on pages 260-261. Then for each of the words listed below collect or compose twenty or more sentences in which the word is used. As largely as possible, take them from actual experience. In doing this you must listen to the use of the word in everyday talk. After you have made your list of sentences as varied and extensive as you can, try to substitute synonyms that will express the idea more accurately. Note whether a knowledge of the attend-

MANY-SIDED WORDS

ant circumstances is necessary to an understanding of the original word, to an understanding of the word substituted for it.

| Bad | Fine | Matter | Affair |
| Nice | Common | Case | Boost |

K

Analyze each of the words given below into its various uses or applications. Then for it in each of these applications assemble as many synonyms as you can unaided. Finally, have recourse to a dictionary or book of synonyms for the further extension of your lists.

(By way of illustration, let us take the word *quiet*. Through meditation and analysis we discover that it may be applied (a) to water or any liquid not in motion, (b) to a place that is without sound, (c) to a place shut off from activity or bustle, (d) to a person who is not demonstrative or forward in manner. We think of all the words we can that can be substituted for it in each of these uses. No matter how incompletely or unsatisfactorily we feel we are performing this task, we must not give it over until we have found every word we can summon. Then we turn to a dictionary or book of synonyms. Thus for *quiet* we shall assemble such synonyms as (a) calm, still, motionless, placid, tranquil, serene, smooth, unruffled, undisturbed, pacific, stagnant; (b) silent, still, noiseless, mute, hushed, voiceless; (c) secluded, sequestered, solitary, isolated, unfrequented, unvisited, peaceful, untrodden, retired; (d) demure, sedate, staid, reserved, meek, gentle, retiring, unobtrusive, modest, unassuming, timid, shrinking, shy.)

Barren	Keep	Pure	Solid
Certain	Liberal	Rare	Sorry
Cold	Light (adjective)	Rich	Spread
Cool	Light (noun)	Right	Straight
Deep	Long	Rude	Still
Dry	Low	Short	Sure
Easy	Mean	Simple	Thick
Foul	Narrow	Slow	Thin
Full	New	Small	Tender
Gentle	Obscure	Smooth	True
Grand	Odd	Sober	Warm
Heavy	Particular	Soft	Yield
Keen			

Literal vs. Figurative Applications

One of the most interesting things to watch in the study of words is their development from a literal to a figurative application. The first man who broke away from the confines of the literal meaning of a word and applied the word to something that only in a figurative sense had qualities analogous to the original meaning, was creating poetry. He was making an imaginative flight comparable in daring to the Wright brothers' first aeronautic flight. But as the word was used over and over in this figurative way the imaginative flight became more and more commonplace. At last it ceased to be imaginative at all; through frequent repetition it had settled into the matter of course. A glance at the *concise* group on page 194 will show you that with time the comparison which was once the basis and the life of the figurative use of words is dulled, obscured, even lost.

As a further enforcement of this fact, let us analyze the word *rough*. In its literal application, it may designate any surface that has ridges, projections, or inequalities and is therefore uneven, jagged, rugged, scraggy, or scabrous. Now frequently a man's face or head is rough because unshaved or uncombed; also the fur of an animal is rough. Hence the term could be used for unkempt, disheveled, shaggy, hairy, coarse, bristly. "The child ran its hand over its father's rough cheek" and "The bear had a rough coat" are sentences that even the most unimaginative mind can understand. We speak of rough timber because its surface has not been planed or made smooth. We speak of a rough diamond because it is unpolished, uncut. Note that all these uses are literal, that in each instance some unevenness of surface is referred to.

But man, urged on by the desire to say what he means with more novelty, strikingness, or force, applied the word to ideas that have no surfaces to be uneven. He imagined what these ideas would be like if they had surfaces. Of course in putting these conceptions into language he was creating figures of speech, some of them startlingly apt, some of them merely far-fetched. He said a man had a *rough* voice, as though the voice were like a cactus in its prickly irregularities. By *rough* he meant what his fellows meant when they spoke of the voice as harsh, grating, jarring, discordant, inharmonious, strident, raucous, or unmusical. Going farther, that early poet said the weather was *rough*. He thought of clement weather as being smooth and even, but of inclement, severe, stormy, tempestuous, or violent weather as being full of projections to rend and harass one. Thus an everyday use of the term today was once wrenched and immoderate speech. Possibly the first man who heard of rough weather was puzzled for a moment, then amused or delighted as he caught the figure. It did not require great originality to think of a crowd as *rough* in its movements. But our poet applied the idea to an individual. To him a rude, uncivil, impolite, ungracious, uncourteous, unpolished, uncouth, boorish, blunt, bluff, gruff, brusk, or burly person was as the unplaned lumber or the unpolished gem; and we imitative moderns still call such a man *rough*. But we do not think of the man as covered with projections that need to be taken off, unless forsooth we receive *rough* treatment at his hands. And note how far we have journeyed from the original idea of the word when we say "I gave the report a *rough* glance," meaning cursory, hasty, superficial, or incomplete consideration.

Many very simple words, including several of those already treated in this chapter, are two-sided in that they are both literal and figurative.

Exercise
L

Trace each of the following words from its literal to its figurative applications, giving synonyms for each of its uses.

Open	Bright	Stiff	Hard
Low	Cool	Sharp	Flat
Keen	Strong	Dull	Raw
Small	Odd	Warm	Deep
Eccentric			

Imperfectly Understood Facts and Ideas

Thus far in this chapter we have been considering many-sided words. We must now turn to a certain class of facts and ideas that deserve better understanding and closer analysis than we usually accord them.

These facts and ideas are supposed to be matters of common knowledge. And in their broad scope and purport they are. Because acquaintance with them is taken for granted it behooves us to know them. Yet they are in reality complicated, and when we attempt to deal with them in detail, our assurance forsakes us. All of us have our "blind sides" intellectually—quake to have certain areas of discussion entered, because we foresee that we must sit idly by without power to make sensible comment. Unto as many as possible of these blind sides of ourselves we should pronounce the blessed words, "Let there be light." We have therefore to consider certain matters and topics which are supposed to belong to the common currency of social information, but with which our familiarity is less thoroughgoing than it should be.

What are these facts and topics? Take for illustration the subject of aeronautics. Suppose we have but the vaguest conception of the part played or likely to be played by aircraft in war, commerce, and pleasure. Suppose we are not aware that some craft are made to float and others to be driven by propellers. Suppose such terms as Zeppelin, blimp, monoplane, biplane, hydroplane, dirigible have no definite import for us. Does not our knowledge fall short of that expected of well-informed men in this present age?

Or take military terms. Everybody uses them—clergymen, pacifists, clubmen, social reformers, novelists, tramps, brick-layers, Big-Stickers. We cannot escape them if we would. We ourselves use them. But do we use them with precise and masterly understanding? You call one civilian colonel and another major; which have you paid the higher compliment? You are uncertain whether a given officer is a colonel or a major, and you wish to address him in such fashion as will least offend his sensitiveness as to rank and nomenclature; which title—colonel or major—is the less perilous? You are told that a major has command of a battalion; does that tell you anything about him? You are told that he has command of a squadron, of a brigade, of a platoon;

do these changes in circumstances have any import for you? If not, you have too faltering a grasp upon military facts and terminology.

The best remedy for such shortcomings is to be insatiably curious on all subjects. This of course is the ideal; nobody ever fully attains it. Nevertheless Exercise M will set you to groping into certain broad matters relevant to ordinary needs. Thereafter, if your purpose be strong enough, you will carry the same methods there acquired into other fields of knowledge.

You may object that all this is as much mental as linguistic—that what is proposed will result in as large accessions of general information as of vocabulary. Let this be admitted. Deficiencies of language are often, perhaps almost invariably, linked with deficiencies of knowledge. To repair the one we must at the same time repair the other. This may seem a hard saying to those who seek, or would impart, mere glibness of phrase without regard for the substance—who worship "words, words, words" without thought of "the matter." There is such a thing as froth of utterance, but who has respect therefor or is deceived thereby? Speech that is not informed is like a house without a foundation. You should not desire to possess it. Abroad in this world of ours already are too many people who darken counsel by words without knowledge.

Exercise

M

A second lieutenant is the commissioned officer of lowest grade in the United States army. Name all the grades from second lieutenant to the grade that is highest.

MANY-SIDED WORDS

An admiral is the officer of highest grade in the United States navy. Name all the grades down to that which is lowest.

Name as many as possible of the different ranks of the clergy in the Roman Catholic Church, in the Church of England.

Give ascendingly the five titles in the British nobility.

Name the different kinds of vehicles.

Name the different kinds of schools.

Name all the different kinds of boats and ships (both ancient and modern) you can think of.

Give the nautical term for the right side of a ship, for the left side of a ship, for the front, for the rear, for the forward portion, for the rear portion.

Name the various kinds of bodies of water (oceans, rivers, lagoons, etc.)

Give all the terms of relationship of persons, both by blood and by marriage. What relation to you is your grandfather's brother? your cousin's daughter?

Name all the bones of the human head.

Give the names of the different parts of a typical flower.

Name as many elements as you can. What is the number usually given? What was the last element discovered, and by whom?

Name the elements of which water is composed. Name the principal elements in the composition of the air.

Make as long a list as possible (up to thirty) of words that appeal to the sense of sight (especially color words and motion words), to the sense of hearing, of smell, of taste, of touch.

Find words descriptive of various expressions in the human face.

Name all the terms you can associated with law, with medicine, with geology.

Name the planets, the signs of the zodiac, as many constellations as you can.

Name the seven colors of the spectrum, and for each name give all the synonyms you can. What are the primary colors? the secondary colors?

Give the various races into which mankind has been divided, and the color of each.

Name every kind of tree you can think of, every kind of flower, every kind of animal, every kind of bird.

X
SUPPLEMENTARY LIST OF WORDS

YOU have already mastered many words, but a glance at any page of the dictionary will convince you that you have not mastered all. Nor will you, ever. Their number is too great, and too many of them are abstrusely technical.

Nevertheless there remain many words that you should bring into your vocabulary. Most of them are not extremely usual; on the other hand they are not so unusual that you would encounter them but once in a lifetime. The majority of them are familiar to you, perhaps; that is, you will have a general feeling that you have seen them before. But this is not enough. Do you know exactly what they mean? Can you, when the occasion comes, use them?—use them promptly and well? This is the test.

Many of the words are absolutely new so far as this book is concerned. They have not been discussed or attached to any list. Many are not entirely new. They have appeared, but not received such emphasis that they are sure to stand fast in your memory. Or some cognate form of them may have been mastered, yet they themselves may remain unknown. Thus you may know *commendation* but not *commendatory, credulous* but not

SUPPLEMENTARY LIST OF WORDS

incredulity, invalid but not *invalidate* or *invalidity*. One of the best of all ways to extend your vocabulary is to make each word of your acquaintance introduce you to its immediate kinsmen, those grouped with it on the same page of the dictionary.

This chapter puts you on your mettle. Hitherto you have been given instructions as to the way to proceed. Now you must shift for yourself. The words, to be sure, are corraled for you. But you must tame them and break them, in order that on them you may ride the ranges of human intercourse. If you have not yet learned how to subdue them to your will and use, it would be futile to tell you how. You have been put in the way of mastering words. The task that henceforth confronts you is your own. You must have at it unaided.

It is true that, in the exercise that follows, specific help is given you on a limited number of the words. But this help is only toward discovering the words for yourself before you have seen them in a list. And for most of the words not even this meager assistance is given.

Exercise

Each of the following groups of words is preceded by sentences in which blanks should be filled by words from that group. But do your best to fill these blanks properly before you consult the group at all. You must learn to think of, or think up, the right word instead of having it pointed out to you.

These benefits were not inherent in the course he had taken; they were purely ——. Anything which existed before Noah's flood is called ——. His left hand, which had ceased to grow during his childhood, was now withered from its long ——. Certain books once belonging to the Bible have been discarded by the Protestants as ——. When Shakespeare makes Hector quote Aristotle, who lived long after the siege of Troy, he is guilty of an ———. Whatever causes the lips to pucker, as alum or a green persimmon, is spoken of as ———.

Abash, abbreviate, abduct, aberrant, aberration, abeyance, abhorrent, abject, abjure, aboriginal, abortive, abrade, abrasion, abrogate, absolution, abstemious, abstention, abstruse, accelerate, accentuate, acceptation, accessary, accession, accessory, acclamation, acclivity, accolade, accomplice, accost, acerbity, acetic, achromatic, acidulous, acme, acolyte, acoustics, acquiescence, acquisitive, acrimonious, acumen, adage, adamantine, addict, adduce, adhesive, adipose, adjudicate, adolescence, adulation, adulterate, advent, adventitious, aerial, affability, affidavit, affiliate, affinity, agglomerate, agglutinate, aggrandizement, agnostic, alignment, aliment, allegorical, alleviate, altercation, altruistic, amalgamate, amatory, ambiguity, ambrosial, ameliorate, amenable, amenity, amity, amnesty, amulet, anachronism, analytical, anathema, anatomy, animadversion, annotate, anomalous, anonymous, antediluvian, anterior, anthology, anthropology, antinomy, antiquarianism, antiseptic, aphorism, apocryphal, aplomb, apostasy, apparatus, apparition, appellate, appertain, appetency, apposite, approbation, appurtenance, aquatic, aqueous, aquiline, arbitrary, archaic, arduous, aromatic, arrear, articulate, ascetic, asperity, asphyxiate, asseverate, assiduity, assimilate, astringent, astute, atrophy, attenuate, auditory, augury, auscultation, austerity, authenticate, authenticity, auxiliary, avidity.

The man wished to fight; he was in ——— mood. There is only a handful of these things; yes, a mere———. Slight mishaps

SUPPLEMENTARY LIST OF WORDS

like these lead to quips and mutual ——. His conduct is odd, grotesque, ——.

Baccalaureate, badinage, bagatelle, baleful, ballast, banality, baneful, beatitude, bellicose, belligerent, benefaction, beneficent, benison, betide, bibulous, bigotry, bizarre, bombastic, burlesque.

This effect was not obtained all at once; it was ——. These subjects belong to the same general field of knowledge as those; the two sets are ——. He is a skilled judge of art, a ——. The Southern states were unwilling to remain in the Union; they could be kept only by ——. Monks take upon themselves the vow of ——. No, this animal does not live on vegetation; it is a —— animal.

Cacophonous, cadaverous, cadence, callow, calumny, capillary, captious, cardinal, carnal, carnivorous, castigate, cataclysm, catastrophe, category, causality, cavernous, celebrity, celibacy, censorious, ceramics, cerebration, certitude, cessation, charlatan, chimerical, chronology, circuitous, circumlocution, citation, clandestine, clarify, clemency, coadjutor, coagulate, coalesce, coercion, cogency, cognizant, cohesion, coincidence, collusion, colossal, comatose, combustible, commendatory, commensurate, commiserate, communal, compatibility, compendium, complaisant, comport, composite, compulsive, compulsory, computation, concatenate, concentric, concessive, concomitant, condign, condiment, condolence, confiscatory, confute, congeal, congenital, conglomerate, congruity, connivance, connoisseur, connubial, consensus, consistence, consort, constriction, construe, contentious, context, contiguity, contiguous, contingent, contortion, contravene, contumacious, contumacy, contumelious, convergent, conversant, convivial, correlate, corrigible, corroborate,

278 CENTURY VOCABULARY BUILDER

corrosive, cosmic, covenant, crass, credence, crescent, criterion, critique, crucial, crucible, cryptic, crystalline, culmination, culpable, cumulative, cupidity, cursive, cursory, cutaneous, cynosure.

> His course was not prescribed for him by superiors; his powers were ———. The suppression of these anarchistic tendencies has required ——— measures. She was just entering society and was proving herself a popular ———. Yes, this tree loses its leaves every year; it is a ——— tree. He pretends that his ——— are sound, because he can read the stars.

Debilitate, debonair, débutante, decadence, decapitate, deciduous, declivity, decompose, decorous, dedicatory, deduction, deferential, deficiency, deglutition, dehiscence, delectable, delete, deleterious, delineate, deliquescent, demarcation, demimonde, demoniac, denizen, dénouement, deprecate, depreciate, derelict, derogatory, despicable, desuetude, desultory, deteriorate, diacritical, diagnosis, diaphanous, diatribe, didactic, diffusive, dilatory, dilettante, dipsomania, dirigible, discommode, discretionary, discursive, disintegrate, disparity, dispensable, disseminate, dissimulation, dissonant, distain, divagation, divination, divulge, dolor, dorsal, drastic, dubiety, duress, dynamic.

> These facts do not circulate except among a limited group of people; they are therefore ———. The departure of the children of Israel from Egypt was a general ———. His philosophy, instead of conforming to a single system, was ———. Lamb wrote admirable letters; he has a delightful ——— style. The period at which our days and nights are of equal length is the ——— period.

Ebullient, ecclesiastical, echelon, eclectic, ecstatic, edict, eerie, effervescent, efficacious, effrontery, effulgence, effusion, egregious, eleemosynary, elicit, élite, elucidate,

SUPPLEMENTARY LIST OF WORDS

embellish, embryonic, emendation, emissary, emission, emollient, empiric, empyreal, emulous, encomium, endue, enervate, enfilade, enigmatic, ennui, enunciate, environ, epicure, epigram, episode, epistolary, epitome, equestrian, equilibrium, equinoctial, equity, equivocate, eradicate, erosion, erotic, erudition, eruptive, eschew, esoteric, espousal, estrange, ethereal, eulogistic, euphonious, evanescent, evangelical, evict, exacerbate, excerpt, excommunicate, excoriate, excruciate, execrable, exegesis, exemplary, exhalation, exhilarate, exigency, exodus, exonerate, exorbitant, exotic, expectorate, expeditious, explicable, explicit, expunge, extant, extemporaneous, extrinsic.

He deceives himself by this argument, for the argument is utterly ———. No complicated action can be planned in absolute detail; much must depend on ——— circumstance.

Fabricate, fabulous, facetious, factitious, fallacious, fallible, fastidious, fatuous, feasible, feculence, fecundity, felicitous, felonious, fetid, feudal, fiducial, filament, filtrate, finesse, flaccid, flagitious, floriculture, florid, fluctuate, foible, forfeiture, fortuitous, fractious, franchise, frangible, frontal, froward, furtive.

The advice was both unasked and unwelcome; it was purely ———. Throughout the World War the ——— of Germany over the other Central European powers was unquestioned. Buffaloes naturally go together in herds; they are ———.

Galaxy, galleon, garrulity, gesticulate, gormand, granivorous, grandiloquent, gravamen, gratuitous, gregarious, habitué, hallucination, harbinger, hardihood, heckle, hectic, hedonist, hegemony, heinous, herbivorous, heretic, hermaphrodite, heterodox, heterogeneous, hibernate, histrionic, hoidenism, homiletics, homogeneous, hydraulic, hypothesis.

> We cannot understand God's ways; they are ——. Nor need we expect to change them; they are ——. If an animal has no backbone, it is ——. A boy so confirmed in his faults that we cannot correct them is ——.

Idiosyncrasy, illicit, immaculate, immanent, imminent, immobile, immure, immutable, impalpable, impeccable, impecunious, imperturbable, impervious, implacable, implicit, impolitic, imponderable, importunate, imprecation, impromptu, improvise, imputation, inadvertent, inamorata, inanity, incarcerate, inchoate, incidence, incision, incongruent, inconsequential, incontinent, incorporeal, incorrigible, incredulity, incumbent, indecorous, indigenous, indigent, indite, indomitable, ineluctable, inexorable, inexplicable, inferential, infinitesimal, infinitude, infraction, infusion, inhibit, innocuous, innuendo, inopportune, insatiable, inscrutable, insidious, inspissated, insulate, intangible, integral, integument, interdict, internecine, intractable, intransigent, intrinsic, inure, invalidate, inveigh, inveigle, invertebrate, invidious, irrefragable, irrefutable, irrelevant, irreparable, irrevocable, iterate.

> He overpraised people; he was always engaged in extravagant —— of somebody or other. The small man who has written a book becomes pretentious at once and regards himself as one of the ——. Thatcher is always engaged in lawsuits; he is the most —— man I ever saw.

Jocose, jocund, jurisprudence, juxtaposition, kaleidoscopic, labyrinth, lacerate, lackadaisical, lacrimal, laity, lambent, lampoon, largess, lascivious, laudable, laudation, lavation, legionary, lethargic, licentious, lineal, lingual,

SUPPLEMENTARY LIST OF WORDS

literati, litigious, loquacity, lubricity, lucent, lucre, lucubration, lugubrious.

> Those soldiers are fighting, not for principle, but for pay; they are ———. Iron that is not heated cannot be hammered into shape; it is not ———.

Machination, macrocosm, magisterial, magniloquent, maladroit, malfeasance, malignity, malleable, mandate, matutinal, medieval, mephitic, mercenary, mercurial, meretricious, metamorphose, meticulous, microcosm, misanthropic, misogyny, misprision, mitigate, monitor, mortuary, mundane, mutable.

> It is a government by the few; therefore an ———. All the men of influence in the state give offices to their kinsmen; the system is one of ———. Yes, grandfather is eighty years old today; he has become an ———.

Nebulous, nefarious, negation, neophyte, nepotism, neurotic, noisome, nomenclature, nonchalant, non sequitur, nucleus, nugatory, obdurate, objurgation, obligatory, obloquy, obsequious, obsession, obsolete, obstreperous, obtrusive, obtuse, obverse, obviate, occult, octogenarian, officious, olfactory, oleaginous, oligarchy, ominous, onomatopœia, opacity, opaque, opprobrious, oracular, orthodox, oscillate, osculate, ostensible, ostentation, ostracize, outré, ovation, overture.

> In England the eldest son inherits the title and the estate, but Americans do not take to a system of ———. You are always putting off until tomorrow what you could do today; do you think it pays to ——— thus? An ambassador whose powers are unlimited is called an ambassador ———. Beasts or men that are given to plundering are ———.

Pabulum, pageantry, paginate, palatial, palliate, palpable, panacea, panegyric, panorama, paradoxical, paramount, parasite, parochial, paroxysm, parsimonious, parturition, patois, patriarchal, patrician, patrimony, peccadillo, pecuniary, pedantic, pellucid, pendulous, penultimate, penurious, peregrination, perfunctory, peripatetic, periphery, persiflage, perspicacious, perspicuity, pertinacious, pharmaceutic, phenomenal, phlegmatic, phraseology, pictorial, piquant, pique, plagiarize, platitudinous, platonic, plebeian, plenipotentiary, plethora, pneumatic, poignant, polity, poltroon, polyglot, pontifical, portentous, posterior, posthumous, potent, potential, pragmatic, preamble, precarious, precocious, precursor, predatory, predestination, predicament, preëmptory, prelate, preliminary, preposterous, prerequisite, prerogative, presentiment, primogeniture, probation, probity, proclivity, procrastinate, prodigal, prodigious, prodigy, profligate, progenitor, proletarian, prolific, prolix, promiscuous, promissory, propaganda, propensity, prophylactic, propinquity, propitiatory, propitious, proprietary, prorogue, proselyte, prototype, protuberant, provender, proximity, prurient, psychical, psychological, puerile, pugnacious, puissant, punctilious, pungent, punitive, pusillanimous, putrescent, pyrotechnics.

The coil of wire, being ———, instantly resumed its original shape. Some one must arrange these papers for publication; will you be their ———? Poe's mind had a bent toward ———; it could reason out a whole chain of circumstances from one or two known facts. He showed a disposition not to comply with these instructions; yes, he was ———.

Rabbinical, rancorous, rapacious, ratiocination, rational, raucous, recalcitrant, recant, recapitulate, recession, reciprocal, reciprocate, recluse, recondite, recreant, recrudescence, rectilinear, rectitude, recumbent, redactor,

SUPPLEMENTARY LIST OF WORDS

redress, redound, refractory, refulgent, rejuvenate, relevant, rendezvous, rendition, reparation, repercussion, repertory, replenish, replete, replevin, reprehend, reprobate, repulsive, requisite, rescind, residue, residuum, resilient, resplendent, resurgence, resuscitate, reticulate, retribution, retrograde, retrospect, rigorous, risible, rodomontade, rudimentary, ruminate.

> His position carries no responsibility; it is a ———. The moon revolves about the earth, and is therefore the earth's ———. His work keeps him at his desk all day; it is ——— work. Your words incite men to disorder and rebellion; they are ———.

Saccharine, sacerdotal, sacrament, sacrilege, salient, salubrious, sardonic, satellite, saturnine, schism, scurrilous, sectarian, secular, sedative, sedentary, seditious, sedulous, segregate, seismograph, senescent, sententious, septuagenarian, sequester, sibilant, similitude, sinecure, sinuous, solicitous, solstice, somnolent, sophisticated, sophistry, sorcery, spasmodic, specious, spirituelle, splenetic, spontaneity, sporadic, spurious, stipend, stipulate, stoical, stricture, stringency, stultify, stupendous, sublimity, suborn, subpœna, subsidiary, subsidy, substratum, subtend, subterfuge, subterranean, subvention, subvert, sudorific, supercilious, supernal, supervene, supine, supposititious, surreptitious, surrogate, surveillance, susceptible, sustenance, sycophantic, syllogism, sylvan, symmetrical, symposium, synchronize, synonymous, synopsis, synthesis.

> The small stream flows into the larger one and is its ———. The thick glass roof lets through sufficient light for us to see by; it is ———. You will not find him hard to manage; he has spirit enough, yet is ———.

Tactile, tangible, tantamount, temerity, tenable, tenacious, tentative, tenuous, termagant, terrestrial, testimentary, thaumaturgic, therapeutic, titular, torso, tortuous, tractable, traduce, transcendent, transfiguration, transient, transitory, translucent, transverse, travesty, tribulation, tributary, truculent, truncate, turbid, turpitude, tyro.

> He is so extravagantly fond of his wife that I should call him ———. Christ died for others; it was a ——— death. The most notable quality in Defoe's narrative is its likeness to actual facts, or in a word, its ———.

Ubiquity, ulterior, ululation, umbrage, unanimous, undulate, urbanity, usurious, uxorious, vacillate, vacuous, vandalism, variegate velocity, venal, venereal, venial, venous, veracious, verdant, verisimilitude, vernacular, versatile, vestal, vibratory, vicarious, vicissitude, virulence, viscid, viscous, vitiate, vitreous, vituperate, vivacious, volatile, volition, voluminous, voluptuary, voluptuous, voracious, votive, vulnerable, whimsical, zealot.

XI

RETROSPECT

DO you never, while occupying a dental chair and deploring the necessity that drives you to that uncomfortable seat, admire the skill of the dentist in the use of his instruments? A great many of these instruments lie at his hand. To you they appear bewildering, so slightly different are they from each other. Yet with unerring readiness the dentist lays hold of the one he needs. Now this facility of his is not a blessing with which a gracious heaven endowed him. It is the consequence and reward of hard study, and above all of work, hard work.

You have been ambitious of like skill in the manipulation of words. Had you not been, you would never have undertaken this study. You have perceived that when you speak or write, words are your instruments. You have wished to learn how to use them. Now for every idea you shall ever have occasion to express await throngs of vocables, each presenting its claims as a fit medium. These you must pass in instantaneous review, these you must expertly appraise, out of these you must choose the words that will best serve your purpose. With practice, you will make your selections unconsciously. You will never, of course, quite attain the infallibility of the dentist; for linguistic instruments are more numerous than dental, and far more complex. But you will more and more nearly approximate the ideal, will more and more nearly find that right expression has become second nature with you.

All this is conditioned upon labor faithful and steadfast. Without labor you will never be adept. At the outset of our study together we warned you that, though we should gather the material and point the way, you yourself must do the work. This book is not one to glance through. It is one to dwell with, to toil with. It exacts much of you—makes you, for each page you turn, pay with the sweat of your brain.

But, assuming that you have done your part, what have you gained? Without answering this question at all fully, we may at this juncture engage in a brief retrospect.

First of all, you have rid yourself of the notion that words are dead things, unrealities worthy of no more than wooden and mechanical employment. As much as anything else in the world, words are alive and responsive, are fraught with unmeasured possibilities of good or ill. You have taken due cognizance of the fact that words must be considered in the aggregate as well as individually, and have reckoned with the pitfalls and dangers as well as with the advantages of their use in combination. But the basis of everything is a keener knowledge of words severally. You have therefore come to study words with the zest and insight you exhibit (or should exhibit) in studying men. Incidentally, you have acquired the habit of looking up dictionary definitions, not merely to satisfy a present need, but also to add permanently to your linguistic resources.

RETROSPECT

You have carried the study of individuals farther. You have come to know words inside and out. Such knowledge not only assists you in your dealings with your contemporaries; it illuminates for you great literature of the past that otherwise would remain obscure. How much keener, for example, is your understanding of Shakespeare's passage on the Seven Ages of Man because of your thorough acquaintance with the single word *pantaloon!* How quickly does the awe for big words slip from you when you perceive that *precocious* is in origin the equivalent of *half-baked!* What intimacy of insight into words you feel when you find that a *companion* is a *sharer of one's bread!* What a linking of language with life you discover when you learn the original signification of *presently,* of *idiot,* of *rival,* of *sandwich,* of *pocket handkerchief!* And what revelations as into a mystic fraternalism with words do you obtain when you confront such a phrase as "the bank *teller*" or "cut to the *quick*"!

Not only have words become more like living beings to you; you have learned to think of them in relations analogous to the human. You can detect the blood kinship, for example, between *prescribe* and *manuscript,* and know that the strain of *fact* or *fic* or *fy* in a word is pretty sure to betoken making or doing. You know that there are elaborate intermarriages among words. You recognize *phonograph,* for example, as a married couple; you even have confidential word as to the dowry brought by each of the contracting parties to the new verbal household.

You have discovered, further, that the language actually swarms with "pairs"—words joined with each other not in blood or by marriage but through meaning. You have so familiarized yourself with hundreds of these pairs that to think of one word is to call the other to mind.

Finally, and in many respects most important of all, you have acquired a vast stock of synonyms. You have had it brought to your attention that the number of basic ideas in the world is surprisingly small; that for each of these ideas there is in our language one generic word; that most people use this one word constantly instead of seeking the subsidiary term that expresses a particular phase of the idea; and that you as a builder of your vocabulary must, while holding fast to the basic idea with one hand, reach out with the other for the fit, sure material of specific words. Nor have you rested in the mere perception of theory. You have had abundant practice, have yourself covered the ground foot by foot. You can therefore proceed with reasonable freedom from the commoner ideas of the human mind to that expression of definite aspects of them which is anything but common.

You have not, of course, achieved perfection. There still is much for you to do. There always will be. Nevertheless in the ways just reviewed, and in various other ways not mentioned in this chapter, you have made yourself verbally rich. You are one of the millionaires of language. When you speak, it is not with stammering incompetence, but with confident readiness. When you write, it is with energy and assurance in the very flow of the ink. Where you had long been a slave, you have become a freeman and can look your fellows in the eye. You have the best badge of culture a human being can possess. You have power at your tongue's end. You have the proud satisfaction of having wrought well, and the inspiration of knowing that whatever verbal need may arise, you are trained and equipped to grapple with it triumphantly.

APPENDICES

Appendix 1

THE DRIFT OF OUR RURAL POPULATION CITYWARD

(An editorial)

To an individual who from whatever motives of personal advantage or mere curiosity has made himself an observer of current tendencies, the drift of our rural population cityward gives food for serious reflection. This drift is one of the most pronounced of the social and economic phenomena of the day. Its consequences upon the life, welfare, and future of the great nation to which we are proud to acknowledge our whole-hearted allegiance are matters of such paramount importance to all concerned that we should turn aside more often than we do from the distracting exactions of our ordinary activities to give them prolonged and earnest consideration.

A generation or so ago human beings were content to spend the full term of their earthly existence amid rural surroundings, or if in their declining days they longed for more of the comforts and associations which are among the cravings of mortality, it was an easy proposition to move to the nearest village or, if they were too high and mighty for this simple measure to satisfy them, they could indulge in the more grandiose performance of residing in the county seat. But nowadays our people want more. Rich or poor, tall or dumpy, tottering grandmothers or babies in swaddling-clothes, they long for ampler pastures. Their brawny arms or hoary heads must bedeck nothing less than the metropolis itself, and perchance put shoulders to the wheel in the incessant grind of the urban treadmill. Can you beat it? Unquestioned profit does not attend the migration. It stands to reason that some of the very advantages sought have been sacrificed on the altar of the drift cityward. Let us say you have your individual domicile or the cramped and sunless apartment you dub your habitation within corporate limits. Does that mean that the privileges of the city are at your disposal, so that you have merely to reach forth your hand and pluck them? Well, hardly! You certainly do not reside in the downtown section, or if you do, you wish to heaven you didn't. And you can reach this section only with delay and inconvenience, whether in the hours of business or in the subsequent period devoted to the glitter of nocturnal revelry and amusement.

But whatever the disadvantages of the city, the people who endure them are convinced that to go back to the vines and figtrees of their native heath would be jumping out of the frying pan into the fire. Why? Well, for one thing, there is no such thing as leisure in the areas that lie beyond those vast aggregations of humanity which constitute our cities. Not only are there innumerable and seemingly interminable chores that must follow the regular occupations of the day, but a thousand emergencies due to chance, weather, or the natural cussedness of things must be disposed of as they arise, regardless of what plans the rustic swain cherishes for the use of his spare time. Urban laborers have contrived by one means or another to bring about a limitation of the number of hours per diem they are forced to toil. To the farmers such an alleviation of their hardships is not within the realm of practicability. They kick about it of course. They say it's a blooming nuisance. But neither their heartburnings nor their struggles can efface it as a fact.

Again, the means of entertainment are more limited, and that by a big lot, with the farmer than with those who dwell in the cities. It is all very well to talk about the blessings of the rural telephone, rural free delivery, and the automobile. These things do make communication easier than it used to be, but after all they're only a drop in the bucket and do little to stop the drift cityward. We may remark just here that if you live a thousand miles from nowhere and are willing to drive your Tin Lizzie into town for "the advantages," you aren't likely to get much even along the line of the movies, and you'll get less still if what you're after is an A-1 school for your progeny.

Finally, the widespread impression that the farmer is a bloated and unscrupulous profiteer has done much to disgust him with his station and employment in life. We don't say he's the one and only when it comes to the virtues. Maybe he hasn't sprouted any wings yet. What if he hasn't? The cities, with their brothels, their big business, and their municipal governments—you wouldn't have the face to say that there's anything wrong with them, now would you? Oh, no! Of course not! The farmer pays high for his machinery and goes clear to the bottom of his pocketbook when he has to buy shoes or a sack of flour, but let him have a steer's hide or a wagon load of wheat to sell, and it's somebody else's ox that's gored. Consumers pay big prices for farm products, goodness knows, but they don't pay them to the farmer. Not on your tintype. The middleman gets his, you needn't question that. We beg pardon a thousand times. We mean the middle*men*. There's no end to those human parasites.

And so farmer after farmer breaks up the old homestead and contributes his mite to the drift cityward. What will be the result that comes out of it all? The effect upon the farmer deserves an editorial all to itself. Here we must limit ourselves to the effects on the future of our beloved American nation. And even these we can now do no more than mention; we lack space to elaborate them. One effect, if the tendency continues, will be such a reduction in home-produced foodstuffs that we shall have to import from other countries lying abroad a good portion of the means of our physical sustenance, and shall face such an increase in the cost of the same that thousands and thousands of our people will find it increasingly harder as the years pass by to maintain their relative economic position. Another effect will be that our civilization, which to this point has sprawled over broad acres, will become an urban civilization, penned in amid conditions, restraints, privations, and perhaps also opportunities unprecedented in our past history and unknown to the experience we have had hitherto. A final effect will be that our most conservative class, the rural populace, will no longer present resistance that is formidable to the innovations which those who hold extreme views are forever exhorting us to embrace; and the result may well be that the disintegration of this staying and stabilizing element in our citizenship—one that retards and mollifies if it does not inhibit change—will produce consequences in its train which may be as dire as they are difficult to foretell.

Appendix 2

CAUSES FOR THE AMERICAN SPIRIT OF LIBERTY

(From the *Speech on Conciliation with the Colonies*)

By Edmund Burke

In this character of the Americans, a love of freedom is the predominating feature which marks and distinguishes the whole; and as an ardent is always a jealous affection, your

Colonies become suspicious, restive, and untractable whenever they see the least attempt to wrest from them by force, or shuffle from them by chicane, what they think the only advantage worth living for. This fierce spirit of liberty is stronger in the English Colonies probably than in any other people of the earth, and this from a great variety of powerful causes; which, to understand the true temper of their minds and the direction which this spirit takes, it will not be amiss to lay open somewhat more largely.

First, the people of the Colonies are descendants of Englishmen. England, Sir, is a nation which still, I hope, respects, and formerly adored, her freedom. The Colonists emigrated from you when this part of your character was most predominant; and they took this bias and direction the moment they parted from your hands. They are therefore not only devoted to liberty, but to liberty according to English ideas, and on English principles. Abstract liberty, like other mere abstractions, is not to be found. Liberty inheres in some sensible object; and every nation has formed to itself some favorite point, which by way of eminence becomes the criterion of their happiness. It happened, you know, Sir, that the great contests for freedom in this country were from the earliest times chiefly upon the question of taxing. Most of the contests in the ancient commonwealths turned primarily on the right of election of magistrates; or on the balance among the several orders of the state. The question of money was not with them so immediate. But in England it was otherwise. On this point of taxes the ablest pens, and most eloquent tongues, have been exercised; the greatest spirits have acted and suffered. In order to give the fullest satisfaction concerning the importance of this point, it was not only necessary for those who in argument defended the excellence of the English Constitution to insist on this privilege of granting money as a dry point of fact, and to prove that the right had been acknowledged in ancient parchments and blind usages to reside in a certain body called a House of Commons. They went much farther; they attempted to prove, and they succeeded, that in theory it ought to be so, from the particular nature of a House of Commons as an immediate representative of the people, whether the old records had delivered this oracle or not. They took infinite pains to inculcate, as a fundamental principle, that in all monarchies the people must in effect themselves, mediately or immediately, possess the power of granting their own money, or no shadow of liberty can subsist. The Colonies draw from you, as with their life-blood, these ideas and principles. Their love of liberty, as with you, fixed and attached on this specific point of taxing. Liberty might be safe, or might be endangered, in twenty other particulars, without their being much pleased or alarmed. Here they felt its pulse; and as they found that beat, they thought themselves sick or sound. I do not say whether they were right or wrong in applying your general arguments to their own case. It is not easy, indeed, to make a monopoly of theorems and corollaries. The fact is, that they did thus apply those general arguments; and your mode of governing them, whether through lenity or indolence, through wisdom or mistake, confirmed them in the imagination that they, as well as you, had an interest in these common principles.

They were further confirmed in this pleasing error by the form of their provincial legislative assemblies. Their governments are popular in an high degree; some are merely popular; in all, the popular representative is the most weighty; and this share of the people in their ordinary government never fails to inspire them with lofty sentiments, and with a strong aversion from whatever tends to deprive them of their chief importance.

If anything were wanting to this necessary operation of the form of government, religion would have given it a complete effect. Religion, always a principle of energy, in this new people is no way worn out or impaired; and their mode of professing it is also one main cause of this free spirit. The people are Protestants; and of that kind which is the most adverse to all implicit submission of mind and opinion. This is a persuasion not only favorable to liberty, but built upon it. I do not think, Sir, that the reason of this averseness in the dissenting churches from all that looks like absolute government is so much to be sought in their religious tenets, as in their history. Every one knows that the Roman Catholic religion is at least coeval with most of the governments where it prevails; that it has generally gone hand in hand with them, and received great favor and every kind of support from authority. The Church of England too was formed from her cradle under the nursing care of regular government. But the dissenting interests have sprung up in direct opposition to all the ordinary powers of the world, and could justify that opposition only on a strong claim to natural liberty. Their very existence depended on the powerful and unremitted assertion of that claim. All Protestantism, even the most cold and passive, is a sort of dissent. But the religion most prevalent in our Northern Colonies is a refinement on the principle of resistance; it is the dissidence of dissent, and the protestantism of the Protestant religion. This religion, under a variety of denominations agreeing in nothing but in the communion of the spirit of liberty, is predominant in most of the Northern Provinces, where the Church of England, notwithstanding its legal rights, is in reality no more than a sort of private sect, not composing most probably the tenth of the people. The Colonists left England when this spirit was high, and in the emigrants was the highest of all; and even that stream of foreigners which has been constantly flowing into these Colonies has, for the greatest part, been composed of dissenters from the establishments of their several countries, who have brought with them a temper and character far from alien to that of the people with whom they mixed.

Sir, I can perceive by their manner that some gentlemen object to the latitude of this description, because in the Southern Colonies the Church of England forms a large body, and has a regular establishment. It is certainly true. There is, however, a circumstance attending these Colonies which, in my opinion, fully counterbalances this difference, and makes the spirit of liberty still more high and haughty than in those to the northward. It is that in Virginia and the Carolinas they have a vast multitude of slaves. Where this is the case in any part of the world, those who are free are by far the most proud and jealous of their freedom. Freedom is to them not only an enjoyment, but a kind of rank and privilege. Not seeing there, that freedom, as in countries where it is a common blessing and as broad and general as the air, may be united with much abject toil, with great misery, with all the exterior of servitude; liberty looks, amongst them, like something that is more noble and liberal. I do not mean, Sir, to commend the superior morality of this sentiment, which has at least as much pride as virtue in it; but I cannot alter the nature of man. The fact is so; and these people of the Southern Colonies are much more strongly, and with an higher and more stubborn spirit, attached to liberty than those to the northward. Such were all the ancient commonwealths; such were our Gothic ancestors; such in our days were the Poles; and such will be all masters of slaves, who are not slaves themselves. In such a people the haughtiness of domination combines with the spirit of freedom, fortifies it, and renders it invincible.

Permit me, Sir, to add another circumstance in our Colonies which contributes no mean part towards the growth and effect of this untractable spirit. I mean their education. In no country perhaps in the world is the law so general a study. The profession itself is numerous and powerful; and in most provinces it takes the lead. The greater number of the deputies sent to the Congress were lawyers. But all who read, and most do read, endeavor to obtain some smattering in that science. I have been told by an eminent bookseller, that in no branch of his business, after tracts of popular devotion, were so many books as those on the law exported to the Plantations. The Colonists have now fallen into the way of printing them for their own use. I hear that they have sold nearly as many of Blackstone's Commentaries in America as in England. General Gage marks out this disposition very particularly in a letter on your table. He states that all the people in his government are lawyers, or smatterers in law; and that in Boston they have been enabled, by successful chicane, wholly to evade many parts of one of your capital penal constitutions. The smartness of debate will say that this knowledge ought to teach them more clearly the rights of legislature, their obligations to obedience, and the penalties of rebellion. All this is mighty well. But my honorable and learned friend on the floor, who condescends to mark what I say for animadversion, will disdain that ground. He has heard, as well as I, that when great honors and great emoluments do not win over this knowledge to the service of the state, it is a formidable adversary to government. If the spirit be not tamed and broken by these happy methods, it is stubborn and litigious. *Abeunt studia in mores.* This study renders men acute, inquisitive, dexterous, prompt in attack, ready in defence, full of resources. In other countries, the people, more simple, and of a less mercurial cast, judge of an ill principle in government only by an actual grievance; here they anticipate the evil, and judge of the pressure of the grievance by the badness of the principle. They augur misgovernment at a distance, and snuff the approach of tyranny in every tainted breeze.

The last cause of this disobedient spirit in the Colonies is hardly less powerful than the rest, as it is not merely moral, but laid deep in the natural constitution of things. Three thousand miles of ocean lie between you and them. No contrivance can prevent the effect of this distance in weakening government. Seas roll, and months pass, between the order and the execution; and the want of a speedy explanation of a single point is enough to defeat a whole system. You have, indeed, winged ministers of vengeance, who carry your bolts in their pounces to the remotest verge of the sea. But there a power steps in that limits the arrogance of raging passions and furious elements, and says, *So far shalt thou go, and no farther.* Who are you, that you should fret and rage, and bite the chains of nature? Nothing worse happens to you than does to all nations who have extensive empire; and it happens in all the forms into which empire can be thrown. In large bodies the circulation of power must be less vigorous at the extremities. Nature has said it. The Turk cannot govern Egypt and Arabia and Kurdistan as he governs Thrace; nor has he the same dominion in Crimea and Algiers which he has at Brusa and Smyrna. Despotism itself is obliged to truck and huckster. The Sultan gets such obedience as he can. He governs with a loose rein, that he may govern at all; and the whole of the force and vigor of his authority in his center is derived from a prudent relaxation in all his borders. Spain, in her provinces, is, perhaps, not so well obeyed as you are in yours. She complies, too; she submits; she watches times. This is the immutable condition, the eternal law of extensive and detached empire.

Then, Sir, from these six capital sources—of descent, of form of government, of religion in the Northern Provinces, of manners in the Southern, of education, of the remoteness of situation from the first mover of government—from all these causes a fierce spirit of liberty has grown up. It has grown with the growth of the people in your Colonies, and increased with the increase of their wealth; a spirit that unhappily meeting with an exercise of power in England which, however lawful, is not reconcilable to any ideas of liberty, much less with theirs, has kindled this flame that is ready to consume us.

Appendix 3

PARABLE OF THE SOWER

(Matthew 13:3-8 and 18-23)

And he spake many things unto them in parables, saying, Behold, a sower went forth to sow;

And when he sowed, some seeds fell by the way side, and the fowls came and devoured them up:

Some fell upon stony places, where they had not much earth: and forthwith they sprung up, because they had no deepness of earth:

And when the sun was up, they were scorched; and because they had no root, they withered away.

And some fell among thorns; and the thorns sprung up, and choked them:

But other fell into good ground, and brought forth fruit, some an hundredfold, some sixtyfold, some thirtyfold.

. . . .

Hear ye therefore the parable of the sower.

When any one heareth the word of the kingdom, and understandeth it not, then cometh the wicked one, and catcheth away that which was sown in his heart. This is he which received seed by the way side.

But he that received the seed into stony places, the same is he that heareth the word, and anon with joy receiveth it;

Yet he hath not root in himself, but dureth for a while: for when tribulation or persecution ariseth because of the word, by and by he is offended.

He also that received seed among the thorns is he that heareth the word; and the care of this world, and the deceitfulness of riches, choke the word, and he becometh unfruitful.

But he that received seed into the good ground is he that heareth the word, and understandeth it; which also beareth fruit, and bringeth forth, some an hundredfold, some sixty, some thirty.

Appendix 4

THE SEVEN AGES OF MAN

(*As You Like It,* II, vii, 139–166)

By William Shakespeare

All the world's a stage,
And all the men and women merely players:
They have their exits and their entrances;
And one man in his time plays many parts,
His acts being seven ages. At first the infant,
Mewling and puking in the nurse's arms.
And then the whining school-boy, with his satchel,
And shining morning face, creeping like snail
Unwillingly to school. And then the lover,
Sighing like furnace, with a woful ballad
Made to his mistress' eyebrow. Then a soldier,
Full of strange oaths, and bearded like the pard,
Jealous in honor, sudden and quick in quarrel,
Seeking the bubble reputation
Even in the cannon's mouth. And then the justice,
In fair round belly with good capon lin'd,
With eyes severe, and beard of formal cut,
Full of wise saws and modern instances;
And so he plays his part. The sixth age shifts

Into the lean and slipper'd pantaloon,
With spectacles on nose and pouch on side,
His youthful hose well sav'd, a world too wide
For his shrunk shank; and his big manly voice,
Turning again toward childish treble, pipes
And whistles in his sound. Last scene of all,
That ends this strange eventful history,
Is second childishness and mere oblivion,
Sans teeth, sans eyes, sans taste, sans everything.

Appendix 5

THE CASTAWAY

(From *Robinson Crusoe*)

By Daniel Defoe

And now our case was very dismal indeed; for we all saw plainly that the sea went so high that the boat could not escape, and that we should be inevitably drowned. As to making sail, we had none, nor, if we had, could we have done anything with it; so we worked at the oar towards the land, though with heavy hearts, like men going to execution; for we all knew that when the boat came near the shore, she would be dashed in a thousand pieces by the beach of the sea. However, we committed our souls to God in the most earnest manner; and the wind driving us towards the shore, we hastened our destruction with our own hands, pulling as well as we could towards land.

What the shore was, whether rock or sand, whether steep or shoal, we knew not; the only hope that could rationally give us the least shadow of expectation, was if we might happen into some bay or gulf, or the mouth of some river, where by great chance we might have run our boat in, or got under the lee of the land, and perhaps made smooth water. But there was nothing of this appeared; but as we made nearer and nearer the shore, the land looked more frightful than the sea.

After we had rowed, or rather driven, about a league and a half, as we reckoned it, a raging wave, mountain-like, came rolling astern of us, and plainly bade us expect the *coup de grâce*. In a word, it took us with such a fury that it overset the boat at once; and separating us as well from the boat as from one another, gave us not time hardly to say, "O God!" for we were all swallowed up in a moment.

Nothing can describe the confusion of thought which I felt,

when I sank into the water; for though I swam very well, yet I could not deliver myself from the waves so as to draw breath, till that wave having driven me, or rather carried me, a vast way on towards the shore, and having spent itself, went back, and left me upon the land almost dry, but half dead with the water I took in. I had so much presence of mind, as well as breath left, that seeing myself nearer the mainland than I expected, I got upon my feet, and endeavored to make on towards the land as fast as I could, before another wave should return and take me up again; but I soon found it was impossible to avoid it; for I saw the sea come after me as high as a great hill, and as furious as an enemy, which I had no means or strength to contend with: my business was to hold my breath, and raise myself upon the water, if I could; and so by swimming to preserve my breathing, and pilot myself towards the shore if possible; my greatest concern now being that the wave, as it would carry me a great way toward the shore when it came on, might not carry me back again with it when it gave back towards the sea.

The wave that came upon me again buried me at once twenty or thirty feet deep in its own body, and I could feel myself carried with a mighty force and swiftness towards the shore a very great way; but I held my breath, and assisted myself to swim still forward with all my might. I was ready to burst with holding my breath, when as I felt myself rising up, so, to my immediate relief, I found my head and hands shoot out above the surface of the water; and though it was not two seconds of time that I could keep myself so, yet it relieved me greatly, gave me breath and new courage. I was covered again with water a good while, but not so long but I held it out; and finding the water had spent itself, and began to return, I struck forward against the return of the waves, and felt ground again with my feet. I stood still a few moments to recover breath, and till the waters went from me, and then took to my heels, and ran with what strength I had, farther towards the shore. But neither would this deliver me from the fury of the sea, which came pouring in after me again; and twice more I was lifted up by the waves and carried forwards as before, the shore being very flat.

The last time of these two had well-nigh been fatal to me; for the sea having hurried me along, as before, landed me, or rather dashed me, against a piece of a rock, and that with such force as it left me senseless, and indeed helpless, as to my own deliverance; for the blow, taking my side and breast, beat the breath as it were quite out of my body; and had it returned again immediately, I must have been strangled in the water; but I recovered a little before the return of the waves, and seeing I should be covered again with the water, I resolved to hold fast by a piece of the rock, and so to hold my breath, if possible, till the wave went back. Now, as the waves were not so high as at first, being nearer land, I held my hold till the wave abated, and then fetched another run, which brought me so near the shore that the next wave though it went over me, yet did not so swallow me up as to carry me away; and the next run I took I got to the mainland; where, to my great comfort, I clambered up the cliffs of the shore, and sat me down upon the grass, free from danger and quite out of the reach of the water.

I was now landed, and safe on shore, and began to look up and thank God that my life was saved, in a case wherein there was some minutes before scarce any room to hope. I believe it is impossible to express, to the life, what the ecstasies and transports of the soul are when it is so saved, as I may say, out of the very grave: and I do not wonder now at that custom, when a malefactor, who has the halter about his neck, is tied up, and just going to be turned off, and has a reprieve brought to him—I say, I do not wonder that they bring a surgeon with it, to let him blood that very moment they tell him of it, that the surprise may not drive the animal spirits from the heart, and overwhelm him.

"For sudden joys, like griefs, confound at first."

I walked about on the shore, lifting up my hands, and my whole being, as I may say, wrapt up in a contemplation of my deliverance; making a thousand gestures and motions, which I cannot describe; reflecting upon all my comrades that were drowned, and that there should not be one soul saved but myself; for, as for them, I never saw them afterwards, or any sign of them, except three of their hats, one cap, and two shoes that were not fellows.

I cast my eyes to the stranded vessel, when, the breach and froth of the sea being so big, I could hardly see it, it lay so far off; and considered, Lord! how was it possible I could get on shore?

After I had solaced my mind with the comfortable part of my condition, I began to look round me, to see what kind of place I was in, and what was next to be done: and I soon found my comforts abate, and that, in a word, I had a dreadful deliverance: for I was wet, had no clothes to shift me, nor anything either to eat or drink, to comfort me; neither did I see any prospect before me but that of perishing with hunger, or being devoured by wild beasts: and that which was particularly afflicting to me was, that I had no weapon, either to hunt and kill any creature for my sustenance, or to defend myself against any other creature that might desire to kill me for theirs. In a word, I had nothing about me but a knife, a tobacco-pipe, and a little tobacco in a box. This was all my provision; and this threw me into terrible agonies of mind, that for awhile I ran about like a madman. Night coming upon me, I began with a heavy heart, to consider what would be my lot if there were any ravenous beasts in that country, seeing at night they always come abroad for their prey.

All the remedy that offered to my thoughts, at that time, was to get up into a thick bushy tree, like a fir, but thorny, which grew near me, and where I resolved to sit all night, and consider the next day what death I should die, for as yet I saw no prospect of life. I walked about a furlong from the shore, to see if I could find any fresh water to drink, which I did to my great joy; and having drunk, and put a little tobacco in my mouth to prevent hunger, I went to the tree, and getting up into it, endeavored to place myself so that if I should sleep I might not fall. And having cut me a short stick, like a truncheon, for my defense, I took up my lodging; and being excessively fatigued, I fell fast asleep, and slept as comfortably as, I believe, few could have done in my condition, and found myself more refreshed with it than I think I ever was on such an occasion.

When I waked it was broad day, the weather clear, and the storm abated, so that the sea did not rage and swell as before; but that which surprised me most was, that the ship was lifted off in the night from the sand where she lay, by the swelling of the tide, and was driven up almost as far as the rock which I at first mentioned, where I had been so bruised by the wave dashing me against it. This being within about a mile from the shore where I was, and the ship seeming to stand upright still, I wished myself on board, that at least I might save some necessary things for my use.

When I came down from my apartment in the tree, I looked about me again, and the first thing I found was the boat, which lay, as the wind and sea had tossed her up, upon the land, about two miles on my right hand. I walked as far as I could upon the shore to have got to her; but found a neck, or inlet, of water between me and the boat, which was about half a mile broad; so I came back for the present, being more intent upon getting at the ship, where I hoped to find something for my present subsistence.

A little after noon I found the sea very calm, and the tide ebbed so far out, that I could come within a quarter of a mile of the ship. And here I found a fresh renewing of my grief; for I saw evidently that if we had kept on board, we had been all safe: that is to say, we had all got safe on shore, and I had not been so miserable as to be left entirely destitute of all comfort and company, as I now was. This forced tears to my eyes again; but as there was little relief in that, I resolved, if possible, to get to the ship; so I pulled off my clothes, for the weather was hot to extremity, and took the water. But when I came to the ship, my difficulty was still greater to know how to get on board; for, as she lay aground, and high out of the water, there was nothing within my reach to lay hold of. I swam round her twice, and the second time I espied a small piece of rope, which I wondered I did not see at first, hanging down by the fore-chains so low that, with great difficulty, I got hold of it, and by the help of that rope got up into the forecastle of the ship. Here I found that the ship was bulged, and had a great deal of water in her hold; but that she lay so on the side of a bank of hard sand, or rather earth, that her stern lay lifted up upon the bank, and her head low, almost to the water. By this means all her quarter was free, and all that was in that part was dry; for you may be sure my first work was to search, and to see what was spoiled and what was free. And, first, I found that all the ship's provisions were dry and untouched by the water, and being very well disposed to eat, I went to the bread-room, and filled my pockets with biscuit, and ate it as I went about other things, for I had no time to lose. I also found some rum in the great cabin, of which I took a large dram, and which I had, indeed, need enough of to spirit me for what was before me. Now I wanted nothing but a boat, to furnish myself with many things which I foresaw would be very necessary to me.

It was in vain to sit still and wish for what was not to be had; and this extremity roused my application. We had several spare yards, and two or three large spars of wood, and a spare topmast or two in the ship: I resolved to fall to work with these, and I flung as many of them overboard as I could manage for their weight, tying every one with a rope, that they might not drive away. When this was done I went down the ship's side, and pulling them to me I tied four of them together at both ends, as well as I could, in the form of a raft, and laying two or three short pieces of plank upon them, crossways, I found I could walk upon it very well, but that it was not able to bear any great weight, the pieces being too light. So I went to work, and with the carpenter's saw I cut a spare topmast into three lengths, and added them to my raft, with a great deal of labor and pains. But the hope of furnishing myself with necessaries encouraged me to go beyond what I should have been able to have done upon another occasion.

My raft was now strong enough to bear any reasonable weight. My next care was what to load it with, and how to preserve what I laid upon it from the surf of the sea: but I was not long considering this. I first laid all the planks or boards upon it that I could get, and having considered well what I most wanted, I first got three of the seamen's chests, which I had broken open and emptied, and lowered them down upon my raft; the first of these I filled with provisions—viz., bread, rice, three Dutch cheeses, five pieces of dried goat's flesh (which we lived much upon), and a little remainder of European corn, which had been laid by for some fowls which we brought to sea with us, but the fowls were killed. There had been some barley and wheat together; but, to my great disappointment, I found afterwards that the rats had eaten or spoiled it all. As for liquors, I found several cases of bottles belonging to our skipper, in which were some cordial waters; and, in all, about five or six gallons of arrack. These I stowed by themselves, there being no need to put them into the chest, nor any room for them. While I was doing this, I found the tide began to flow, though very calm; and I had the mortification to see my coat, shirt, and waistcoat, which I had left on shore upon the sand, swim away. As for my breeches, which were only linen, and open-kneed, I swam on board in them and my stockings. However, this put me upon rummaging for clothes, of which I found enough, but took no more than I wanted for present use, for I had other things which my eye was more upon; as, first, tools to work with on shore: and it was after long searching that I found out the carpenter's chest, which was indeed a very useful prize to me, and much more valuable than a ship-lading of gold would have been at that time. I got it down to my raft, whole as it was, without losing time to look into it, for I knew in general what it contained.

My next care was for some ammunition and arms. There were two very good fowling-pieces in the great cabin, and two pistols. These I secured first, with some powder-horns, a small bag of shot, and two old rusty swords. I knew there were three barrels of powder in the ship, but knew not where our gunner had stowed them; but with much search I found them, two of them dry and good, the third had taken water. Those two I got to my raft, with the arms. And now I thought myself pretty well freighted, and began to think how I should get to shore with them, having neither sail, oar, nor rudder; and the least capful of wind would have overset all my navigation.

I had three encouragements: first, a smooth, calm sea; secondly, the tide rising, and setting in to the shore; thirdly, what little wind there was blew me towards the land. And thus, having found two or three broken oars, belonging to the boat, and besides the tools which were in the chest, two saws, an axe, and a hammer, with this cargo I put to sea. For a mile, or thereabouts, my raft went very well, only that I found it drive a little distant from the place where I had landed before: by which I perceived that there was some indraught of the water, and consequently, I hoped to find some creek or river there, which I might make use of as a port to get to land with my cargo.

As I imagined, so it was. There appeared before me a little opening of the land. I found a strong current of the tide set into it; so I guided my raft as well as I could, to keep in the middle of the stream.

But here I had like to have suffered a second shipwreck, which, if I had, I think verily would have broken my heart; for, knowing nothing of the coast, my raft ran aground at one end of it upon a shoal, and not being aground at the other end, it wanted but a little that all my cargo had slipped off towards the end that was afloat, and so fallen into the water. I did my utmost, by setting my back against the chests, to keep them in their places, but could not thrust off the raft with all my strength; neither durst I stir from the posture I was in; but holding up the chests with all my might, I stood in that manner near half an hour, in which time the rising of the water brought me a little more upon a level; and a little after, the water still rising, my raft floated again, and I thrust her off with the oar I had into the channel, and then driving up higher, I at length found myself in the mouth of a little river, with land on both sides, and a strong current or tide running up. I looked on both sides for a proper place to get to shore, for I was not willing to be driven too high up the river; hoping in time to see some ship at sea, and therefore resolved to place myself as near the coast as I could.

At length I spied a little cove on the right shore of the creek, to which, with great pain and difficulty, I guided my raft, and at last got so near, that reaching ground with my oar, I could thrust her directly in. But here I had like to have dipped all my cargo into the sea again; for that shore lying pretty steep—that is to say, sloping—there was no place to land but where one end of my float, if it ran on shore, would lie so high, and the other sink lower, as before, that it would endanger my cargo again. All that I could do was to wait till the tide was at the highest, keeping the raft with my oar like an anchor, to hold the side of it fast to the shore, near a flat piece of ground, which

I expected the water would flow over; and so it did. As soon as I found water enough, for my raft drew about a foot of water, I thrust her upon that flat piece of ground, and there fastened or moored her, by sticking my two broken oars into the ground—one on one side, near one end, and one on the other side, near the other end; and thus I lay till the water ebbed away, and left my raft and all my cargo safe on shore.

Appendix 6

READING LISTS

One of the best ways to *know* words is through seeing them used by the masters. For this reason, as well as for many others, you should read extensively in good literature. The following lists of prose works may prove useful for your guidance. They are not intended to be exclusive, not intended to designate "the hundred best books." Rather do they name some good books of fairly varied types. These are not all of equal merit, even in their use of words. Some use words with nice discrimination, some with splendid vividness and force. For each author only one or two books are named, but in many instances you will wish to read further in the author, perhaps indeed his entire works.

Biography and Autobiography

Boswell, James: *Life of Samuel Johnson*
Bradford, Gamaliel: *Lee the American; American Portraits, 1875–1900*
Franklin, Benjamin: *Autobiography*
Grant, U. S.: *Personal Memoirs*
Irving, Washington: *Life of Goldsmith*
Paine, A. B.: *Life of Mark Twain*
Walton, Izaak: *Lives*

Essays, Adventure, etc.

Addison, Joseph: *Spectator Papers*
Bryce, Sir James: *The American Commonwealth*
Burke, Edmund: *Speech on Conciliation*
Burroughs, John: *Wake Robin*

Chesterton, G. K.: *Heretics*
Crothers, S. M.: *The Gentle Reader*
Dana, R. H., Jr.: *Two Years Before the Mast*
Darwin, Charles: *Origin of Species*
Emerson, R. W.: *Essays*
Irving, Washington: *Sketch Book*
Lincoln, Abraham: *Speeches and Addresses*
Lucas, E. V.: *Old Lamps for New*
Macaulay, T. B.: *Essays*
Muir, John: *The Mountains of California*
Thoreau, H. D.: *Walden*
Twain, Mark: *Life on the Mississippi*

Fiction

Allen, James Lane: *The Choir Invisible*
Austen, Jane: *Pride and Prejudice*
Barrie, Sir James M.: *Sentimental Tommie*
Bennett, Arnold: *The Old Wives' Tale*
Blackmore, R. D.: *Lorna Doone*
Bunyan, John: *Pilgrim's Progress*
Cable, G. W.: *Old Creole Days*
Conrad, Joseph: *The Nigger of the Narcissus*
Defoe, Daniel: *Robinson Crusoe*
Dickens, Charles: *David Copperfield*
Eliot, George: *Adam Bede*
Galsworthy, John: *The Patrician*
Goldsmith, Oliver: *The Vicar of Wakefield*
Hardy, Thomas: *The Return of the Native*
Harte, Bret: *The Luck of Roaring Camp* (short story)
Hawthorne, Nathaniel: *The Scarlet Letter*
Hergesheimer, Joseph: *Java Head*
Hudson, W. H.: *Green Mansions*
Kingsley, Charles: *Westward Ho!*
Kipling, Rudyard: *Plain Tales from the Hills* (short stories)
London, Jack: *The Call of the Wild*
Merrick, Leonard: *The Man Who Understood Women* (volume of short stories); *The Actor Manager*
Mitchell, S. Weir: *Hugh Wynne, Free Quaker*
Norris, Frank: *The Octopus*
Poe, Edgar Allan: *The Fall of the House of Usher* (short story)
Poole, Ernest: *The Harbor*
Scott, Sir Walter: *Ivanhoe*
Smith, F. Hopkinson: *Colonel Carter of Cartersville*

APPENDICES

Stevenson, R. L.: *Treasure Island*
Tarkington, Booth: *Monsieur Beaucaire*
Thackeray, W. M.: *Vanity Fair*
Twain, Mark: *Huckleberry Finn*
Wells, H. G.: *Tono Bungay*
Wharton, Edith: *Ethan Frome*
Wister, Owen: *The Virginian*

INDEX

The index comprises, besides miscellaneous items, four large classes of matter: (1) topics, including many minor ones not given separate textual captions; (2) all individual words and members of pairs explained or commented on in the text; (3) the key syllables, but not the separate words, of family groups; (4) the first or generic term, but not the other terms, in all assemblies of synonyms; hence, this book can be used as a handbook of ordinarily used synonyms.

Abandon, Synonyms of, 189
Abase, Synonyms of, 189-190
Abettor, Synonyms of, 250
Abolish, Synonyms of, 220
Abridge, 170
Abstract vs. concrete terms, 27-30. Also see *Words*
Absurd, 79
Accumulate, 78
Acknowledge, Synonyms of, 250
Acquit, Synonyms of, 220
Act family, 105
Active, Synonyms of, 250
Advise, Synonyms of, 250
Aeronautics, Familiar terms in, 271
Affair, 67
Affect, 149, 150
Affecting, Synonyms of, 250
Affront, Synonyms of, 243-244
Afraid, Synonyms of, 221
Ag family, 105
Agnostic, Synonyms of, 250
Allay, Synonyms of, 221
Allopath, 147
Allow, Synonyms of, 221
Altitude, 167
Amicable, 168
Amuse, Synonyms of, 250
Analysis. See *Vocabulary* and *Synonyms*
Analysis, Rhetorical, 47-48, 51-52, 56
Anglo-Saxon words in modern English. See *Native words*
Anim family, 124
Anni, annu family, 124
Announce, Synonyms of, 250
Answer, Synonyms of, 190-191
Antipathy, Synonyms of, 250
Antonyms, 176, 177
Appreciate, 77
Apprehend, 79

Apricot, 79
Ardor, 77
Argument, 47, 48, 52, 56
Artful, 82
Artifice, Synonyms of, 250
Ascend, 168
Ascend, Synonyms of, 250
Ascribe, 91-92
Ascribe, Synonyms of, 221
Ask, Synonyms of, 191-193
Assail, 79
Associate, Synonyms of, 250
Attach, Synonyms of, 250
Attack, Synonyms of, 250
Attention, 80
Audi, auri family, 124
Audience, Adapting discourse to, 54-58
Auto family, 124
Avert, 78
Awkward, Synonyms of, 221

Backhanded, 79
Bald heads, 35
Bare, 262
Base, 266
Bear, 262
Bedlam, 84
Beef, 159
Begin, Synonyms of, 250
Belief, Synonyms of, 250
Belittle, Synonyms of, 251
Bind, Synonyms of, 251
Bit, Synonyms of, 251
Bite, Synonyms of, 222
Blood relationships between words, 91-94, 274-275. Small groups of words so related, 93, 134-135, 135-144. Also see *Words*
Bluff, Synonyms of, 251
Boast, Synonyms of, 251

311

INDEX

Body, Synonyms of, 251
Bold, 262
Bombastic, Synonyms of, 251
Books of synonyms, List of, 177-178
Boor, 83
Boorish, Synonyms of, 251
Booty, Synonyms of, 251
Boys, Kinds of, 181-182
Brand, brun family, 106
Break, 170
Break, Synonyms of, 222
Breakfast, 78
Bridegroom, 80
Bright, 262
Brittle, Synonyms of, 251
Brotherly, 166
Building, Synonyms of, 251
Burke, Edmund. See *Causes for the American Spirit of Liberty*
Burn family, 106
Burn, Synonyms of, 193
Burn with indignation, 79
Busy, Synonyms of, 193-194
By and by, 81

Cad family, 106
Calf, 159, 160
Call, Synonyms of, 251
Calm, Synonyms of, 251
Cant family, 124
Cap(t) family, 107
Capricious, 79
Care, Synonyms of, 251
Careful, Synonyms of 222
Cart before the horse, 79
Cas family, 106
"Castaway, The" (Defoe), 300-307. Comments and assignments on, 11, 23, 26, 30, 31, 33-34
"Causes for the American Spirit of Liberty" (Burke), 293-298. Comments and assignments on, 10, 26, 29-30, 31-32, 34, 37, 46, 97
Cede, ceed, cess family, 106
Ceive, ceit, cept family, 107
Celebrate, Synonyms of, 251
Celibates, Verbal, 59-88
Censure, 81
Cent family, 125
Cent family, 124
Charm (noun), Synonyms of, 251
Charm (verb), Synonyms of, 251
Chant family, 124
Cheat, Synonyms of, 251
Child. See *How a child becomes acquainted*, etc.
Choke, Synonyms of, 251
Choose, Synonyms of, 251
Chron family, 125
Church, 164
Churl, 83

Cid family, 106
Cide family, 107
Cigar, 67-68
Cip family, 107
Circumstances, 80
Cis(e) family, 107
Classes of words, in general, 25 (also see *Words*); in your own vocabulary, 63-65
Classic words, distinguished from native, 160; in modern English, 135, 158-175
Clear, 262-263
Clodhopper, 83
Close, 263
Close the door to, 78
Coax, Synonyms of, 251
Cold, 166-167
Coleridge, S. T., Quotation from, 32
Color, Synonyms of, 251
Combine, Synonyms of, 251
Comfort, Synonyms of, 251
Common, 82
Companion, 80, 287
Complain, Synonyms of, 251
Conchology, 98-101, 102-103
Concise, Synonyms of, 194-195
Condescend, Synonyms of, 222
Condition, 67
Confirm, Synonyms of, 222
Confirmed, Synonyms of, 251
Confound, 81
Congregate, 79
Connect, Synonyms of, 251
Connotation, 5, 35-39
Constable, 80
Contagious, 149, 150
Continual, Synonyms of, 251
Continuous, continual, 149
Contract, Synonyms of, 251
Conversation, 168
Copy, Synonyms of, 251
Cordiality, 77
Corp(s) family, 125
Corrode, 79
Corrupt, Synonyms of, 251
Costly, Synonyms of, 251
Coterie, Synonyms of, 251
Counterfeit, 80
Courage, Synonyms of, 223
Course family, 107
Coxcomb, 78
Crafty, 82
Crease, cresce, cret, crue family, 125
Cred, creed family, 125
Crestfallen, 78
Crisscross, 80
Critical, Synonyms of, 251
Criticism, 81
Crooked, Synonyms of, 251
Cross, 79

INDEX

Cross, Synonyms of, 251
Crowd, Synonyms of, 252
Crowsfeet, 79
Crude, 79
Cruel, Synonyms of, 223
Cry, 183
Cry, Synonyms of, 223
Cunning, 82
Cur family, 107
Cure family, 126
Curious, Synonyms of, 252
Cut, Synonyms of, 224

Daily, 166
Dainty, Synonyms of, 252
Daisy, 78
Dandelion, 78
Danger, Synonyms of, 252
Darken, Synonyms of, 252
Dead, Synonyms of, 252
Deadly, Synonyms of, 224
Death, Synonyms of, 195-196
Decay, Synonyms of, 252
Deceit, Synonyms of, 252
Deceptive, Synonyms of, 252
Decorate, Synonyms of, 252
Decorous, Synonyms of, 252
Deface, Synonyms of, 252
Defeat, Synonyms of, 224
Defect, Synonyms of, 252
Definitions, of words, 66-69; Dictionary vs. informal, 67, 145; How to look up in a dictionary, 69-74
Defoe, Daniel. See *The Castaway*
Degrade, 78
Delay, Synonyms of, 252
Demean, 149
Democrat, 5
Demon, 80
Demoralize, Synonyms of, 252
Deny, Synonyms of, 224-225
Deportment, Synonyms of, 252
Deprive, Synonyms of, 252
Description, 27, 47, 49, 53-54, 56
Despise, Synonyms of, 252
Despondency, Synonyms of, 252
Destroy, Synonyms of, 225
Detach, Synonyms of, 252
Determined, Synonyms of, 252
Deviate, 79
Devilish, 164
Devout, Synonyms of, 252
Dexterity, 80
Dic, dict family, 108
Dictionaries, List of, 70; How to use, 69-74
Die, Synonyms of, 225
Differ, 79
Difficulty, Synonyms of, 252
Dign family, 126

Dilapidated, 78
Dip, Synonyms of, 225-226
Dirty, Synonyms of, 252
Disaster, 78
Discernment, Synonyms of, 252
Discharge, 263
Discords, Verbal, 24-39
Discourse, at first hand, 46-54; adapted to audience, 54-58
Disease, Synonyms of, 226
Disgraceful, Synonyms of, 252
Disgusting, Synonyms of, 252
Dishonor, Synonyms of, 244
Disloyal, Synonyms of, 226
Dispel, Synonyms of, 252
Dissatisfied, Synonyms of, 252
Diurnal, 166
Divide, Synonyms of, 252
Do, Synonyms of, 226
Doctrine, Synonyms of, 252
Doom, Doomsday, 81
Dream, Synonyms of, 252
Dress, Synonyms of, 226-227
"Drift of Our Rural Population Cityward, The" (Editorial), 291-293. Comments and assignments on, 10, 19, 26, 30, 34, 46
Drink, Synonyms of, 227
Drip, Synonyms of, 252
Drunk, Synonyms of, 252
Dry, Synonyms of, 252
Duc, duct family, 108
Dull, 263
Dur(e) family, 126

Early, Synonyms of, 196
Eat, Synonyms of, 252
Editorial. See *The Drift of Our Rural Population Cityward*
Effect, 149, 150
Egregious, 79
Ejaculate, 79
Elicit, Synonyms of, 227
Embarrass, Synonyms of, 227-228
Embrace, 170
Encroach, Synonyms of, 252
End, Synonyms of, 252
Enemy, 169
Enemy, Synonyms of, 253
Engine, 102
Enni family, 124
Enormity, enormousness, 149
Enough, Synonyms of, 253
Entice, Synonyms of, 253
Erase, Synonyms of, 253
Error family, 108
Error, Synonyms of, 253
Estimate, Synonyms of, 253
Eternal, Synonyms of, 253
Eu family, 101-103
Eugenics, 101-103

INDEX

Ex family, 96-97
Examination, Synonyms of, 253
Example, Synonyms of, 253
Exceed, Synonyms of, 253
Exclude, 78
Excuse, Synonyms of, 228
Expand, Synonyms of, 253
Expel, Synonyms of, 253
Experiment, Synonyms of, 253
Explain, Synonyms of, 228
Explanation (Exposition), 27, 47, 49-51, 52, 56
Explicit, Synonyms of, 253
Expression, 80

Face, Synonyms of, 197
Fact family, 109, 287
Faculty, Synonyms of, 253
Failing, Synonyms of, 253
Fair, 263
False, 263
Fame, Synonyms of, 244-246
Families, Verbal, 89-144
Famous, Synonyms of, 253
Fashion, Synonyms of, 253
Fast, 263
Fast, Synonyms of, 253
Fasten, Synonyms of, 253
Fat, Synonyms of, 228
Fate, Synonyms of, 253
Fatherly, 163
Fawn, Synonyms of, 253
Fear, Synonyms of, 228-229
Feat, fect, feit family, 109
Feign, Synonyms of, 253
Fellow, 84
Feminine, Synonyms of, 229
Fer family, 109
Fertile, Synonyms of, 253
Fic(e) family, 109, 287
Fiddle, 35
Fide family, 110
Fie, 81
Fiendish, Synonyms of, 253
Fight, Synonyms of, 229
Financial, Synonyms of, 197-198
Fin(e) family, 126
Firm, 263
Fit, Synonyms of, 253
Flag, The, 5
Flame, Synonyms of, 253
Flat, 264
Flat, Synonyms of, 253
Flatter, Synonyms of, 253
Flect, flex family, 126
Flee, Synonyms of, 198
Fleeting, Synonyms of, 229
Flexible, Synonyms of, 253
Flit, Synonyms of, 253
Flock, Synonyms of, 253
Flock together, 79

Flow, Synonyms of, 253
Flu, fluence, flux family, 126
Foe, 169
Follow, Synonyms of, 253
Follower, Synonyms of, 253
Fond, 80
Fond, Synonyms of, 253
Force, Synonyms of, 253
Foretell, Synonyms of, 198-199
Fort family, 127
Fossils in modern English, List of, 87-88
Found family, 127
Fract, frag family, 127
Fracture, 170
Frank, Synonyms of, 230
Franklin, Benjamin, and *Spectator Papers*, 45
Fraternal, 166
Free, 264
Free, Synonyms of, 253
French and Norman-French words occurring in modern English, 135, 158-160
Freshen, Synonyms of, 253
Fret, 81
Friendly, 168
Friendly, Synonyms of, 254
Frighten, Synonyms of, 254
Frigid, 166-167
Frown, Synonyms of, 254
Frugal, Synonyms of, 254
Frustrate, Synonyms of, 230
Fug(e) family, 127
Fuse family, 127
Fy family, 109, 287

Game, Synonyms of, 254
Gather, Synonyms of, 254
Gen family, 101-103
General facts and ideas with which acquaintance assumed, 270-273
General ideas, as best basis for study of synonyms, 180-182, 288
General vs. specific terms, 27-30, 180-182, 288. Also see *Words*
Genus and species, 67-68, 180-182
Ger, gest family, 128
Germanic words in modern English, 135, 158-159
Get, Synonyms of, 199-200
Get on to, 78
"Gettysburg Address" (Lincoln), Comments on, 16
Ghost, 169
Ghost, Synonyms of, 254
Gift, Synonyms of, 254
Give, Synonyms of, 200
Glad, Synonyms of, 230
Go out of one's way, 79
Good, 260-261

INDEX

Good family, 91
Goodby, 78
Grade family, 110
Gram family, 95-96
Grand, Synonyms of, 254
Graph family, 95-96, 287
Gray hair, 35
Great, 264
Greedy, 169
Greek prefixes, List of, 144
Greek stems, List of, 141-143
Greek words in modern English, 135, 141, 159
Greet, Synonyms of, 254
Gress family, 110
Grief, Synonyms of, 254
Grieve, Synonyms of, 254
Groom, 80
Grudgingly, 67
Guard, Synonyms of, 254
Guileless, 83

Hab family, 110
Habit, Synonyms of, 230-231
Habitation, Synonyms of, 254
Hale family, 110
Half-baked, 79, 287
Harass, Synonyms of, 231
Hard, 264
Harmful, Synonyms of, 254
Harsh, 264
Haste, Synonyms of, 201
Hate, Synonyms of, 201-202
Hatred, Synonyms of, 246-247
Have, Synonyms of, 254
Hayseed, 83
Head foremost, 79
Headstrong, Synonyms of, 254
Heal family, 110
Healthful, Synonyms of, 202-203
Heathen, 80
Heavy, Synonyms of, 203
Height, 167-168
Help (noun), Synonyms of, 254
Help (verb), Synonyms of, 254
Hesitate, Synonyms of, 254
Hib family, 110
Hide, Synonyms of, 254
High, Synonyms of, 254
Highstrung, 79
Hinder, Synonyms of, 231
Hint, Synonyms of, 254
Hol family, 110
Hole, Synonyms of, 231-232
Holy, Synonyms of, 254
Home, 35, 163
Homeopath, 147
Homesickness, 168
Hopeful, Synonyms of, 254
Hopeless, Synonyms of, 254
Hose, 76

House, 35
How a child becomes acquainted with the complexity of life and of language, 180-182
Hug, 170
Humor, 77
Hussy, 83

Idiot, 82, 287
Idle, Synonyms of, 232
Ig family, 105
Ignorant, Synonyms of, 232-233
Imp, 83
Imperfectly understood facts and ideas, 270-273
Impolite, Synonyms of, 254
Importance, Synonyms of, 254
Imposter, Synonyms of, 254
Imprison, Synonyms of, 254
Improper, Synonyms of, 254
Impure, Synonyms of, 254
In a minute, 82
Inborn, Synonyms of, 254
Incense, 79
Incite, Synonyms of, 254
Incline, Synonyms of, 233
Inclose, Synonyms of, 254
Increase, Synonyms of, 254
Indecent, Synonyms of, 255
Infantry, 82
Infectious, 149, 150
Ingenious, 102
Inner, 167
Innocent, 83
Innuendo, 80
Insane, Synonyms of, 255
Insanity, Synonyms of, 255
Insinuate, 79
Insipid, Synonyms of, 255
Instances, 75
Instigate, 79
Insult, 79
Intention, Synonyms of, 255
Internal, 167
Interpose, Synonyms of, 255
Investigate, 79
Irreligious, Synonyms of, 255
Irritate, Synonyms of, 255
It family, 111
"Ivanhoe" (Scott), Quotation from, 159-160

Ject family, 111
Join, Synonyms of, 255
Journey, Synonyms of, 233
Jud family, 111
Jump on, 79
Junct family, 111
Jur, jus family, 111
Jure family, 112
Just, 264

INDEX

Key-syllables, Variations in form of, 103-104; Misleading resemblance between, 104-105; Lists of, 105-143
Kick, 79
Kill, Synonyms of, 219
Kind, Synonyms of, 233
Kindle, Synonyms of, 255
Kinships between words. See Blood relationships between words, Marriages between words, Words
Knave, 82
Knowledge, 149, 150

Lack, Synonyms of, 255
Lame, Synonyms of, 255
Large, Synonyms of, 255
Late family, 128
Latin prefixes, List of, 140-141
Latin stems, List of, 135-140
Latin words in modern English. See Classic words
Laugh, Synonyms of, 186-187
Laughable, Synonyms of, 255
Lead, Synonyms of, 255
Lect, leg family, 112
Lengthen, Synonyms of, 255
Lessen, Synonyms of, 255
Lewd, 82
Liberal, Synonyms of, 203
Lie (noun), Synonyms of, 255
Lie (verb), Synonyms of, 255
Lig family, 112
Likeness, Synonyms of, 255
Limp, Synonyms of, 255
List, Synonyms of, 255
Literal vs. figurative terms and applications, 31-35, 268-270. Also see Words
Loc, loco, local, locate family, 128
Locu family, 128
Log family, 98-101, 102-103
Look, Synonyms of, 187-189
Loose use of words, 12, 86, 88, 176
Loquy family, 128
Lord, 78
Lose steam, 79
Loud, Synonyms of, 255
Love, 183
Love, Synonyms of, 234
Low, Synonyms of, 255
Loyal, Synonyms of, 255
Luc, lum, lus family, 112
Lude, lus family, 128
Lunatic, 78
Lurk, Synonyms of, 255
Lust, 80

Make, Synonyms of, 255

Make one's pile, 78
Man, as a generic term, 181
Man, manu family, 92
Mand family, 113
Manifest, Synonyms of, 255
Manly, 167, 203
Many, Synonyms of, 255
Many-sided words, 260-270
Margin, Synonyms of, 234
Marriage, Synonyms of, 247
Marriages between words, 94-97. Also see Words
Marshal, 80
Masculine, Synonyms of, 203-204
Matinée, 84
Matrimonial, Synonyms of, 234
Meaning, Synonyms of, 255
Meet, Synonyms of, 255
Meeting, Synonyms of, 255
Melt, Synonyms of, 256
Memory, Synonyms of, 256
Mercy, Synonyms of, 247-248
Mere, merely, 75, 76
Meter, metri family, 129
Military terms, Familiar, 271-272
Mis(e), mit family, 113
Misrepresent, Synonyms of, 256
Mix, Synonyms of, 256
Mob family, 113
Model, Synonyms of, 256
Modern, 75
Mono family, 129
Mort family, 129
Mortal, 266
Mortify, 81
Mot(e) family, 113
Mother, 5
Motive, Synonyms of, 256
Move family, 113
Move, Synonyms of, 256
Mut(e) family, 129

Name, Synonyms of, 204-205
Narration, 27, 47, 49, 52-53, 56
Nasturtium, 78
Nat(e) family, 129
Native words, distinguished from classic, 160; in modern English, 135, 158-175
Near, Synonyms of, 256
Neat, Synonyms of, 256
Needful, Synonyms of, 256
Negligence, Synonyms of, 256
New, Synonyms of, 256
Nice, Synonyms of, 256
Nickname, 83
Noble family, 130
Noise, 83
Noisy, Synonyms of, 256
Nostalgia, 168
Nostril, 80

INDEX

Nostrum, 80
Not(e), nor(e) family, 130
Noticeable, Synonyms of, 256

Objective, 147-148
Occupation, Synonyms of, 234-235
Offspring, 169
Old, Synonyms of, 205-206
Ology family, 98-101, 102-103
Omen, ominous, 81
Opposites, 145, 146-148
Order (noun), Synonyms of, 256
Order (verb), Synonyms of, 256
Oversight, Synonyms of, 256
Ox, 159

Pacify, Synonyms of, 235
Pagan, 80
Pairs, Three types of, 145; Lists of or assignments in, 146-175; as Synonyms, 176
Pale, Synonyms of, 256
Pan family, 130
Pantaloon, 76, 287
"Parable of the Sower," 298-299; Comments and assignments on, 10, 19, 29, 33, 46
"Parable of the Prodigal Son," Comments on, 16, 28, 30, 36
Parallels, 145, 158-175
Paraphrasing, 45-46
Pard, 75, 76
Parlor, 80
Parson, 84
Part, Synonyms of, 235
Parts of Speech, Wrong, 12-13
Pass, path family, 114
Pastor, 80, 211
Paternal, 163
Patience, Synonyms of, 256
Patter, 78
Pay (noun), Synonyms of, 235
Pay (verb), Synonyms of, 206-208
Ped family, 114
Pedigree, 79
Pell family, 114
Pen, 80
Pend, pense family, 115
Penetrate, Synonyms of, 256
Perspiration, 163
Pet family, 115
Petit, petty family, 130
Petr, peter family, 130
Phil(e) family, 130
Phone family, 95-96, 287
Pin-money, 79
Pity, Synonyms of, 248
Place, Synonyms of, 256
Plain, 264
Plan, Synonyms of, 256
Playful, Synonyms of, 256

Plentiful, Synonyms of, 256
Plic(ate), ply family, 115
Plunder, Synonyms of, 256
Pocket handkerchief, 84, 287
Pod family, 114
Poli family, 131
Polite, 79
Polite, Synonyms of, 235-236
Pond family, 115
Ponder, 79
Pone, pose family, 116
Poor, 264
Porcine, 266
Pork, 159, 160
Port family, 96-97
Portent, portentous, 81
Poten(t) family, 131
Poverty, Synonyms of, 248-249
Precocious, 79, 287
Prehend family, 116
Preposterous, 79
Presbyterian, 5
Presently, 81, 287
Pretty, Synonyms of, 256
Prise family, 116
Prob family, 116
Prod up, 79
Profitable, Synonyms of, 256
Progeny, 169
Prompt, Synonyms of, 256
Proud, Synonyms of, 208-209
Pull, Synonyms of, 256
Pulse family, 114
Punish, Synonyms of, 209-210
Push, Synonyms of, 256
Put(e) family, 131
Puzzle, Synonyms of, 256

Qualm, 81
Quarrel, Synonyms of, 236
Quean, 83
Queer, Synonyms of, 256
Quick, 265
Quickly, Dame, 21-22, 31
Quiet, 267
Quotations from literature embodying old senses of words, 86-87

Raise, Synonyms of, 236
Rash, Synonyms of, 256
Reading Lists, 307-309
Rebellion, Synonyms of, 256
Recant, 79
Recover, Synonyms of, 256
Recrudescence, 79
Reflect, Synonyms of, 256
Refuse, 79
Regret, Synonyms of, 249
Relate, Synonyms of, 256
Relinquish, Synonyms of, 236

318 INDEX

Renounce, Synonyms of, 237
Replace, Synonyms of, 257
Reprove, Synonyms of, 237
Republican, 5
Repulsive, Synonyms of, 257
Requital, Synonyms of, 257
Residence, 163
Responsible, Synonyms of, 257
Reveal, Synonyms of, 257
Reverence, Synonyms of, 257
Rich, Synonyms of, 210
Ridicule, Synonyms of, 257
Right, 261-262
Ripe, Synonyms of, 257
Rise, 168
Rise, Synonyms of, 257
Rival, 84, 287
Robber, Synonyms of, 237
Rog, rogate family, 131
Rogue, Synonyms of, 257
Rough, 268-270
Round, Synonyms of, 257
Routine, 78
Rub, Synonyms of, 257
Ruminate, 79
Run, Synonyms of, 237-238
Rupt family, 117
Rural, Synonyms of, 210-211

Sabotage, 82
Sad, Synonyms of, 257
Sal, sail family, 131
Salary, 79
Sandwich, 84, 287
Sans, 76
Sarcasm, 79
Satiate, Synonyms of, 257
Saws, 75, 76
Say, Synonyms of, 238
Scandinavian words in modern English, 135, 158-159
Science, scit(e) family, 132
Scoff, Synonyms of, 257
Scott, Sir Walter, Quotation from, 159-160
Scribe, script family, 91-92, 287
Secret, Synonyms of, 257
Sect family, 132
Secu, sequ family, 117
Sed family, 117
See, Synonyms of, 219
Seep, Synonyms of, 257
Sell, 168
Sell, Synonyms of, 257
Sens(e), sent family, 132
Serious, 265
"Seven Ages of Man, The" (Shakespeare), 299-300; Comments and assignments on, 10, 19, 26, 29, 33, 37, 46, 75-76
Severe, 266

Shakespeare, William. See *The Seven Ages of Man*
Shamefaced, 80
Shape, Synonyms of, 257
Share, Synonyms of, 257
Sharp, 265
Sharp, Synonyms of, 257
Shear family, 117
Shine, Synonyms of, 238
Shore family, 117
Shore, Synonyms of, 257
Shorten, 170
Shorten, Synonyms of, 257
Show (noun), Synonyms of, 257
Show (verb), Synonyms of, 257
Shrink, Synonyms of, 257
Shun, Synonyms of, 257
Shy, Synonyms of, 257
Side, 36
Sid(e) family, 117
Sidetrack, 78
Sign family, 118
Sign, Synonyms of, 257
Silent, Synonyms of, 211-212
Silly, 83
Simple, Synonyms of, 257
Sing, Synonyms of, 212-213
Sing another tune, 79
Sinister, 79
Sist family, 119
Skilful, Synonyms of, 257
Skin, Synonyms of, 257
Slander, Synonyms of, 238
Slang, 14-15
Sleep, Synonyms of, 220
Sleepy, Synonyms of, 257
Slovenliness, 11-15
Slovenly, Synonyms of, 257
Sly, Synonyms of, 257
Smell, Synonyms of, 239
Smile, Synonyms of, 257
Smoke in one's pipe, 79
Solitary, Synonyms of, 257
Solve, *solu* family, 118
Song, Synonyms of, 239
Soon, 81
Sources for modern English, Variety of, 94, 158-159
Sour, Synonyms of, 258
Sow, 159
Speak, Synonyms of, 239
Spect, spic(e) family, 118
"Spectator Papers, The" (Addison), 45
Speech, Synonyms of, 258
Spend, Synonyms of, 240
Spire, spirit family, 119
Spirit, 169
Spond, spons(e) family, 132
Spot, Synonyms of, 240
Spruce, Synonyms of, 258

INDEX

Sta, sti family, 119
Stale, Synonyms of, 258
Stay, Synonyms of, 240
Stead family, 120
Steal, Synonyms of, 240-241
Steep, Synonyms of, 258
Stiff, 265
Stingy, Synonyms of, 258
Stirrup, 80
Storm, Synonyms of, 258
Straight, Synonyms of, 258
Strain, string, strict family, 120
Strange, Synonyms of, 258
Strike, Synonyms of, 241
Strong, 265
Strong, Synonyms of, 258
Struct, stru(e) family, 132
Stubborn, Synonyms of, 249-250
Stupid, Synonyms of, 258
Suave, Synonyms of, 213
Subjective, 147-148
Succeed, Synonyms of, 258
Succession, Synonyms of, 258
Sue family, 117
Sullen, Synonyms of, 241
Sult family, 131
Superfluous details, 21-23
Supernatural, Synonyms of, 258
Suppose, Synonyms of, 258
Surprise, Synonyms of, 258
Swearing, Synonyms of, 258
Sweat, 163
Swine, 159
Synonyms, Necessity for, 176-177;
Similar not identical in meaning, 72, 177; List of books of, 177-178; How to acquire, 178-183; Analysis of your use of, 179-180; Progress from the general to the specific, 180-182, 288; Pertinent rather than comprehensive, 182-183; Lists of, or assignments in, 184-270 (also see *Pairs*)

Tact family, 120
Tail family, 120
Tain family, 121
Take down a notch, 78
Take hold of, 79
Take the hide off, 79
Take umbrage, 78
Talk (noun), 168
Talk (verb), Synonyms of, 241-242
Talkative, Synonyms of, 214-215
Tameness, 8-11
Tang family, 120
Teach, Synonyms of, 258
Tear, Synonyms of, 242
Telegrams and night letters, 19-21
Ten, tent family, 104-105

Tend, tens, tent, ten family, 104-105
Tender, 105
Tennyson, Alfred, Quotation from, 32
Tension, 72-74, 77, 79, 90
Term, termin family, 121
Ter(re), terra family, 133
Thank your lucky stars, 78
Thesis, theme family, 133
Thing(s), 67, 261
Thoughtful, Synonyms of, 258
Throw, Synonyms of, 242
Throw in the shade, 79
Throw out a remark, 79
Tin family, 104-105
Tire, Synonyms of, 258
Tool, Synonyms of, 258
Tone, 105
Tone, Unity of. See *Discords Verbal*
Tort family, 121
Track, 79
Tract, tra(i) family, 121
Translation, 44-45
Trifle, Synonyms of, 258
Triteness, 13-14
Trivial, 82
Trust, Synonyms of, 258
Truth, 169-170
Try, Synonyms of, 258
Tum family, 133
Turb family, 133
Turn, Synonyms of, 258

Ugly, Synonyms of, 258
Umpire, 83
Understood, 78
Unsophisticated, 83
Unwilling, Synonyms of, 258

Vade, vasion family, 133
Vail, val(e) family, 134
Vain, 265
Vapid, 79
Veal, veau, 159, 160
Vend, 168
Vene, vent family, 122
Veracity, 169-170
Vers(e), vert family, 122
Vid family, 103-104
Villain, 83
Vince, vict family, 122
Vinegar, 80
Violin, 35
Vir family, 134
Virile, 167, 204
Virtue, 80
Vis family, 103-104
Viv(e) family, 134
Voc, voke family, 123

INDEX

Vocabulary, Ready, wide, or accurate, 40-42; Speaking or writing, 43-44; Analysis of your own, 62-66, 179-180
Volve, volute family, 123
Voluntary, 168-169
Voracious, 169
Vulgar, 82

Walk, Synonyms of, 184-186
Watchful, Synonyms of, 258
Wave (noun), Synonyms of, 258
Wave (verb), Synonyms of, 258
Weak, 265
Weak, Synonyms of, 215-216
Weariness, Synonyms of, 258
Wearisome, Synonyms of, 258
Wench, 83
Wet (adjective), Synonyms of, **258**
Wet (verb), Synonyms of, 258
Wheedle, 78
Whim, Synonyms of, 258
Whip, Synonyms of, 242
Whole family, 110
Wicked, Synonyms of, 243
Wild, 266
Willing, 168-169
Wind, Synonyms of, 258
Wind (verb), Synonyms of, 258
Winding, Synonyms of, **258**
Wis, wit family, 103-104
Wisdom, 149, 150
Wise, Synonyms of, 216-217
Wizard, 82
Wonderful, Synonyms of, **258**

Wordiness, 15-23
Words, as realities, 4-5; as instruments, 4-6, 285-286; to be learned in various ways, 7; like people, 7, 60-61, 75, 89-91, 97; in combination, 7-58; Individual, 59-144; to learn first, 61-62; The past of, 75-88; Buried meanings of, 76-77; Poetry of, 78; Dignified and unassuming, 76-79; Literal, concrete, and specific, 79-81; General, 80-81; Exaggerative, 81-82; Debased, 82-83; as celibates, 59-88; related in blood or by marriage, 89-144, 274-275; examined for relationships, 97-103; related in meaning, 145-157; often confused, 145, 149-157; Native and classic, 158-175; Many-sided, 260-270; Supplementary list of, 274-284. Also see *Classes of words, Abstract vs. concrete terms, Literal vs. figurative terms, General vs. specific terms, Slang, Vocabulary, Synonyms, Fossils, Loose use of words*
Work, Synonyms of, 217
Workman, Synonyms of, 258
Worm in, 79
Write, Synonyms of, 258
Writing as an aid to memory, 66, 179
Wrong, 80

Yearn, Synonyms of, 258
Young, Synonyms of